HOSPITALITY CRISIS AND EMERGENCY MANAGEMENT

Dayanand Prasad

CENTRUM PRESS
NEW DELHI-110002 (INDIA)

CENTRUM PRESS

H.O.: 4360/4, Ansari Road, Daryaganj,
New Delhi-110002 (India)
Tel: 23278000, 23261597, 23255577, 23286875

B.O.: No. 1015, Ist Main Road, BSK IIIrd Stage,
IIIrd Phase, IIIrd Block, Bengaluru-560085 (INDIA)
Tel: 080-41723429

Email: centrumpress@gmail.com
Visit us at: www.centrumpress.com

Hospitality Crisis and Emergency Management

First Edition, 2013

ISBN 978-93-81460-15-3

PRINTED IN INDIA

Printed at Balaji Offset, Delhi.

Contents

Preface

An effective emergency response and good family assistance will reduce the frustrations that many people experience when caught up in the aftermath of a major incident. Besides going a long way to ensuring effective crisis management, it is also a humane, caring and compassionate way to respond. Few crises will seem as dramatic as New York or Bali-unless it is your own. When your crisis occurs, the hardest part of dealing with it can involve answering the public call for information-as personified by a TV correspondent or newspaper reporter who shows up on your doorstep or on your telephone line to get the story. How well you respond depends on how well you are prepared. While the existence of some of the above components may be based on the assumption of the pre-existence of a structured and experienced emergency services (police, fire and ambulance), this would be an unrealistic expectation. in many situations.

The strategies to manage risk include transferring the risk to another party, avoiding the risk, reducing the negative effect or probability of the risk, ov even accepting some or all of the consequences of a particular risk. Certain aspects of many of the risk management standards have come under criticism for having no measurable improvement on risk, whether the confidence in estimates and decisions seem to increase. This section provides an introduction to the principles of risk management. The vocabulary of risk management is defined in ISO Guide 73, "Risk management. Vocabulary." In ideal risk management, a prioritization process is followed whereby the risks with the greatest loss and the greatest probability of occurring are handled first, and risks with lower probability of occurrence and lower loss are handled in descending order. In practice the process can be very difficult, and balancing between risks with a high probability of occurrence but lower loss versus a risk with high loss but lower probability of occurrence can often be mishandled.

Intangible risk management identifies a new type of a risk that has a 100% probability of occurring but is ignored by the organization due to a lack of identification ability. For example, when deficient knowledge is applied to a situation, a knowledge risk materializes. Relationship risk appears when ineffective collaboration occurs. Process-engagement risk may be an issue when ineffective operational procedures are applied. These risks directly reduce the productivity of knowledge workers, decrease cost effectiveness, profitability, service, quality, reputation, brand value, and earnings quality. Intangible risk management allows risk management to create immediate value from the identification and reduction of risks that reduce productivity.

Risk management also faces difficulties in allocating resources. This is the idea of opportunity cost. Resources spent on risk management could have been spent on more profitable activities. Again, ideal risk management minimizes spending and minimizes the negative effects of risks.

It not only covers all the important topics that is required in a textbook, but also introduces the reader with latest developments and information.

—Author

1

Introduction

Risk management is the identification, assessment, and prioritization of risks (defined in ISO 31000 as *the effect of uncertainty on objectives*, whether positive or negative) followed by coordinated and economical application of resources to minimize, monitor, and control the probability and/or impact of unfortunate events or to maximize the realization of opportunities. Risks can come from uncertainty in financial markets, project failures (at any phase in development, production, or sustainment life-cycles), legal liabilities, credit risk, accidents, natural causes and disasters as well as deliberate attack from an adversary or events of uncertain root-cause. Several risk management standards have been developed including the Project Management Institute, the National Institute of Science and Technology, actuarial societies, and ISO standards. Methods, definitions and goals vary widely according to whether the risk management method is in the context of project management, security, engineering, industrial processes, financial portfolios, actuarial assessments, or public health and safety.

The strategies to manage risk include transferring the risk to another party, avoiding the risk, reducing the negative effect or probability of the risk, ov even accepting some or all of the consequences of a particular risk.

Certain aspects of many of the risk management standards have come under criticism for having no measurable improvement on risk, whether the confidence in estimates and decisions seem to increase.

This section provides an introduction to the principles of risk management. The vocabulary of risk management is defined in

ISO Guide 73, "Risk management. Vocabulary." In ideal risk management, a prioritization process is followed whereby the risks with the greatest loss and the greatest probability of occurring are handled first, and risks with lower probability of occurrence and lower loss are handled in descending order. In practice the process can be very difficult, and balancing between risks with a high probability of occurrence but lower loss versus a risk with high loss but lower probability of occurrence can often be mishandled.

Intangible risk management identifies a new type of a risk that has a 100% probability of occurring but is ignored by the organization due to a lack of identification ability. For example, when deficient knowledge is applied to a situation, a knowledge risk materializes.

Relationship risk appears when ineffective collaboration occurs. Process-engagement risk may be an issue when ineffective operational procedures are applied. These risks directly reduce the productivity of knowledge workers, decrease cost effectiveness, profitability, service, quality, reputation, brand value, and earnings quality. Intangible risk management allows risk management to create immediate value from the identification and reduction of risks that reduce productivity.

Risk management also faces difficulties in allocating resources. This is the idea of opportunity cost. Resources spent on risk management could have been spent on more profitable activities. Again, ideal risk management minimizes spending and minimizes the negative effects of risks.

Method

For the most part, these methods consist of the following elements, performed, more or less, in the following order.

1. identify, characterize, and assess threats
2. assess the vulnerability of critical assets to specific threats
3. determine the risk (i.e. the expected consequences of specific types of attacks on specific assets)
4. identify ways to reduce those risks
5. prioritize risk reduction measures based on a strategy.

Principles of Risk Management

The International Organization for Standardization (ISO) identifies the following principles of risk management:

Risk management should:

- create value
- be an integral part of organizational processes
- be part of decision making
- explicitly address uncertainty and assumptions
- be systematic and structured
- be based on the best available information
- be tailorable
- take into account human factors
- be transparent and inclusive
- be dynamic, iterative and responsive to change
- be capable of continual improvement and enhancement.

Process

According to the standard ISO 31000 "Risk management — Principles and guidelines on implementation," the process of risk management consists of several steps as follows:

Establishing the Context

Establishing the context involves:

1. Identification of risk in a selected domain of interest
2. Planning the remainder of the process.
3. Mapping out the following:
   - o the social scope of risk management
   - o the identity and objectives of stakeholders
   - o the basis upon which risks will be evaluated, constraints.
4. Defining a framework for the activity and an agenda for identification.
5. Developing an analysis of risks involved in the process.

6. Mitigation or Solution of risks using available technological, human and organizational resources.

Identification

After establishing the context, the next step in the process of managing risk is to identify potential risks. Risks are about events that, when triggered, cause problems. Hence, risk identification can start with the source of problems, or with the problem itself.

- Source analysis Risk sources may be internal or external to the system that is the target of risk management.

Examples of risk sources are: stakeholders of a project, employees of a company or the weather over an airport.

- Problem analysis Risks are related to identified threats For example: the threat of losing money, the threat of abuse of privacy information or the threat of accidents and casualties. The threats may exist with various entities, most important with shareholders, customers and legislative bodies such as the government.

When either source or problem is known, the events that a source may trigger or the events that can lead to a problem can be investigated. For example: stakeholders withdrawing during a project may endanger funding of the project; privacy information may be stolen by employees even within a closed network; lightning striking an aircraft during takeoff may make all people on board immediate casualties.

The chosen method of identifying risks may depend on culture, industry practice and compliance. The identification methods are formed by templates or the development of templates for identifying source, problem or event. Common risk identification methods are:

- Objectives-based risk identification Organizations and project teams have objectives. Any event that may endanger achieving an objective partly or completely is identified as risk.
- Scenario-based risk identification In scenario analysis different scenarios are created. The scenarios may be the alternative ways to achieve an objective, or an analysis of the interaction of forces in, for example, a market or battle.

Any event that triggers an undesired scenario alternative is identified as risk.

- Taxonomy-based risk identification The taxonomy in taxonomy-based risk identification is a breakdown of possible risk sources. Based on the taxonomy and knowledge of best practices, a questionnaire is compiled. The answers to the questions reveal risks.
- Common-risk checking In several industries, lists with known risks are available. Each risk in the list can be checked for application to a particular situation.
- Risk charting This method combines the above approaches by listing resources at risk, threats to those resources, modifying factors which may increase or decrease the risk and consequences it is wished to avoid. Creating a matrix under these headings enables a variety of approaches. One can begin with resources and consider the threats they are exposed to and the consequences of each. Alternatively one can start with the threats and examine which resources they would affect, or one can begin with the consequences and determine which combination of threats and resources would be involved to bring them about.

Assessment

Once risks have been identified, they must then be assessed as to their potential severity of impact (generally a negative impact, such as damage or loss) and to the probability of occurrence. These quantities can be either simple to measure, in the case of the value of a lost building, or impossible to know for sure in the case of the probability of an unlikely event occurring. Therefore, in the assessment process it is critical to make the best educated decisions in order to properly prioritize the implementation of the risk management plan.

Even a short-term positive improvement can have long-term negative impacts. Take the "turnpike" example. A highway is widened to allow more traffic. More traffic capacity leads to greater development in the areas surrounding the improved traffic capacity. Over time, traffic thereby increases to fill available capacity. Turnpikes thereby need to be expanded in a seemingly endless cycles. There are many other engineering examples where expanded capacity (to do any function) is soon filled by increased demand. Since expansion comes at a cost, the resulting growth could become unsustainable without forecasting and management.

The fundamental difficulty in risk assessment is determining the rate of occurrence since statistical information is not available on all kinds of past incidents. Furthermore, evaluating the severity of the consequences (impact) is often quite difficult for intangible assets. Asset valuation is another question that needs to be addressed. Thus, best educated opinions and available statistics are the primary sources of information. Nevertheless, risk assessment should produce such information for the management of the organization that the primary risks are easy to understand and that the risk management decisions may be prioritized. Thus, there have been several theories and attempts to quantify risks.

Composite Risk Index

The above formula can also be re-written in terms of a Composite Risk Index, as follows:

Composite Risk Index = Impact of Risk event x Probability of Occurrence

The impact of the risk event is commonly assessed on a scale of 1 to 5, where 1 and 5 represent the minimum and maximum possible impact of an occurrence of a risk (usually in terms of financial losses). However, the 1 to 5 scale can be arbitrary and need not be on a linear scale.

The probability of occurrence is likewise commonly assessed on a scale from 1 to 5, where 1 represents a very low probability of the risk event actually occurring while 5 represents a very high probability of occurrence. This axis may be expressed in either mathematical terms (event occurs once a year, once in ten years, once in 100 years etc.) or may be expressed in "plain english"- event has occurred here very often; event has been known to occur here; event has been known to occur in the industry etc.). Again, the 1 to 5 scale can be arbitrary or non-linear depending on decisions by subject-matter experts.

The Composite Index thus can take values ranging (typically) from 1 through 25, and this range is usually arbitrarily divided into three sub-ranges. The overall risk assessment is then Low, Medium or High, depending on the sub-range containing the calculated value of the Composite Index. For instance, the three sub-ranges could be defined as 1 to 8, 9 to 16 and 17 to 25.

Note that the probability of risk occurrence is difficult to estimate, since the past data on frequencies are not readily available, as mentioned above. After all, probability does not imply certainty.

Likewise, the impact of the risk is not easy to estimate since it is often difficult to estimate the potential loss in the event of risk occurrence.

Further, both the above factors can change in magnitude depending on the adequacy of risk avoidance and prevention measures taken and due to changes in the external business environment. Hence it is absolutely necessary to periodically re-assess risks and intensify/relax mitigation measures, or as necessary. Changes in procedures, technology, schedules, budgets, market conditions, political environment, or other factors typically require re-assessment of risks.

Risk Options

Risk mitigation measures are usually formulated according to one or more of the following major risk options, which are:

1. Design a new business process with adequate built-in risk control and containment measures from the start.
2. Periodically re-assess risks that are accepted in ongoing processes as a normal feature of business operations and modify mitigation measures.
3. Transfer risks to an external agency (e.g. an insurance company)
4. Avoid risks altogether (e.g. by closing down a particular high-risk business area).

Later research has shown that the financial benefits of risk management are less dependent on the formula used but are more dependent on the frequency and how risk assessment is performed.

In business it is imperative to be able to present the findings of risk assessments in financial, market, or schedule terms. Robert Courtney Jr. (IBM, 1970) proposed a formula for presenting risks in financial terms. The Courtney formula was accepted as the official risk analysis method for the US governmental agencies. The formula proposes calculation of ALE (annualised loss expectancy) and compares the expected loss value to the security control implementation costs (cost-benefit analysis).

Potential Risk Treatments

Once risks have been identified and assessed, all techniques to manage the risk fall into one or more of these four major categories:

- Avoidance (eliminate, withdraw from or not become involved)
- Reduction (optimize-mitigate)
- Sharing (transfer-outsource or insure)
- Retention (accept and budget).

Ideal use of these strategies may not be possible. Some of them may involve trade-offs that are not acceptable to the organization or person making the risk management decisions. Another source, from the US Department of Defence, Defence Acquisition University, calls these categories ACAT, for Avoid, Control, Accept, or Transfer. This use of the ACAT acronym is reminiscent of another ACAT (for Acquisition Category) used in US Defence industry procurements, in which Risk Management figures prominently in decision making and planning.

Risk Avoidance

This includes not performing an activity that could carry risk. An example would be not buying a property or business in order to not take on the legal liability that comes with it. Another would be not flying in order not to take the risk that the airplane were to be hijacked. Avoidance may seem the answer to all risks, but avoiding risks also means losing out on the potential gain that accepting (retaining) the risk may have allowed. Not entering a business to avoid the risk of loss also avoids the possibility of earning profits.

Hazard Prevention

Hazard prevention refers to the prevention of risks in an emergency. The first and most effective stage of hazard prevention is the elimination of hazards. If this takes too long, is too costly, or is otherwise impractical, the second stage is mitigation.

Risk Reduction

Risk reduction or "optimization" involves reducing the severity of the loss or the likelihood of the loss from occurring. For example, sprinklers are designed to put out a fire to reduce the risk of loss by fire. This method may cause a greater loss by water damage and therefore may not be suitable. Halon fire suppression systems may mitigate that risk, but the cost may be prohibitive as a strategy.

Acknowledging that risks can be positive or negative, optimising risks means finding a balance between negative risk and the benefit of the operation or activity; and between risk reduction and effort applied. By an offshore drilling contractor effectively applying HSE Management in its organisation, it can optimise risk to achieve levels of residual risk that are tolerable.

Modern software development methodologies reduce risk by developing and delivering software incrementally. Early methodologies suffered from the fact that they only delivered software in the final phase of development; any problems encountered in earlier phases meant costly rework and often jeopardized the whole project. By developing in iterations, software projects can limit effort wasted to a single iteration.

Outsourcing could be an example of risk reduction if the outsourcer can demonstrate higher capability at managing or reducing risks. For example, a company may outsource only its software development, the manufacturing of hard goods, or customer support needs to another company, while handling the business management itself. This way, the company can concentrate more on business development without having to worry as much about the manufacturing process, managing the development team, or finding a physical location for a call center.

Risk Sharing

Briefly defined as "sharing with another party the burden of loss or the benefit of gain, from a risk, and the measures to reduce a risk."

The term of 'risk transfer' is often used in place of risk sharing in the mistaken belief that you can transfer a risk to a third party through insurance or outsourcing. In practice if the insurance company or contractor go bankrupt or end up in court, the original risk is likely to still revert to the first party.

As such in the terminology of practitioners and scholars alike, the purchase of an insurance contract is often described as a "transfer of risk." However, technically speaking, the buyer of the contract generally retains legal responsibility for the losses "transferred", meaning that insurance may be described more accurately as a post-event compensatory mechanism. For example, a personal injuries insurance policy does not transfer the risk of a car accident to the insurance company. The risk still lies with the policy holder namely the person who has been in the accident. The insurance policy simply provides that if an accident (the event) occurs involving the policy holder then some compensation may be payable to the policy holder that is commensurate to the suffering/damage.

Some ways of managing risk fall into multiple categories. Risk retention pools are technically retaining the risk for the group, but spreading it over the whole group involves transfer among individual members of the group. This is different from traditional insurance, in that no premium is exchanged between members of the group up front, but instead losses are assessed to all members of the group.

Risk Retention

Involves accepting the loss, or benefit of gain, from a risk when it occurs. True self insurance falls in this category. Risk retention is a viable strategy for small risks where the cost of insuring against the risk would be greater over time than the total losses sustained. All risks that are not avoided or transferred are retained by default. This includes risks that are so large or catastrophic that they either cannot be insured against or the premiums would be infeasible. War is an example since most property and risks are not insured against war, so the loss attributed by war is retained by the insured. Also any amounts of potential loss (risk) over the amount insured is retained risk. This may also be acceptable if the chance of a very large loss is small or if the cost to insure for greater coverage amounts is so great it would hinder the goals of the organization too much.

Create a Risk Management Plan

Select appropriate controls or countermeasures to measure each risk. Risk mitigation needs to be approved by the appropriate level of management. For instance, a risk concerning the image of the organization should have top management decision behind it whereas IT management would have the authority to decide on computer virus risks.

The risk management plan should propose applicable and effective security controls for managing the risks. For example, an observed high risk of computer viruses could be mitigated by acquiring and implementing antivirus software. A good risk management plan should contain a schedule for control implementation and responsible persons for those actions.

According to ISO/IEC 27001, the stage immediately after completion of the risk assessment phase consists of preparing a Risk Treatment Plan, which should document the decisions about how each of the identified risks should be handled. Mitigation of risks often means selection of security controls, which should be documented in a Statement of Applicability, which identifies which particular control objectives and controls from the standard have been selected, and why.

Implementation

Implementation follows all of the planned methods for mitigating the effect of the risks. Purchase insurance policies for the risks that have been decided to be transferred to an insurer, avoid all risks that can be avoided without sacrificing the entity's goals, reduce others, and retain the rest.

Review and Evaluation of the Plan

Initial risk management plans will never be perfect. Practice, experience, and actual loss results will necessitate changes in the plan and contribute information to allow possible different decisions to be made in dealing with the risks being faced.

Risk analysis results and management plans should be updated periodically. There are two primary reasons for this:

1. to evaluate whether the previously selected security controls are still applicable and effective, and

2. to evaluate the possible risk level changes in the business environment. For example, information risks are a good example of rapidly changing business environment.

Limitations

If risks are improperly assessed and prioritized, time can be wasted in dealing with risk of losses that are not likely to occur. Spending too much time assessing and managing unlikely risks can divert resources that could be used more profitably. Unlikely events do occur but if the risk is unlikely enough to occur it may be better to simply retain the risk and deal with the result if the loss does in fact occur. Qualitative risk assessment is subjective and lacks consistency. The primary justification for a formal risk assessment process is legal and bureaucratic.

Prioritizing the *risk management processes* too highly could keep an organization from ever completing a project or even getting started. This is especially true if other work is suspended until the risk management process is considered complete.

It is also important to keep in mind the distinction between risk and uncertainty. Risk can be measured by impacts x probability.

Areas of Risk Management

As applied to corporate finance, risk management is the technique for measuring, monitoring and controlling the financial or operational risk on a firm's balance sheet.

The Basel II framework breaks risks into market risk (price risk), credit risk and operational risk and also specifies methods for calculating capital requirements for each of these components.

Enterprise Risk Management

In enterprise risk management, a risk is defined as a possible event or circumstance that can have negative influences on the enterprise in question. Its impact can be on the very existence, the resources (human and capital), the products and services, or the customers of the enterprise, as well as external impacts on society, markets, or the environment. In a financial institution, enterprise risk management is normally thought of as the combination of credit risk, interest rate risk or asset liability management, market risk, and operational risk.

In the more general case, every probable risk can have a pre-formulated plan to deal with its possible consequences (to ensure *contingency* if the risk becomes a *liability*). From the information above and the average cost per employee over time, or cost accrual ratio, a project manager can estimate:

- the cost associated with the risk if it arises, estimated by multiplying employee costs per unit time by the estimated time lost (*cost impact, C* where C = *cost accrual ratio* * *S*).
- the probable increase in time associated with a risk (*schedule variance due to risk, Rs* where Rs = P * S):
  - o Sorting on this value puts the highest risks to the schedule first. This is intended to cause the greatest risks to the project to be attempted first so that risk is minimized as quickly as possible.
  - o This is slightly misleading as *schedule variances* with a large P and small S and vice versa are not equivalent. (The risk of the RMS *Titanic* sinking vs. the passengers' meals being served at slightly the wrong time).
- the probable increase in cost associated with a risk (*cost variance due to risk, Rc* where Rc = P*C = P*CAR*S = P*S*CAR)
  - o sorting on this value puts the highest risks to the budget first.

Risk in a project or process can be due either to Special Cause Variation or Common Cause Variation and requires appropriate treatment. That is to re-iterate the concern about extremal cases not being equivalent in the list immediately above.

Risk Management Activities as Applied to Project Management

In project management, risk management includes the following activities:

- Planning how risk will be managed in the particular project. Plans should include risk management tasks, responsibilities, activities and budget.
- Assigning a risk officer-a team member other than a project manager who is responsible for foreseeing potential project problems. Typical characteristic of risk officer is a healthy skepticism.

- Maintaining live project risk database. Each risk should have the following attributes: opening date, title, short description, probability and importance. Optionally a risk may have an assigned person responsible for its resolution and a date by which the risk must be resolved.
- Creating anonymous risk reporting channel. Each team member should have possibility to report risk that he/she foresees in the project.
- Preparing mitigation plans for risks that are chosen to be mitigated. The purpose of the mitigation plan is to describe how this particular risk will be handled – what, when, by who and how will it be done to avoid it or minimize consequences if it becomes a liability.
- Summarizing planned and faced risks, effectiveness of mitigation activities, and effort spent for the risk management.

Risk Management for Megaprojects

Megaprojects (sometimes also called "major programs") are extremely large-scale investment projects, typically costing more than US$1 billion per project. Megaprojects include bridges, tunnels, highways, railways, airports, seaports, power plants, dams, wastewater projects, coastal flood protection schemes, oil and natural gas extraction projects, public buildings, information technology systems, aerospace projects, and defence systems. Megaprojects have been shown to be particularly risky in terms of finance, safety, and social and environmental impacts. Risk management is therefore particularly pertinent for megaprojects and special methods and special education have been developed for such risk management.

Risk Management of Information Technology

Information technology is increasing pervasive in modern life in every sector.

IT risk is a risk related to information technology. This relatively new term due to an increasing awareness that information security is simply one facet of a multitude of risks that are relevant to IT and the real world processes it supports.

A number of methodologies have been developed to deal with this kind of risk. ISACA's Risk IT framework ties IT risk to Enterprise risk management.

Risk Management Techniques in Petroleum and Natural Gas

For the offshore oil and gas industry, operational risk management is regulated by the safety case regime in many countries. Hazard identification and risk assessment tools and techniques are described in the international standard ISO 17776:2000, and organisations such as the IADC (International Association of Drilling Contractors) publish guidelines for HSE Case development which are based on the ISO standard. Further, diagrammatic representations of hazardous events are often expected by governmental regulators as part of risk management in safety case submissions; these are known as bow-tie diagrams. The technique is also used by organisations and regulators in mining, aviation, health, defence, industrial and finance.

Risk Management and Business Continuity

Risk management is simply a practice of systematically selecting cost effective approaches for minimising the effect of threat realization to the organization. All risks can never be fully avoided or mitigated simply because of financial and practical limitations. Therefore all organizations have to accept some level of residual risks.

Whereas risk management tends to be preemptive, business continuity planning (BCP) was invented to deal with the consequences of realised residual risks. The necessity to have BCP in place arises because even very unlikely events will occur if given enough time. Risk management and BCP are often mistakenly seen as rivals or overlapping practices. In fact these processes are so tightly tied together that such separation seems artificial. For example, the risk management process creates important inputs for the BCP (assets, impact assessments, cost estimates etc.). Risk management also proposes applicable controls for the observed risks. Therefore, risk management covers several areas that are vital for the BCP process. However, the BCP process goes beyond risk management's preemptive approach and assumes that the disaster will happen at some point.

Risk Communication

Risk communication is a complex cross-disciplinary academic field. Problems for risk communicators involve how to reach the intended audience, to make the risk comprehensible and relatable to other risks, how to pay appropriate respect to the audience's values related to the risk, how to predict the audience's response to the communication, etc. A main goal of risk communication is to improve collective and individual decision making. Risk communication is somewhat related to crisis communication.

Bow Tie Diagrams

A popular solution to the quest to communicate risks and their treatments effectively is to use bow tie diagrams. These have been effective, for example, in a public forum to model perceived risks and communicate precautions, during the planning stage of offshore oil and gas facilities in Scotland. Equally, the technique is used for HAZID (Hazard Identification) workshops of all types, and results in a high level of engagement. For this reason (amongst others) an increasing number of government regulators for major hazard facilities (MHFs), offshore oil & gas, aviation, etc. welcome safety case submissions which use diagrammatic representation of risks at their core.

Communication advantages of bow tie diagrams:

- Visual illustration of the hazard, its causes, consequences, controls, and how controls fail.
- The bow tie diagram can be readily understood at all personnel levels.
- "A picture paints a thousand words."

Seven Cardinal rules for the practice of risk communication

- Accept and involve the public/other consumers as legitimate partners.
- Plan carefully and evaluate your efforts with a focus on your strengths, weaknesses, opportunities, and threats.
- Listen to the public's specific concerns.
- Be honest, frank, and open.
- Coordinate and collaborate with other credible sources.

- Meet the needs of the media.
- Speak clearly and with compassion.

Aviation Security Threats and Realities

Over the past few weeks, aviation security — specifically, enhanced passenger-screening procedures — has become a big issue in the media; the discussion of the topic has become even more fervent as we enter Thanksgiving weekend, which is historically one of the busiest travel periods of the year.

As this discussion has progressed, we have been asked repeatedly by readers and members of the press for our opinion on the matter.

We have answered such requests from readers, and we have done a number of media interviews, but we've resisted writing a fresh analysis on aviation security because, as an organization, our objective is to lead the media rather than follow the media regarding a particular topic. We want our readers to be aware of things before they become pressing public issues, and when it comes to aviation-security threats and the issues involved with passenger screening, we believe we have accomplished this. Many of the things now being discussed in the media are things we've written about for years.

When we were discussing this topic internally and debating whether to write about it, we decided that since we have added so many new readers over the past few years, it might be of interest to our expanding readership to put together an analysis that reviews the material we've published and that helps to place the current discussion into the proper context. We hope our longtime readers will excuse the repetition.

We believe that this review will help establish that there is a legitimate threat to aviation, that there are significant challenges in trying to secure aircraft from every conceivable threat, and that the response of aviation security authorities to threats has often been slow and reactive rather than thoughtful and proactive.

Threats

Commercial aviation has been threatened by terrorism for decades now. From the first hijackings and bombings in the late

1960s to last month's attempt against the UPS and FedEx cargo aircraft, the threat has remained constant. As we have discussed for many years, jihadists have long had a fixation with attacking aircraft. When security measures were put in place to protect against Bojinka-style attacks in the 1990s – attacks that involved modular explosive devices smuggled onto planes and left aboard – the jihadists adapted and conducted 9/11-style attacks.

When security measures were put in place to counter 9/11-style attacks, the jihadists quickly responded by going to onboard suicide attacks with explosive devices concealed in shoes. When that tactic was discovered and shoes began to be screened, they switched to devices containing camouflaged liquid explosives. When that plot failed and security measures were altered to restrict the quantity of liquids that people could take aboard aircraft, we saw the jihadists alter the paradigm once more and attempt the underwear-bomb attack last Christmas.

In a special edition of Inspire magazine released last weekend, al Qaeda in the Arabian Peninsula (AQAP) noted that, due to the increased passenger screening implemented after the Christmas Day 2009 attempt, the group's operational planners decided to employ explosive devices sent via air cargo (we have written specifically about the vulnerability of air cargo to terrorist attacks).

Finally, it is also important to understand that the threat does not emanate just from jihadists like al Qaeda and its regional franchises. Over the past several decades, aircraft have been attacked by a number of different actors, including North Korean intelligence officers, Sikh, Palestinian and Hezbollah militants and mentally disturbed individuals like the Unabomber, among others.

Realities

While understanding that the threat is very real, it is also critical to recognize that there is no such thing as absolute, foolproof security. This applies to ground-based facilities as well as aircraft. If security procedures and checks have not been able to keep contraband out of high-security prisons, it is unreasonable to expect them to be able to keep unauthorized items off aircraft, where (thankfully) security checks of crew and passengers are far less invasive than they are for prisoners. As long as people, luggage and cargo are allowed aboard aircraft, and as long as people on the ground crew and the flight crew have access to aircraft, aircraft will remain vulnerable to a number of internal and external threats.

This reality is accented by the sheer number of passengers that must be screened and number of aircraft that must be secured. According to figures supplied by the Transportation Security Administration (TSA), in 2006, the last year for which numbers are available, the agency screened 708,400,522 passengers on domestic flights and international flights coming into the United States. This averages out to over 1.9 million passengers per day.

Another reality is that, as mentioned above, jihadists and other people who seek to attack aircraft have proven to be quite resourceful and adaptive. They carefully study security measures, identify vulnerabilities and then seek to exploit them. Indeed, last September, when we analysed the innovative designs of the explosive devices employed by AQAP, we called attention to the threat they posed to aviation more than three months before the Christmas 2009 bombing attempt. As we look at the issue again, it is not hard to see, as we pointed out then, how their innovative efforts to camouflage explosives in everyday items and hide them inside suicide operatives' bodies will continue and how these efforts will be intended to exploit vulnerabilities in current screening systems.

As we wrote in September 2009, getting a completed explosive device or its components by security and onto an aircraft is a significant challenge, but it is possible for a resourceful bombmaker to devise ways to overcome that challenge. The latest issue of Inspire magazine demonstrated how AQAP has done some very detailed research to identify screening vulnerabilities. As the group noted in the magazine: "The British government said that if a toner weighs more than 500 grams it won't be allowed on board a plane. Who is the genius who came up with this suggestion? Do you think that we have nothing to send but printers?"

AQAP also noted in the magazine that it is working to identify innocuous substances like toner ink that, when X-rayed, will appear similar to explosive compounds like PETN, since such innocuous substances will be ignored by screeners. With many countries now banning cargo from Yemen, it will be harder to send those other items in cargo from Sanaa, but the group has shown itself to be flexible, with the underwear-bomb operative beginning his trip to Detroit out of Nigeria rather than Yemen. In the special edition of Inspire, AQAP also specifically threatened to work with allies to launch future attacks from other locations.

Drug couriers have been transporting narcotics hidden inside their bodies aboard aircraft for decades, and prisoners frequently hide drugs, weapons and even cell phones inside body cavities. It is therefore only a matter of time before this same tactic is used to smuggle plastic explosives or even an entire non-metallic explosive device onto an aircraft — something that would allow an attacker to bypass metal detectors and backscatter X-ray inspection and pass through external pat-downs.

Look for the Bomber, Not Just the Bomb

This ability to camouflage explosives in a variety of different ways, or hide them inside the bodies of suicide operatives, means that the most significant weakness of any suicide-attack plan is the operative assigned to conduct the attack. Even in a plot to attack 10 or 12 aircraft, a group would need to manufacture only about 12 pounds of high explosives — about what is required for a single, small suicide device and far less than is required for a vehicle-borne improvised explosive device. Because of this, the operatives are more of a limiting factor than the explosives themselves; it is far more difficult to find and train 10 or 12 suicide bombers than it is to produce 10 or 12 devices.

A successful attack requires operatives who are not only dedicated enough to initiate a suicide device without getting cold feet; they must also possess the nerve to calmly proceed through airport security checkpoints without alerting officers that they are up to something sinister. This set of tradecraft skills is referred to as demeanor, and while remaining calm under pressure and behaving normally may sound simple in theory, practicing good demeanor under the extreme pressure of a suicide operation is very difficult.

Demeanor has proved to be the Achilles' heel of several terror plots, and it is not something that militant groups have spent a great deal of time teaching their operatives. Because of this, it is frequently easier to spot demeanor mistakes than it is to find well-hidden explosives. Such demeanor mistakes can also be accentuated, or even induced, by contact with security personnel in the form of interviews, or even by unexpected changes in security protocols that alter the security environment a potential attacker is anticipating and has planned for.

There has been much discussion of profiling, but the difficulty of creating a reliable and accurate physical profile of a jihadist, and the adaptability and ingenuity of the jihadist planners, means that any attempt at profiling based only on race, ethnicity or religion is doomed to fail. In fact, profiling can prove counterproductive to good security by blinding people to real threats. They will dismiss potential malefactors who do not fit the specific profile they have been provided.

In an environment where the potential threat is hard to identify, it is doubly important to profile individuals based on their behaviour rather than their ethnicity or nationality — what we refer to as focusing on the "how" instead of the "who." Instead of relying on physical profiles, which allow attack planners to select operatives who do not match the profiles being selected for more intensive screening, security personnel should be encouraged to exercise their intelligence, intuition and common sense. A Caucasian U.S. citizen who shows up at the U.S. Embassy in Nairobi or Dhaka claiming to have lost his passport may be far more dangerous than some random Pakistani or Yemeni citizen, even though the American does not appear to fit the profile for requiring extra security checks.

However, when we begin to consider traits such as intelligence, intuition and common sense, one of the other realities that must be faced with aviation security is that, quite simply, it is not an area where the airlines or governments have allocated the funding required to hire the best personnel. Airport screeners make far less than FBI special agents or CIA case officers and receive just a fraction of the training. Before 9/11, most airports in the United States relied on contract security guards to conduct screening duties. After 9/11, many of these same officers went from working for companies like Wackenhut to being TSA employees. There was no real effort made to increase the quality of screening personnel by offering much higher salaries to recruit a higher caliber of candidate.

There is frequent mention of the need to make U.S. airport security more like that employed in Israel. Aside from the constitutional and cultural factors that would prevent American airport screeners from ever treating Muslim travellers the way they are treated by El Al, another huge difference is simply the amount of money spent on salaries and training for screeners and other security personnel. El Al is also aided by the fact that it has a very small fleet of aircraft that fly only a small number of passengers to a handful of destinations.

Additionally, airport screening duty is simply not glamorous work. Officers are required to work long shifts conducting monotonous checks and are in near constant contact with a travelling public that can at times become quite surly when screeners follow policies established by bureaucrats at much higher pay grades. Granted, there are TSA officers who abuse their authority and do not exhibit good interpersonal skills, but anyone who travels regularly has also witnessed fellow travellers acting like idiots.

While it is impossible to keep all contraband off aircraft, efforts to improve technical methods and procedures to locate weapons and IED components must continue. However, these efforts must not only be reacting to past attacks and attempts but should also be looking forward to thwart future attacks that involve a shift in the terrorist paradigm. At the same time, the often-overlooked human elements of airport security, including situational awareness, observation and intuition, need to be emphasized now more than ever. It is those soft skills that hold the real key to looking for the bomber and not just the bomb.

Hotel Crisis Management Needs Moving to the Next Level

The Tohoku disaster shows how important is for hoteliers to move beyond the traditional crisis management approaches and plan how they will be able to continue to operate under the immediate aftermath's adverse conditions. Oxford Brookes' Alexandros Paraskevas explains the basic components of a hotel's business continuity plan.

The ongoing tragedy in Japan shows that the crisis we are facing today and increasingly tomorrow are far from being linear; they are becoming more complex, interconnected and transboundary. In this situation we have a unique in magnitude earthquake that hit Japan's infrastructure, followed by a devastating tsunami flooding its coastline and threatening countries ranging from the Philippines, Taiwan and Korea to Hawaii, the North and South American coasts. But the disaster did not stop there: the meltdown at the Fukushima Daiichi nuclear power plant near the town of Okuma is complicating even further an already complex disaster by adding a series of severe energy disruptions in the best case and the threat of a nuclear disaster far worse than the one we faced in Chernobyl in 1986.

Crisis situations like this underline the need for carefully designed crisis management plans that go beyond the standard evacuation processes that are normally practised and tested by hotels. Having wardens and assembly points in a safe distance somewhere in the perimeter of the property and persons assigned to have lists with guest and employee names is not enough any more.

In the case of an evacuation for example, apart from the logistics of the evacuation per se, hoteliers need to also consider the "what then?" question. Where do we take the evacuees? Is there a plan for alternative accommodation sites or we leave them in their fate? What happens to their luggage and personal effects left behind? Do we have a process in place for moving these to their new accommodation sites? How do we keep our employees help us in managing the process? What about their families?

The Tohoku earthquake of last week left most hotels with minor or no damages at all but nevertheless affected in a number of ways. Some can not be evacuated because of the floods; others have to accommodate stranded guests and evacuees from other areas; all of them will have to deal with continuous energy disruptions and water shortages in addition to protecting their facility from a potential radioactive fallout. Regardless of the level of disruption to their operations from this disaster, these hotels and business units must resume their functions and address their customers' needs in a properly organised manner. The better they are prepared for these challenges the faster they will bounce back to 'business as usual' and this will give them a valuable competitive advantage.

Therefore crisis management planning has to go beyond dealing with the disaster itself and move to the level of 'business continuity' which is concerned with how we are going to continue our basic operations under disaster conditions. There are three basic components that need to be considered: people, facilities and processes.

The people component will be looking at staff and guest welfare in case of a major disruption, especially when they move to alternate locations or if there are victims. In the pre-disruption period, the planning should be looking at the chain-of-command in the hotel, including the notification process and the call trees. Necessary for this task will be an up-to-date contact information database. In the aftermath of a disruption, depending on its severity, the planning should be looking at the creation of an information/ support system for guests' and staff's families, the co-ordination of victim counselling, and to ensure that appropriate duty of care is in place.

The facilities component, apart from the checks on structural integrity, security and full compliance with safety standards (both company and regulatory) should include plans for alternate easily accessible accommodation for guests during the period of disruption. Periodic tests should also be planned and records kept of evacuation procedures and safety and security measures in place on site.

The process component will be concerned with the availability, resumption, continuity and recovery of all those processes and services deemed necessary for the operation of the hotel (check-in, check-out, guest accounts, housekeeping, food and beverage) as well as the resources necessary for them (staffing levels, alternative energy sources, lighting, heating, water supply and pressure, etc).

In a disaster like in Japan, therefore the primary concern would be employee and guest safety. All guests and employees should be accounted for and emergency 'skeleton staff' should be assigned with specific duties in shifts, so that they can check their own families as well as get some rest. In the broader area of the affected region (Miyagi, Iwate and Fukushima) temporary shelters should be made available to hotel guests, if hotels suffered structural damage, and guests provided with basic necessities such as food, water and blankets. Due to power disruption there is a high risk for the hotels' food supplies to deteriorate soon therefore it is suggested that they are all cooked in the shelter and distributed to guests and to the local community as a gesture of solidarity.

Expected aftershocks of 7.7R suggest that shelters should be located in higher ground since another tsunami is possible. In co-ordination with local authorities, given that the Sendai airport remains closed and the Shinkansen (high speed rail) out of operation, possible evacuation routes towards Nigatta and Tokyo or other major cities should be explored. Conventional rail lines are expected to be in operation relatively soon and these may provide a window of opportunity-as long as it lasts. Same routes would serve to bring in food, water and other supplies (e.g., propane gas bottles) necessary for the resumption of basic hotel processes and services. These can be sourced by unaffected suppliers or by sister hotels (if any) outside the affected region.

Properties outside the impacted region will maintain their operation but will have to be able to withstand aftershocks (therefore structural inspections are strongly recommended) and an overflow of evacuees as well as existing guests who cannot leave the country. Provision must be made for major disruption in utility services and the management needs to 'train' both guests and staff in safety procedures not only for the expected aftershocks but also for the case of a nuclear emergency. Since, apart from the Fukushima power plant, five more plants are reported to be under 'severe stress' the possibility of more meltdowns is high. Hotel management and staff need to be prepared for such a possibility and take the necessary protective measures if and when needed. In the absence of a specific CBRN (Chemical, Biological, Radiological, Nuclear) policy, the hotel may follow the processes planned for a pandemic or seek advice from the local authorities.

By planning these three components (people, facilities and processes) for the immediate aftermath of a disaster, hoteliers will have made an important step to the next level of crisis management and build up their property's resilience to disasters, regardless of their severity and complexity.

2

Crisis Management

We live in ever-changing times, where consumers are increasingly aware, lawyers are ever more litigious and the media increasingly willing to expose any weakness in a hospitality organisation or tourist destination.

A company or region in the midst of a crisis cannot completely control these factors, as events in Asia Pacific have demonstrated loud and clear over the past 12 months.

However, sufficient preparation and effective management can take the edge off the above factors. Companies and destinations are now realising that they not only have a moral obligation, but also may need to take a legal stance to be prepared to cope with incidents that involve their clients.

Planning, though critical, is not the only component. Training, conducting drills, testing procedures and providing additional external resources are other important functions.

By doing the above, organisations can go a long way to emerging from such incidents with their reputations and/or corporate image intact. Good crisis management can be divided in four sections, as shown in the chart below. The lessons learned in Bali are manifold and must be now used to prepare other destinations, as well as all their stakeholders-including hotels-for future crises.

In essence, the following "components" are required in order to handle any crisis situation effectively:

* Leadership (crisis coordination);

* Adequate emergency response (ambulance/paramedics/ medical support);
* Victim identification;
* Media relations;
* Family assistance;
* Information dissemination;
* Internal and external communications.

An effective emergency response and good family assistance will reduce the frustrations that many people experience when caught up in the aftermath of a major incident. Besides going a long way to ensuring effective crisis management, it is also a humane, caring and compassionate way to respond.

Few crises will seem as dramatic as New York or Bali-unless it is your own. When your crisis occurs, the hardest part of dealing with it can involve answering the public call for information-as personified by a TV correspondent or newspaper reporter who shows up on your doorstep or on your telephone line to get the story.

How well you respond depends on how well you are prepared. While the existence of some of the above components may be based on the assumption of the pre-existence of a structured and experienced emergency services (police, fire and ambulance), this would be an unrealistic expectation. in many situations.

However, there are still some basic steps that governments/ regions can look at in order to enhance their level of preparedness.

This involves the triad of:

* Planning (developing written plans);
* Training (selecting and training the initial crisis responders); and
* Regular rehearsals (conducting "major incident" exercises).

Local governments-or, even better, regional organisation like ASEANTA and/or PATA-could take the lead in this, and enhance their image, by;

* Creating awareness amongst the industry;

* Organising training sessions for all stakeholders; and
* Communicating their efforts to the consumer.

The key to success is intensive training, although indepth consultations towards establishing the exact needs of the participants is needed to tailor the final curricula to local, regional and inter-regional training activities.

The focus of the training sessions must be on senior and intermediate levels of management, with the aim that, by the end of the course, all those attending will be knowledgeable about the following :

Stage 1 : Before the Crisis;

* What constitutes a real crisis;
* Why crisis management is necessary;
* Assessing potential crisis issues;
* Crisis-management team responsibilities;
* Setting up the emergency communication system; and
* Major elements of crisis management planning.

Stage 2 : During and after the Crisis;

Structuring the media centre;

* Designating spokespersons;
* Preparing "message points";
* Interview techniques and guidelines;
* Controlling the story; and
* Starting the "back-to-normal" plans.

In almost every instance of successful response to a crisis, management and response activities consisting of sound operating execution, coupled with superior communications, predominate.

Operational response is essential-it's the one that saves lives, property and other assets. The ability to communicate is no less important-it's the one that saves the business. The simple fact is: perception is reality, and public perception of your company's reaction to a crisis is as important as your operating response.

There are no clear boundaries with any crisis. There is rarely a single moment when one can say an incident or issue has transformed into a crisis. Crisis-management experts recommend adopting a low threshold when defining a crisis, erring on the side of caution and assuming that a small episode can escalate into a crisis at warp speed.

The repercussions and impact of crises in tourism is manifested across a series of stakeholders. To avert mismanagement of crises and its consequences, organisations and destinations need to enhance their capacity to understand and respond to crisis situations. We all need to sharpen our skills at predicting and preventing such situations.

In a down market, many hotel revenue managers strive with how best to manage declining demand and the pressures to reduce rate, which caused hotels to re-examine their rates and the potential value they offer. As a result, too many hotels reduce overall rates only to find that lower rates don't create demand and produce lower overall revenue.

Pricing is a crucial revenue management (RM) practice affecting both occupancy and RevPAR (revenue per available room). In order for a RM strategy to succeed, a balance should be maintained between simulating sufficient demand to maximize occupancy, while not leaving money on the table in the form of too-low ADR (average daily rate). In the current environment of price transparency, rates/prices take on an even greater role. Thus, suggesting the right rate to a potential customer has become one of the most important aspects of revenue management.

With the world economy going down, hotels felt the pressure to reduce rates to maintain market share, boost occupancy or stimulate demand, and stay competitive *(as seen in the graph below)*. The continued dropping of prices by competitors has created pricing and marketing challenges. On the one hand, this discounting generated concerns about the impact of discounts on the long-term rate integrity of the hotel and the difficulty that the hotel might face with increasing prices again after an extended period of offering discounted prices. On the other hand, deep discounts can ultimately affect and deteriorate the brand image of a hotel. Customers make associations between price and quality, and perceived quality is a central component to any hotel's brand image. Therefore, a rate discount negatively affects a hotel's brand (However, many hotels define their brand by bargain prices and a high rate does not guarantee positive brand development).

How do we minimize the depth of the fall?

Is Rate the answer? If yes, how low does one go in price discounting?

Price is one of many levers, used alone it will do more *DAMAGE* than good.

Don't drop your trousers!

Few Tips on Price Management

- Don't lower your rates-if you do it now, customers get used to it. It's hard to get back the revenue you are expecting as it will take a long time to get your rates up again.
- Optimize the occasions you have (high seasons, exhibitions...) and watch high as well as low demand periods.
- Examine those channels (GDS, 3rd party distribution channels) that have the highest and lowest ADR.

If discounting is damaging to a hotel's brand, and maintaining one static or fixed rate is equally detrimental to RevPAR and occupancy, then the solution lies in variable pricing, modified in real-time to best match demand conditions, also known as dynamic pricing. This eliminates the possibility or not to engage in across-the board discounting. Instead, the highest rate likely to generate a sale is presented to the right customer at the right time.

The past months and/or year have seen extraordinary change on account of global economic difficulty. Hotels haven't learned that dropping prices will not recover enough revenues to cover the discounting. These just cause price wars in the long run. Thus, hotels need to adapt and update their RM strategy to profit from the current and future economic climate, by maintaining rate integrity, resisting the urge to discount and holding their brand image and values.

How can hotels manage price during an economic downturn? How do they respond to a price war? What are possible approaches to limit long-term damage? Stay tuned for Crisis Management part 2 in the next issue to obtain insights on price and non-price methods.

About h-hotelier.com

h-hotelier is a hospitality services firm that offers a holistic approach to business intelligence solutions, revenue management consultancy, training and development programs among many others.

h-hotelier product h-enigma simplifies the concept of business intelligence, making it affordable and very easy to use and understand, while at the same time keeping its rich aspect as one of its main strong point. h-enigma consist of a reporting tool with a yield, CRM and shopping module incorporated in it.

h-hotelier brings together talented professionals in the hotel industry to help your company streamline its processes to enhance its profitability and improve its overall performance.

Crisis Management Part 2

During the economic downturn, demand declines and market prices decreases adversely impacting profit margins. In this challenging environment, what is the right strategy for managing pricing and demand: a focus on short-term revenue or long-term growth?

As managers are concerned about price-related issues when business slows, they tend to offer more discounts to meet revenue targets. It is important to emphasis that large and non-systematic discounting may harm a business in the short and long run. In the short run, the demand level captured through low prices is not enough to offset the lost revenues as a result of discounting. In the long run, customer expectations are affected as managers' future ability to modify the pricing policies lessens.

There are several levers at hotels' disposal to reduce the decline in revenue per available room (RevPar). These (price and non-price approaches) are discussed below.

Use Better Pricing

Cutting prices across the board is not a key to success as this strategy impacts customers' perceived value of the business, which makes it difficult for hotels to recover their preliminary positioning when better times come around. Rather, hotels must focus on particular market segments and distribution channels as rate decreases should be targeted and differentiated.

Set Intelligent Pricing Strategies

Pricing strategies must be used to result in advantageous redistribution of business such as: use of last minute promotions; open early bird rates at an aggressive level, long in advance; discount contracted rates rather than public rates; and use fencing to support rate differentiation strategies aimed at boosting average room rate (ARR).

These pricing strategies lead customers with specific requirements to certain rate types and conditions.

Develop Smart Customer Loyalty Schemes

A valuable source of information is available through customer profiles that allow hotels to develop loyalty through customized packaging and bundling of their products and services. This strategy results in gains achieved by both the customer and the hotel.

Assess Your Current and Prospective Customers

Price sensitivity of certain market segments and the possible emergence of new segments if new rates are offered are crucial factors to consider. Discounted rates should be directed at price sensitive market segments and rate fences should be created to avoid less price-sensitive customers from purchasing products at discounted rates. In addition, the hotel should recognize potential market segments interested in a selected discount and determine whether it is a market segment that fits in with the hotel brand image and positioning.

Use Opaque Distribution Channels

The use of opaque distribution channels (such as priceline.com and hotwire.com) allows hotels to offer discounts which are hidden to the customer. This strategy protects both the hotel's brand image and customers.

In a crisis situation, doing nothing is not an option. Taking short term actions, which produce modest benefits, might make you feel you are doing something effective and valuable, but consider whether or not they end up damaging the relationship you have and might have in the future with your customers. For the longer term, hotels should focus in retaining and acquiring profitable customers to survive during and prosper after the downturn.

Hotels try to keep profit margins up during hard times and seize this opportunity to attract new customers through intelligent loyalty schemes and appropriate discounting (as discussed above). As a result, hotels expect to retain these customers once the downturn is over.

To conclude, discounting and pricing strategies must be dealt with carefully during a market downturn. Success is established by hotels that are able to define short term pricing improvements through the implementation of some of the key ingredients of successful crisis management such as rate differentiation, fencing, adoption of loyalty programs, smart bundling, opaque distribution channels and development additional market segment.

About h-hotelier.com

h-hotelier is a hospitality services firm that offers a holistic approach to business intelligence solutions, revenue management consultancy, training and development programs among many others.

h-hotelier product h-enigma simplifies the concept of business intelligence, making it affordable and very easy to use and understand, while at the same time keeping its rich aspect as one of its main strong point. h-enigma consist of a reporting tool with a yield, CRM and shopping module incorporated in it.

h-hotelier brings together talented professionals in the hotel industry to help your company streamline its processes to enhance its profitability and improve its overall performance.

A Critical Evaluation of the Human Resource Practices and Policies in an Organisation

A Definition of Human Resource Management

Harvey (1994) suggests that *"human resource management involves the total management of people within the firm, using the notion of people as valuable assets, increasing in value with time, an asset to be used to generate profit or maintain survival in a competitive world."*

Mullins (1997) quotes Willman for whom human resource management is concerned with *"mechanisms through which the organisation attracts candidates for employment, selects them, introduces them to the organisation's structure and culture, motivates them to perform a given set of tasks, pays them for this and seeks to identify their potential for future development. It is then concerned with systems of promotion, manpower planning, succession planning and coping with labour turnover of one form or another."*

Mullins (1997) also said: *"The contributions from an effective personnel function are not always readily apparent and nor are they easy to identify. Over a period of time, however, some quantified measures should provide management with an indication of its effectiveness. Possible examples include labour costs, staff turnover and stability index, complaints from customers, absenteeism/timekeeping, breakages, scrap or waste, accidents at work, promotions and staff development, discipline and grievance procedures and dismissals."*

A Brief Outline of the Nature of the Organization

The organisation described is a privately and closely owned hotel company that owns and manages hotels and catering businesses. There are more than 2,000 people working for the company but it has neither a Personnel Department nor a Human Resources Department. The company's President thought that such departments were unnecessary because their function will cost money without delivering a tangible benefit. However, trying to satisfy its functions, he established that each manager of an hotel or catering business was responsible not only to transmit to its employees "the company's philosophy" but to recruit and to train new employees and motivate all of them, old and new.

Identification and Analysis of the Various Human Resources Management Practices Present in the Organization

The company president's system of management is as described by Likert (1996) as system number 1 *"Exploitive authoritative type where management uses fear and threats, communication is downward; superiors and subordinates are psychologically far apart and the bulk of decisions are taken at the top of the organisation."*

Consequently, there is no written policy relating to the company's strategy, culture, cost, potential, flexibility, etc. The managers of the hotel and catering businesses met the President only once a year during the Company's Annual Convention. At this occasion the President appears accessible and friendly and speaks about the state of the Company's business, and the financial and business targets achieved or not achieved and the goals to strive for in the coming year. He always finishes his speech saying how important the human component is for the company, stressing that for the future growth of the company it is essential that every worker, including himself, performs his or her task in the best way.

Nevertheless, most of the those present at the successive Annual Conventions did not take much notice of the words of the President's speech and all his promises related to the implementation of Human Resources Management, because for many years, there was nobody in the Head Office in charge of developing and implementing it.

Evaluation of the Effectiveness of Each Practice Policy

Despite the fact that there is neither written policy nor a personnel function or human resources department, people working in the Company are sufficiently satisfied with their work because their salary is reasonable and competitive with the market. In most of the cases, it allows the staff to maintain some status outside the company – an extrinsic outcome. However the staff do not have a strong bond towards the company because no one-except their immediate manager-appears to be concerned about them, their work, or if they have needs to grow in their work.

Consequently, the staff does not experience strong intrinsic outcomes. There are some workers for whom pay was the only outcome that they valued. However in the opposite way, there are other workers for whom pay and working conditions were not important enough. They need intrinsic outcomes such as praise or recognition of a job well done. In both cases the staff are not very much committed to the organisation.

Ideas for Improving Human Resource Management Practice & Policy

The implementation in the company of human resources

management is without any doubt of immediate importance especially in view of the deterioration of the firm's performance.

As Mullins (1997) writes: *"The nature of human resources management will determine both business efficiency and the performance of individual members. It is important to think of intangible benefits such as improved morale, job satisfaction and staff development."*

The company needs personnel policies and organisation. Lockwood (1992) sources Peter Drucker saying that he identified five basic "operations" to start implementing human resources management. In the first place, it is necessary to set objectives, deciding what should be done to achieve those objectives and communicating them to the people whose performance is needed to achieve them.

Second, managers organise by dividing work activity into manageable groups. Next, managers motivate and communicate, making a team out of people responsible for various jobs. The fourth element is the job of measurement, analysing, appraising and interpreting performance. Fifth and finally, managers develop and direct people.

Managing people requires some relevant functions as planning and organising, motivating, communicating, leading, and controlling. Within each of these functions different levels of management will undertake different activities. Lockwood (1992) outlined such a ladder of responsibilities for the hospitality industry in the following chart.

As Mullins (1997) said the implementation of human resources management should be based on philosophies of managerial behaviour and the employee relationship.

Those philosophies should include:

- respect for the individual
- the recognition of the staff's needs and expectations at workjustice in treatment and a fair reward systemstability of employmentgood working environment and conditions of serviceopportunities for personnel development and career progression democratic functioning of the organisation full observance of all the laws and codes of conduct relating to empioyment.

Evaluation of the Likely Efectiveness of Ideas

This evaluation of the implementation in the company is done in terms of acceptability to those involved in the business feasibility in terms of finance, resources and systems, and the extent to which the idea would improve organisational effectiveness and contribution to competitive advantage in this company.

The implementation of HR policies and procedures should be very positive and the staff's acceptability very high if the managerial behaviour changes. This change should be a shared and committed responsibility. Everybody should be involved – from the autocratic President down The company should, post-implementation, be trying to achieve the aim to develop the potential of every member of staff, to obtain their best contribution which, obviously will contribute in a very positive way to the company's performance.

It is important to note that the implementation and the daily activity of human resources management will cost money, which could prove to be a major stumbling block as far as the decision-maker, the president, is concerned.

But it is important to say that all the money invested by the company through staffing the organisation, which includes employee training, clarifying aims and objectives and motivating people will get evident benefits for the employees to help the customers thereby enhancing the company's well-being. The company's prestige and thus business will increase because its employees are well trained, friendly, motivated and knowledgeable about their work. Consequently, the customers' satisfaction will rise because the company meets their expectations and demands. Finally, the employees will feel that they work for a company that is concerned about them, their professionalism and their future.

Risk Management Tools

Risk Management is a non-intuitive field of study, where the most simple of models consist of a probability multiplied by an impact. Even understanding individual risks is difficult as multiple probabilities can contribute to Risk total probability, and impacts can be "units" of cost, time, events (for example, a catastrophe), market states, etc. This is further complicated by there being no straightforward approach to consider how multiple risks will influence one another or increase the overall risk of the subject of analysis.

Risk management tools allow planners to explicitly address uncertainty by identifying and generating metrics, parameterizing, prioritizing, and developing mitigations, and tracking risk. These capabilities are very difficult to track without some form of documentation or, with the advent of information technology, software application. Simple risk management tools allow documentation. More sophisticated tools provide a visual display of risks, while the most cutting edge, such as those developed by Air Force Research Laboratory Headquarters, are able to aggregate risks into a coherent picture. A few tools have predictive capability, which, through collaboration between partners allow fair partition of risks and improvement of business relations.

List of Risk Management Tools

Risk-performs risk analysis using Monte Carlo simulation to show many possible outcomes in Microsoft Excel spreadsheet—and predicts how likely they are to occur.

Active Risk Manager-(ARM), addresses enterprise-wide risk management (ERM) and governance, risk and compliance (GRC) requirements, enabling the identification, communication, analysis and mitigation of risks and opportunities in both quantitative and qualitative formats.

The Aggregate Risk Tool-(ART), generates predictive financial data from any probability-impact model.

Bow tie diagrams-a fault identifying visual tool.

Capital asset pricing model-(CAPM) is used to determine the appropriate required rate of return of an asset, if that asset be added to an already well diversified portfolio, based on non-diversifiable risk.

Control Estratégico de Riesgo (CERO)-Software tool with specific tools for each activity of the risk management process. With clients mostly in Latin America.

Cost/Risk Identification & Management System (CRIMS)-Integrated Probabilistic risk assessment model with cost and other variables.

Crystal Ball-performs risk analysis using Monte Carlo simulation, analyzes time series and creates statistical forecasts, and determines the best values of decision variables based on stochastic optimization, all in a Microsoft Excel spreadsheet.

Cura Enterprise-Cura's GRC platform is a highly configurable solution that meets organizational requirements, and provides a balance between qualified and quantified data, all of which can be normalized and reported on across the entire organization.

Cura Quants-Is a quantitative modeling solution designed to integrate with the existing Enterprise GRC Platform. Cura Quants enables customers to quickly and easily quantify the impact of capital and project related risks as well as the effects of accompanying treatment strategies.

Dymonda-Dymonda is a software tool that enables Dynamic Flowgraph Methodology (DFM) modelling and analysis. The model explicitly identifies the cause-and-effect and timing relationships between parameters and states that are best suited to describe a particular system behaviour.

Resolve by RPM'"-Cloud software toolbox to manage, track and audit processes associated with risk and safety areas within corporations.

IBM OpenPages GRC Platform-Integrated enterprise governance, risk and compliance solution that includes modules for operational risk management, policy and compliance management, financial controls management, IT governance, and internal audit management.

Methodware-Methodware's ERA is a GRC solution that is a scalable,and flexible tool to automate, identify and track risk across departments, regions, and business units effectively transparency.

Operational risk management-The continual cyclic process which includes risk assessment, risk decision making, and implementation of risk controls, which results in acceptance, mitigation, or avoidance of risk.

PIMS Risk-Is a complete risk framework for identifying, analysing and evaluate threats and opportunities. Created for and used by major companies in oil and energy sector.

Probabilistic risk assessment (PRA), Probability Consequence (P/C) or Probability Impact Model-Simple model where estimates of probability of occurrence are multiplied by the consequence (cost, schedule delay, etc.). This is the most common tool, examples are RiskNav and RiskMatrix.

Reference class forecasting – Predicts the outcome of a planned, risky action based on actual outcomes in a reference class of similar actions to that being forecast.

RiskAid products-collaborative web/intranet-based risk management software environments for projects, operations and Enterprise Risk Management (ERM), developed by Risk Reasoning.

RiskAoA – A predictive tool used to discriminate between proposals, choices or alternatives, by expressing risk for each as a single number, so a proposal's trade-space between cost, scheduled time and risk from its desired characteristics can be compared instantly. RiskAoA and variations of PRA are the only approved tools for United States Department of Defence Military Acquisition.

RiskComplete-Tracks project risk from planning approached to measuring tasks, from concept to manufacture.

RiskIssue.com-An online risk management tool for business, projects, teams and processes.

RiskLike'Con-A free probabilistic risk assessment tool. Displays risks in the industry-standard matrix; Probability vs. Consequence.

Risk register-A project planning and organizational risk assessment tool. It is often referred to as a Risk Log.

RiskPath-An improvement of RiskAoA, available to the public, where forecasts are quantified for each alternative.

Safety case-An assessment of the potential risks in a project and of the measures to be taken to minimize them.

SAPHIRE-A probabilistic risk and reliability assessment software tool. SAPHIRE stands for Systems Analysis Programs for Hands-on Integrated Reliability Evaluations.

SCHRAM-The Schedule Risk Assessment Manager; allows the generation of risk-adjusted schedules; the time of least risk, consequence of rushed/broken schedules. Allows realistic planning based on operational realities.

TRIMS-Provides insight as a knowledge-based tool that measures technical risk management rather than cost and schedule.

Unified Risk Assessment and Regulatory Compliance-A standards based end-to-end comprehensive cloud service from Unisys that performs model based risk assessment and also provides a real time dashboard for Regulatory & Policy Compliance traceability and transparency.

Xero Risk-Web based enterprise risk governance tool to identify, track and balance risks across an organization using user definable assessment and impact criteria.

Risk Register

A risk register is a tool commonly used in project planning and organisational risk assessments. It is often referred to as a Risk Log.

This tool is widely used within Risk Management for identifying, analysing and managing risks. In this context a project risk is essentially an uncertain event that, should it occur, will have an impact on the project (this could be positive or negative).

It contains the information on the identified and collected project risks that the project team identifies when estimating and adjusting the activity durations for risks.

The project team considers the extent to which the effects of risks are included in the baseline duration estimate for each schedule activity, particularly the risks with high impact.

Example Contents

A wide range of contents for a risk register exist and recommendations are made by the Project Management Institute Body of Knowledge (PMBOK) and PRINCE2 among others. In addition many companies provide software tools that act as risk registers. Typically a risk register contains:

- A description of the risk
- The impact should this event actually occur
- The probability of its occurrence
- Risk score is multiplication of Probability and Impact

- A summary of the planned response should the event occur
- A summary of the mitigation (the actions taken in advance to reduce the probability and/or impact of the event)
- The risks are often given a ranking with the highest priority risks clearly identified to all involved.

Useful Terminology

In a "qualitative" risk register descriptive terms are used: for example a risk might have a "High" impact and a "Medium" probability. In a "quantitative" risk register the descriptions are enumerated: for example a risk might have a "$1m" impact and a "50%" probability.

Contingent response-the actions to be taken should the risk event actually occur.

Contingency-the budget allocated to the contingent response

Trigger-an event that itself results in the risk event occurring (for example the risk event might be "flooding" and "heavy rainfall" the trigger)

Social Risk Management

Social risk management (SRM) is a new conceptual framework assigned and designed by the World Bank. The objective of SRM is to extend the traditional framework of social policy to the non-market based social protection of which its three primary strategies include prevention, mitigation, and coping. It is now well understood that social unrest is positively parallel to the poverty. Assisting individuals, households and communities to elevate living standard above the poverty level will harmonize global economy and strengthen the social security.

Strategies

Prevention Strategies

Prevention strategies are those implemented to avert a risk. Some typical measures could be:

- In the labor market, SRM intervention targets skill training or job function improvement to reduce the risk of un/

under-employment or low wages which are probably man-made.

- In the financial market, SRM emphasize on optimizing macroeconomic policies to reduce the shocks of financial crisis, such as oil price surges, or unpredictable market moves on currencies, indices and blue chip stocks.
- For natural disasters and environment degradation, SRM are gear to deploy a networked warning system or sustainable, renewable and environmental friendly eco-system to minimize the impact of the consequences.
- In health care, SRM focuses on the prevention of pandemic illnesses by implementing vaccination and public health education programs. Setting up rehabilitation centres to help drug addicts.
- In the public social security, establishing a community-based insurance schemes to compensate pensioners, disability or chronic illness person's living expenses. Building up nursing homes for elderlies and setting up public housing for homelesses and orphans.

Mitigation Strategies

Mitigation strategies focus on reducing the risk. Common practices are:

- In the financial market, diversifying portfolios or hedging stocks to decrease the exposure of the financial risks.
- Microfinance to the poor or jobless people.

Coping Strategies

Coping strategies are designed to relieve the impact of the risk event once it has occurred. The typical examples are

- Issuing government relieve fund or publicly raising money.
- Setting up unemployment benefit schemes.

Source of Social Risks

The degree of social risks usually vary from idiosyncratic (micro), regional covariant (meso), to nation-wide covariant (macro).

Risk Governance

Risk governance is a systemic approach to decision making processes associated to natural and technological risks, based on the principles of cooperation, participation, mitigation and sustainability, adopted to achieve more effective risk management, that is convergent with other public and private policies. It seeks to reduce risk exposure and vulnerability by filling gaps in risk policy, in order to avoid or reduce human and economic costs caused by disasters.

Operational Risk Management

The term Operational Risk Management (ORM) is defined as a continual cyclic process which includes risk assessment, risk decision making, and implementation of risk controls, which results in acceptance, mitigation, or avoidance of risk. ORM is the oversight of operational risk, including the risk of loss resulting from inadequate or failed internal processes and systems; human factors; or external events.

Four Principles of ORM

The U.S. Department of Defence summarizes the principles of ORM as follows:

- Accept risk when benefits outweigh the cost.
- Accept no unnecessary risk.
- Anticipate and manage risk by planning.
- Make risk decisions at the right level.

Three Levels of ORM

In Depth : In depth risk management is used before a project is implemented, when there is plenty of time to plan and prepare. Examples of in depth methods include training, drafting instructions and requirements, and acquiring personal protective equipment.

Deliberate : Deliberate risk management is used at routine periods through the implementation of a project or process. Examples include quality assurance, on-the-job training, safety briefs, performance reviews, and safety checks.

Time Critical : Time critical risk management is used during operational exercises or execution of tasks. It is defined as the effective use of all available resources by individuals, crews, and teams to safely and effectively accomplish the mission or task using risk management concepts when time and resources are limited. Examples of tools used includes execution check-lists and change management. This requires a high degree of situational awareness.

ORM Process

In Depth

The International Organization for Standardization defines the risk management process in a four-step model:

1. Establish context
2. Risk assessment
   - o Risk identification
   - o Risk analysis
   - o Risk evaluation
3. Risk treatment
4. Monitor and review.

This process is cyclic as any changes to the situation (such as operating environment or needs of the unit) requires re-evaluation per step one.

Deliberate

The U.S. Department of Defence summarizes the deliberate level of ORM process in a five-step model:

1. Identify hazards
2. Assess hazards
3. Make risk decisions
4. Implement controls
5. Supervise (and watch for changes).

Time Critical

The U.S. Navy summarizes the time critical risk management process in a four-step model:

Assess the Situation

The three conditions of the Assess step are task loading, additive conditions, and human factors.

- Task loading refers to the negative effect of increased tasking on performance of the tasks.
- Additive factors refers to having a situational awareness of the cumulative effect of variables (conditions, etc.).
- Human factors refers to the limitations of the ability of the human body and mind to adapt to the work environment (e.g. stress, fatigue, impairment, lapses of attention, confusion, and wilful violations of regulations).

Balance Your Resources

This refers to balancing resources in three different ways:

- Balancing resources and options available. This means evaluating and leveraging all the informational, labor, equipment, and material resources available.
- Balancing Resources verses hazards. This means estimating how well prepared you are to safely accomplish a task and making a judgement cali.
- Balancing individual verses team effort. This means observing individual risk warning signs. It also means observing how well the team is communicating, knows the roles that each member is supposed to play, and the stress level and participation level of each team member.

Communicate Risks and Intentions

- Communicate hazards and intentions.
- Communicate to the right people.
- Use the right communication style. Asking questions is a technique to opening the lines of communication. A direct and forceful style of communication gets a specific result from a specific situation.

Do and debrief. (Take action and monitor for change.)

This is accomplished in three different phases:

- Mission Completion is a point where the exercise can be evaluated and reviewed in full.

- Execute and Gauge Risk involves managing change and risk while an exercise is in progess.
- Future Performance Improvements refers to preparing a "lessons learned" for the next team that plans or executes a task.

Benefits of ORM

1. Reduction of operational loss.
2. Lower compliance/auditing costs.
3. Early detection of unlawful activities.
4. Reduced exposure to future risks.

Chief Operational Risk Officer

The role of the Chief Operational Risk Officer (CORO) continues to evolve and gain importance. In addition to being responsible for setting up a robust Operational Risk Management function at companies, the role also plays an important part in increasing awareness of the benefits of sound operational risk management.

Most complex financial institutions have a Chief Operational Risk Officer. The position is also required for Banks that fall into the Basel II Advanced Measurement Approach "mandatory" category.

ORM Software

The impact of the Enron failure and the implementation of the Sarbanes-Oxley Act has caused several software development companies to create enterprise-wide software packages to manage risk. These software systems allow the financial audit to be executed at lower cost.

Forrester Research has identified 115 Governance, Risk and Compliance vendors that cover operational risk management projects. Active Agenda is an open source project dedicated to operational risk management.

Risk Management Information Systems

Risk Management Information Systems (RMIS) are typically computerized systems that assist in consolidating property values, claims, policy, and exposure information and provide the tracking and management reporting capabilities to enable you to monitor and control your overall cost of risk.

General Overview

The management of risk data and information is key to the success of any risk management effort regardless of an organization's size or industry sector. Risk management information systems/services (RMIS) are used to support expert advice and cost-effective information management solutions around key processes such as:

- Risk identification and assessment
- Risk control
- Risk financing.

Typically, RMIS facilitates the consolidation of insurance related information, such as claims from multiple sources,property values, policy information, and exposure information, into one system. Often, Risk Management Information Services/Systems (RMIS) applies primarily to "casualty" claims/loss data systems. Such casualty coverages include Auto Liability, Auto Physical Damage, Workers' Compensation, General Liability and Products Liability.

RMIS products are designed to provide their insured organizations and their brokers with basic policy and claim information via electronic access, and most recently, via the Internet. This information is essential for managing individual claims, identifying trends, marketing an insurance program, loss forecasting, actuarial studies and internal loss data communication within a client organization. They may also provide the tracking and management reporting capabilities to enable one to monitor and control overall cost of risk in an efficient and cost-effective manner.

In the context of the acronym RMIS, the word "risk" pertains to an insured or self-insured organization. This is important because prior to the advent of RMIS, insurance company loss information reporting typically organized loss data around insurance policy numbers. The historical focus on insurance policies detracted from a clear, coherent and consolidated picture of a single customer's loss experience. The advent of RMIS in the 1980s was a breakthrough step in the insurance industry's evolution toward persistent and focused understanding of their end-customer needs. Typically, the best solution for your organization depends on whether it is enhancing an existing RMIS system, ensuring the highest level of data quality, or designing and implementing a new system while maintaining a focus on state-of-the-art technology.

Common Types of RMIS

Most major insurance companies (carriers), broker/agents, and Third Party Administrators (TPAs)offer/provide at least one external RMIS product to their insureds (clients) and any brokers involved in the insurance program. Most commonly, RMIS products allow individual claim detail look-up, basic trend report production, policy summaries and ad hoc queries. The resulting information can then be shared throughout the client's organization, usually for insurance program cost allocation, loss prevention and effective claim management at the local level. More advanced products allow multiple claim data sources to be consolidated into one "Master RMIS," which is essential for most large client organizations with complex insurance programs.

The primary users of RMIS are risk/insurance departments of insured organizations and any insurance broker involved. Interestingly, it is much less common for the insured's safety department and vehicle operations department to have access to RMIS despite similar interest in the data. In fact, safety and vehicle operations of larger organizations typically maintain their own separate database systems of "accidents/incidents," many of which will correlate to RMIS claim data.

Insurance companies normally use a different version of externally provided RMIS for internal use, such as by underwriting and loss control personnel. Occasionally, there could be timing or other differences that could cause data discrepancies between the internal system and externally provided RMIS.

Insurance brokers have a similar need for access to their insured client's claim data. Brokers are normally added as an additional user to the RMIS product provided to their clients by the insurance carrier and TPAs. The information available from RMIS is critical to the broker for interfacing effectively with their counterparts in the insurance carrier and TPAs. Additionally, effectively presented RMIS information that shows trends and analysis is essential to successfully marketing their clients' insurance programs. Insurance carrier and Third-Party Administer (TPA) claim adjusters traditionally use claims management systems to collect and manage claim information and to administer claims. Some client organizations, however, may choose to manage certain types of claims or those within a loss retention layer and thus use this type of system as well.

Typically, the claims management system provides the primary data to RMIS products. RMIS products in turn provide an externally accessed view into the client's claims data. RMIS products are commonly available directly from larger insurance carriers and TPAs, but the most advanced systems are often offered by independent RMIS vendors. Independent RMIS vendor systems are most desirable when a client organization needs to consolidate claims data from multiple current insurance programs and/or past programs with current program information.

Key Vendor Attributes and Differences

Along with insurance carriers, broker/agents and TPAs that offer their own proprietary systems, there are a variety of direct RMIS technology companies who sell to direct insureds and even the carriers, broker/agents and TPAs themselves.

Major differences among RMIS vendors include:

- Currency of technology (Internet-based vs. Internet-accessible);
- System speed (response time for screen changes, report generation time, etc.);
- Flexibility in meeting client requirements (custom screen views, client-defined data fields, special reports, etc.);
- Ongoing support service quality (availability of senior/ quality technical support, help desk availability, dedicated staff and stability, etc.);
- Data quality control (data conversion accuracy, data source cleanup, etc.);
- Pricing (first-year cost, ongoing cost, custom programming charges, data record storage fees);

- Availability of related modules (property exposure management, policy management, claim/incident setup, Occupational Safety and Health Administration (OSHA) record keeping, claims audits, etc.);
- Turnaround time for data loads;
- Foreign conversion/support (financial fields, language, fluent support staff, etc.)

RMIS system compatibility varies among carriers, broker/ agents and TPAs. However, quality independent RMIS vendors by design can take almost any claim data source and convert or map the data to their particular system's file structure. A few major insurance carriers offer similar consolidation services, i.e., combining the insured client's current claim data with another carrier's or TPA's data for the same insured client. The other data sources can be for current separate insurance programs or from expired insurance programs. Usually, this type of consolidation service is performed to accommodate their major policyholder organizations. Major TPAs, however, more commonly offer such data consolidation services.

Average RMIS Costs and RMIS Market Drivers

The cost of a typical independent RMIS product varies from $60,000 to $150,000 for the first year, and ongoing annual charges are slightly less. Insurance company RMIS product lines typically average around $50,000 for the first user, but they often offer less expensive light-weight versions for claim look-up only. More costly full-featured products are sometimes available with more advanced reporting systems. The products are usually priced on a per-user basis on a sliding scale for a larger number of users. Insured clients' brokers are given access at no cost or occasionally for a flat annual fee for multiple insured clients with a particular broker.

TPAs commonly include one or two RMIS access IDs within their claims management pricing to encourage both the client's broker and the client to use their claim look-up product. Normally, beyond the first two access IDs, the pricing follows the same per-user range of the insurance companies. The cost drivers of RMIS include:

- Number of user/access IDs

- Number of outside claim data sources that must be converted (carriers and TPAs do not have to convert their own data)
- Frequency of outside claim data updates
- Special programming/report development charges
- Training of users (initial and annual users' conferences).

Clearly, higher cost systems do not always correlate to better performance in terms of both usefulness and speed. While most carrier and TPA RMIS systems are similarly priced, the independent RMIS vendors' price range varies significantly, as previously mentioned.

Crisis Management

Crisis management is the process by which an organization deals with a major event that threatens to harm the organization, its stakeholders, or the general public. Three elements are common to most definitions of crisis: (a) a threat to the organization, (b) the element of surprise, and (c) a short decision time. Venette argues that "crisis is a process of transformation where the old system can no longer be maintained." Therefore the fourth defining quality is the need for change. If change is not needed, the event could more accurately be described as a failure or incident. In contrast to risk management, which involves assessing potential threats and finding the best ways to avoid those threats, crisis management involves dealing with threats after they have occurred. It is a discipline within the broader context of management consisting of skills and techniques required to identify, assess, understand, and cope with a serious situation, especially from the moment it first occurs to the point that recovery procedures start.

Crisis management consists of:

- Methods used to respond to both the reality and perception of crises.
- Establishing metrics to define what scenarios constitute a crisis and should consequently trigger the necessary response mechanisms.
- Communication that occurs within the response phase of emergency management scenarios.

Crisis management methods of a business or an organization are called Crisis Management Plan. Crisis management is occasionally referred to as incident management, although several industry specialists such as Peter Power argue that the term crisis management is more accurate.

The credibility and reputation of organizations is heavily influenced by the perception of their responses during crisis situations. The organization and communication involved in responding to a crisis in a timely fashion makes for a challenge in businesses. There must be open and consistent communication throughout the hierarchy to contribute to a successful crisis communication process. The related terms emergency management and business continuity management focus respectively on the prompt but short lived "first aid" type of response (e.g. putting the fire out) and the longer term recovery and restoration phases (e.g. moving operations to another site). Crisis is also a facet of risk management, although it is probably untrue to say that Crisis Management represents a failure of Risk Management since it will never be possible to totally mitigate the chances of catastrophes occurring.

Types of Crisis

During the crisis management process, it is important to identify types of crises in that different crises necessitate the use of different crisis management strategies. Potential crises are enormous, but crises can be clustered.

Lerbinger categorized seven types of crises;

1. Natural disaster
2. Technological crises
3. Confrontation
4. Malevolence
5. Organizational Misdeeds
6. Workplace Violence
7. Rumours.

Natural Crises

Natural crises, typically natural disasters considered as 'acts of God,' are such environmental phenomena as earthquakes, volcanic eruptions, tornadoes and hurricanes, floods, landslides, tsunamis, storms, and droughths that threaten life, property, and the environment itself.

Example: 2004 Indian Ocean earthquake (Tsunami).

Technological Crises

Technological crises are caused by human application of science and technology. Technological accidents inevitably occur when technology becomes complex and coupled and something goes wrong in the system as a whole (Technological breakdowns). Some technological crises occur when human error causes disruptions (Human breakdowns). People tend to assign blame for a technological disaster because technology is subject to human manipulation whereas they do not hold anyone responsible for natural disaster. When an accident creates significant environmental damage, the crisis is categorized as *megadamage*. Samples include software failures, industrial accidents, and oil spills.

Examples: Chernobyl disaster, Exxon Valdez oil spill

Confrontation Crises

Confrontation crises occur when discontented individuals and/or groups fight businesses, government, and various interest groups to win acceptance of their demands and expectations. The common type of confrontation crises is boycotts, and other types are picketing, sit-ins, ultimatums to those in authority, blockade or occupation of buildings, and resisting or disobeying police.

Example: Rainbow/PUSH's (People United to Serve Humanity) boycott of Nike.

Crises of Malevolence

An organization faces a crisis of malevolence when opponents or miscreant individuals use criminal means or other extreme tactics for the purpose of expressing hostility or anger toward, or seeking gain from, a company, country, or economic system, perhaps with the aim of destabilizing or destroying it. Sample crises include product tampering, kidnapping, malicious rumors, terrorism, and espionage.

Example: 1982 Chicago Tylenol murders

Crises of Organizational Misdeeds

Crises occur when management takes actions it knows will harm or place stakeholders at risk for harm without adequate precautions. Lerbinger specified three different types of crises of organizational misdeeds: crises of skewed management values, crises of deception, and crises of management misconduct.

Crises of Skewed Management Values

Crises of skewed management values are caused when managers favour short-term economic gain and neglect broader social values and stakeholders other than investors. This state of lopsided values is rooted in the classical business creed that focuses on the interests of stockholders and tends to view the interests of its other stakeholders such as customers, employees, and the community.

Example: Sears sacrifices customer trust

Crises of Deception

Crises of deception occur when management conceals or misrepresents information about itself and its products in its dealing with consumers and others.

Example: Dow Corning's silicone-gel breast implant.

Crises of Management Misconduct

Some crises are caused not only by skewed values and deception but deliberate amorality and illegality.

Workplace Violence

Crises occur when an employee or former employee commits violence against other employees on organizational grounds.

Example: DuPont's Lycra.

Rumors

False information about an organization or its products creates crises hurting the organization's reputation. Sample is linking the organization to radical groups or stories that their products are contaminated.

Example: Procter & Gamble's Logo controversy.

Crisis Leadership

Erika Hayes James, an organizational psychologist at the University of Virginia's Darden Graduate School of Business, identifies two primary types of organizational crisis. James defines organizational crisis as "any emotionally charged situation that, once it becomes public, invites negative stakeholder reaction and thereby has the potential to threaten the financial well-being, reputation, or survival of the firm or some portion thereof."

1. Sudden crisis
2. Smoldering crises.

Sudden Crises

Sudden crises are circumstances that occur without warning and beyond an institution's control. Consequently, sudden crises are most often situations for which the institution and its leadership are not blamed.

Smoldering Crises

Smoldering crises differ from sudden crises in that they begin as minor internal issues that, due to manager's negligence, develop to crisis status. These are situations when leaders are blamed for the crisis and its subsequent effect on the institution in question. James categorises five phases of crisis that require specific crisis leadership competencies. Each phase contains an obstacle that a leader must overcome to improve the structure and operations of an organization. James's case study on crisis in the financial services sector, for example, explores why crisis events erode public trust in leadership. James's research demonstrates how leadership competencies of integrity, positive intent, capability, mutual respect, and transparency impact the trust-building process.

1. Signal detection
2. Preparation and prevention
3. Containment and damage control
4. Business recovery
5. Learning.

Signal Detection

Signal detection is the stage in a crisis in which leaders should, but do not always, sense early warning signals (red flags) that suggest the possibility of a crisis. The detection stages of a crisis include: Sense-making: represents an attempt to create order and make sense, retrospectively, of what occurs. Perspective-taking: the ability to consider another person's or group's point of view.

Preparation and Prevention

It is during this stage that crisis handlers begin preparing for or averting the crisis that had been foreshadowed in the signal detection stage. Organizations such as the Red Cross's primary mission is to prepare for and prevent the escalation of crisis events. Walmart has been described as an emergency relief standard bearer after having witnessed the incredibly speedy and well-coordinated effort to get supplies to the Gulf Coast of the United States in anticipation of Hurricane Katrina.

Containment and Damage Control

Usually the most vivid stage, the goal of crisis containment and damage control is to limit the reputational, financial, safety, and other threats to firm survival. Crisis handlers work diligently during this stage to bring the crisis to an end as quickly as possible to limit the negative publicity to the organization, and move into the business recovery phase.

Business Recovery

When crisis hits, organizations must be able to carry on with their business in the midst of the crisis while simultaneously planning for how they will recover from the damage the crisis caused. Crisis handlers not only must engage in continuity planning (determining the people, financial, and technology resources needed to keep the organization running), but will also actively pursue organizational resilience.

Learning

In the wake of a crisis, organizational decision makers adopt a learning orientation and use prior experience to develop new routines and behaviors that ultimately change the way the organization operates. The best leaders recognize this and are purposeful and skillful in finding the learning opportunities inherent in every crisis situation.

Models and Theories Associated with Crisis Management

Crisis Management Model

Successfully defusing a crisis requires an understanding of how to handle a crisis – before they occur. Gonzalez-Herrero and Pratt found the different phases of Crisis Management.

There are 3 phases in any Crisis Management are as below

1. The diagnosis of the impending trouble or the danger signals.
2. Choosing appropriate Turnaround Strategy.
3. Implementation of the change process and its monitoring.

Management Crisis Planning

No corporation looks forward to facing a situation that causes a significant disruption to their business, especially one that stimulates extensive media coverage. Public scrutiny can result in a negative financial, political, legal and government impact. Crisis management planning deals with providing the best response to a crisis.

Contingency Planning

Preparing contingency plans in advance, as part of a crisis management plan, is the first step to ensuring an organization is appropriately prepared for a crisis. Crisis management teams can rehearse a crisis plan by developing a simulated scenario to use as a drill.

The plan should clearly stipulate that the only people to speak publicly about the crisis are the designated persons, such as the company spokesperson or crisis team members. The first hours after a crisis breaks are the most crucial, so working with speed and efficiency is important, and the plan should indicate how quickly each function should be performed. When preparing to offer a statement externally as well as internally, information should be accurate. Providing incorrect or manipulated information has a tendency to backfire and will greatly exacerbate the situation. The contingency plan should contain information and guidance that will help decision makers to consider not only the short-term consequences, but the long-term effects of every decision.

Business Continuity Planning

When a crisis will undoubtedly cause a significant disruption to an organization, a business continuity plan can help minimize the disruption. First, one must identify the critical functions and processes that are necessary to keep the organization running. Then each critical function and or/process must have its own contingency plan in the event that one of the functions/processes ceases or fails. Testing these contingency plans by rehearsing the required actions in a simulation will allow for all involved to become more sensitive and aware of the possibility of a crisisis. As a result, in the event of an actual crisis, the team members will act more quickly and effectively.

Structural-functional Systems Theory

Providing information to an organization in a time of crisis is critical to effective crisis management. Structural-functional systems theory addresses the intricacies of information networks and levels of command making up organizational communication. The structural-functional theory identifies information flow in organizations as "networks" made up of members and "links". Information in organizations flow in patterns called networks.

Diffusion of Innovation Theory

Another theory that can be applied to the sharing of information is Diffusion of Innovation Theory. Developed by Everett Rogers, the theory describes how innovation is disseminated and communicated through certain channels over a period of time. Diffusion of innovation in communication occurs when an individual communicates a new idea to one or several others. At its most elementary form, the process involves: (1) an innovation, (2) an individual or other unit of adoption that has knowledge of or experience with using the innovation, (3) another individual or other unit that does not yet have knowledge of the innovation, and (4) a communication channel connecting the two units. A communication channel is the means by which messages get from one individual to another.

Role of Apologies in Crisis Management

There has been debate about the role of apologies in crisis management, and some argue that apology opens an organization up for possible legal consequences. "However some evidence indicates that compensation and sympathy, two less expensive strategies, are as effective as an apology in shaping people's perceptions of the organization taking responsibility for the crisis because these strategies focus on the victims' needs. The sympathy response expresses concern for victims while compensation offers victims something to offset the suffering."

Crisis Leadership

James identifies six leadership competencies which facilitate organizational restructuring during and after a crisis.

1. Building an environment of trust
2. Reforming the organization's mindset
3. Identifying obvious and obscure vulnerabilities of the organization
4. Making wise and rapid decisions as well as taking courageous action
5. Learning from crisis to effect change.

Crisis leadership research concludes that leadership action in crisis reflects the competency of an organization, because the test of crisis demonstrates how well the institution's leadership structure serves the organization's goals and withstands crisis. Developing effective human resources is vital when building organizational capabilities through crisis management executive leadership.

Unequal Human Capital Theory

James postulates that organizational crisis can result from discrimination lawsuits. James's theory of unequal human capital and social position derives from economic theories of human and social capital concluding that minority employees receive fewer organizational rewards than those with access to executive management.

In a recent study of managers in a *Fortune* 500 company, race was found to be a predictor of promotion opportunity or lack thereof. Thus, discrimination lawsuits can invite negative stakeholder reaction, damage the company's reputation, and threaten corporate survival.

Examples of Successful Crisis Management

Tylenol (Johnson and Johnson)

In the fall of 1982, a murderer added 65 milligrams of cyanide to some Tylenol capsules on store shelves, killing seven people, including three in one family. Johnson & Johnson recalled and destroyed 31 million capsules at a cost of $100 million. The affable CEO, James Burke, appeared in television ads and at news conferences informing consumers of the company's actions. Tamper-resistant packaging was rapidly introduced, and Tylenol sales swiftly bounced back to near pre-crisis levels.

When another bottle of tainted Tylenol was discovered in a store, it took only a matter of minutes for the manufacturer to issue a nationwide warning that people should not use the medication in its capsule form.

Odwalla Foods

When Odwalla's apple juice was thought to be the cause of an outbreak of E. coli infection, the company lost a third of its market value. In October 1996, an outbreak of E. coli bacteria in Washington state, California, Colorado and British Columbia was traced to unpasteurized apple juice manufactured by natural juice maker Odwalla Inc. Forty-nine cases were reported, including the death of a small child. Within 24 hours, Odwalla conferred with the FDA and Washington state health officials; established a schedule of daily press briefings; sent out press releases which announced the recall; expressed remorse, concern and apology, and took responsibility for anyone harmed by their products; detailed symptoms of E. coli poisoning; and explained what consumers should do with any affected products. Odwalla then developed-through the help of consultants-effective thermal processes that would not harm the products' flavours when production resumed. All of these steps were communicated through close relations with the media and through full-page newspaper ads.

Mattel

Mattel Inc., the toy maker, has been plagued with more than 28 product recalls and in Summer of 2007, amongst problems with exports from China, faced two product recall in two weeks. The company "did everything it could to get its message out, earning high marks from consumers and retailers. Though upset by the situation, they were appreciative of the company's response. At Mattel, just after the 7 a.m. recall announcement by federal officials, a public relations staff of 16 was set to call reporters at the 40 biggest media outlets. They told each to check their e-mail for a news release outlining the recalls, invited them to a teleconference call with executives and scheduled TV appearances or phone conversations with Mattel's chief executive. The Mattel CEO Robert Eckert did 14 TV interviews on a Tuesday in August and about 20 calls with individual reporters. By the week's end, Mattel had responded to more than 300 media inquiries in the U.S. alone."

Pepsi

The Pepsi Corporation faced a crisis in 1993 which started with claims of syringes being found in cans of diet Pepsi. Pepsi urged stores not to remove the product from shelves while it had the cans and the situation investigated. This led to an arrest, which Pepsi made public and then followed with their first video news release, showing the production process to demonstrate that such tampering was impossible within their factories. A second video news release displayed the man arrested. A third video news release showed surveillance from a convenience store where a woman was caught replicating the tampering incident. The company simultaneously publicly worked with the FDA during the crisis. The corporation was completely open with the public throughout, and every employee of Pepsi was kept aware of the details. This made public communications effective throughout the crisis. After the crisis had been resolved, the corporation ran a series of special campaigns designed to thank the public for standing by the corporation, along with coupons for further compensation. This case served as a design for how to handle other crisis situations.

Examples of Unsuccessful Crisis Management

Bhopal

The Bhopal disaster in which poor communication before, during, and after the crisis cost thousands of lives, illustrates the importance of incorporating cross-cultural communication in crisis management plans. According to American University's Trade Environmental Database Case Studies (1997), local residents were not sure how to react to warnings of potential threats from the Union Carbide plant. Operating manuals printed only in English is an extreme example of mismanagement but indicative of systemic barriers to information diffusion. According to Union Carbide's own chronology of the incident (2006), a day after the crisis Union Carbide's upper management arrived in India but was unable to assist in the relief efforts because they were placed under house arrest by the Indian government. Symbolic intervention can be counter productive; a crisis management strategy can help upper management make more calculated decisions in how they should respond to disaster scenarios. The Bhopal incident illustrates the difficulty in consistently applying management standards to multi-national operations and the blame shifting that often results from the lack of a clear management plan.

Ford and Firestone Tire and Rubber Company

The Ford-Firestone Tire and Rubber Company dispute transpired in August 2000. In response to claims that their 15-inch Wilderness AT, radial ATX and ATX II tire treads were separating from the tire core—leading to grisly, spectacular crashes—Bridgestone/Firestone recalled 6.5 million tires. These tires were mostly used on the Ford Explorer, the world's top-selling sport utility vehicle (SUV).

The two companies committed three major blunders early on, say crisis experts. First, they blamed consumers for not inflating their tires properly. Then they blamed each other for faulty tires and faulty vehicle design. Then they said very little about what they were doing to solve a problem that had caused more than 100 deaths—until they got called to Washington to testify before Congress.

Exxon

On March 24, 1989, a tanker belonging to the Exxon Corporation ran aground in the Prince William Sound in Alaska. The Exxon Valdez spilled millions of gallons of crude oil into the waters off Valdez, killing thousands of fish, fowl, and sea otters. Hundreds of miles of coastline were polluted and salmon spawning runs disrupted; numerous fishermen, especially Native Americans, lost their livelihoods. Exxon, by contrast, did not react quickly in terms of dealing with the media and the public; the CEO, Lawrence Rawl, did not become an active part of the public relations effort and actually shunned public involvement; the company had neither a communication plan nor a communication team in place to handle the event—in fact, the company did not appoint a public relations manager to its management team until 1993, 4 years after the incident; Exxon established its media center in Valdez, a location too small and too remote to handle the onslaught of media attention; and the company acted defensively in its response to its publics, even laying blame, at times, on other groups such as the Coast Guard. These responses also happened within days of the incident.

Lessons Learned in Crisis Management

Impact of Catastrophes on Shareholder Value

One of the foremost recognized studies conducted on the impact of a catastrophe on the stock value of an organization was completed by Dr Rory Knight and Dr Deborah Pretty (1995, Templeton College, University of Oxford-commissioned by the Sedgewick Group). This study undertook a detailed analysis of the stock price (post impact) of organizations that had experienced catastrophes.

The study identified organizations that recovered and even exceeded pre-catastrophe stock price, (*Recoverers*), and those that did not recover on stock price, (*Non-recoverers*). The average cumulative impact on shareholder value for the recoverers was 5% plus on their original stock value. So the net impact on shareholder value by this stage was actually positive. The non-recoverers remained more or less unchanged between days 5 and 50 after the catastrophe, but suffered a net negative cumulative impact of almost 15% on their stock price up to one year afterwards.

One of the key conclusions of this study is that "Effective management of the consequences of catastrophes would appear to be a more significant factor than whether catastrophe insurance hedges the economic impact of the catastrophe".

While there are technical elements to this report it is highly recommended to those who wish to engage their senior management in the value of crisis management.

Crisis as Opportunity

To address such shareholder impact, management must move from a mindset that manages crisis to one that generates crisis leadership. Research shows that organizational contributory factors affect the tendency of executives to adopt an effective "crisis as opportunity" mindset. Since pressure is both a precipitator and consequence of crisis, leaders who perform well under pressure can effectively guide the organization through such crisis.

James contends that most executives focus on communications and public relations as a reactive strategy. While the company's reputation with shareholders, financial well-being, and survival are all at stake, potential damage to reputation can result from the actual management of the crisis issue.

Additionally, companies may stagnate as their risk management group identifies whether a crisis is sufficiently "statistically significant". Crisis leadership, on the other hand, immediately addresses both the damage and implications for the company's present and future conditions, as well as opportunities for improvement.

Public Sector Crisis Management

Corporate America is not the only community that is vulnerable to the perils of a crisis. Whether a school shooting, a public health crisis or a terrorist attack that leaves the public seeking comfort in the calm, steady leadership of an elected official, no sector of society is immune to crisis. In response to that reality, crisis management policies, strategies and practices have been developed and adapted across multiple disciplines.

Schools and Crisis Management

In the wake of the Columbine High School Massacre, the September 11 attacks in 2001, and shootings on college campuses including the Virginia Tech massacre, educational institutions at all levels are now focused on crisis management.

A national study conducted by the University of Arkansas for Medical Sciences (UAMS) and Arkansas Children's Hospital Research Institute (ACHRI) has shown that many public school districts have important deficiencies in their emergency and disaster plans (The School Violence Resource Center, 2003). In response the Resource Center has organized a comprehensive set of resources to aid schools is the development of crisis management plans.

Crisis management plans cover a wide variety of incidents including bomb threats, child abuse, natural disasters, suicide, drug abuse and gang activities – just to list a few. In a similar fashion the plans aim to address all audiences in need of information including parents, the media and law enforcement officials.

Government and Crisis Management

Historically, government at all levels – local, state, and national – has played a large role in crisis management. Indeed, many political philosophers have considered this to be one of the primary roles of government. Emergency services, such as fire and police departments at the local level, and the United States National Guard at the federal level, often play integral roles in crisis situations.

To help coordinate communication during the response phase of a crisis, the U.S. Federal Emergency Management Agency (FEMA) within the Department of Homeland Security administers the National Response Plan (NRP). This plan is intended to integrate public and private response by providing a common language and outlining a chain-of-command when multiple parties are mobilized. It is based on the premise that incidences should be handled at the lowest organizational level possible. The NRP recognizes the private sector as a key partner in domestic incident management, particularly in the area of critical infrastructure protection and restoration.

The NRP is a companion to the National Incidence Management System that acts as a more general template for incident management regardless of cause, size, or complexity.

FEMA offers free web-based training on the National Response Plan through the Emergency Management Institute.

Common Alerting Protocol (CAP) is a relatively recent mechanism that facilitates crisis communication across different mediums and systems. CAP helps create a consistent emergency alert format to reach geographically and linguistically diverse audiences through both audio and visual mediums.

Elected Officials and Crisis Management

Historically, politics and crisis go hand-in-hand. In describing crisis, President Abraham Lincoln said, "We live in the midst of alarms, anxiety beclouds the future; we expect some new disaster with each newspaper we read."

Crisis management has become a defining feature of contemporary governance. In times of crisis, communities and members of organizations expect their public leaders to minimize the impact of the crisis at hand, while critics and bureaucratic competitors try to seize the moment to blame incumbent rulers and their policies. In this extreme environment, policy makers must somehow establish a sense of normality, and foster collective learning from the crisis experience.

In the face of crisis, leaders must deal with the strategic challenges they face, the political risks and opportunities they encounter, the errors they make, the pitfalls they need to avoid, and the paths away from crisis they may pursue. The necessity for management is even more significant with the advent of a 24-hour news cycle and an increasingly internet-savvy audience with ever-changing technology at its fingertips.

Public leaders have a special responsibility to help safeguard society from the adverse consequences of crisis. Experts in crisis management note that leaders who take this responsibility seriously would have to concern themselves with all crisis phases: the incubation stage, the onset, and the aftermath. Crisis leadership then involves five critical tasks: sense making, decision making, meaning making, terminating, and learning.

A brief description of the five facets of crisis leadership includes:

1. Sense making may be considered as the classical situation assessment step in decision making.
2. Decision making is both the act of coming to a decision as the implementation of that decision.
3. Meaning making refers to crisis management as political communication.
4. Terminating a crisis is only possible if the public leader correctly handles the accountability question.

5. Learning, refers to the actual learning from a crisis is limited. The authors note, a crisis often opens a window of opportunity for reform for better or for worse.

Professional Organizations

There are a number of professional industry associations that provide advice, literature and contacts to turnaround professionals and academics. Some are:

1. Turnaround Management Society (International/Focus on Europe)
2. Institute for Turnaround (England)
3. Turnaround Management Association (International)
4. Institut für die Standardisierung von Unternehmenssanierungen (Germany).

Common Alerting Protocol

The Common Alerting Protocol (CAP) is an XML-based data format for exchanging public warnings and emergencies between alerting technologies. CAP allows a warning message to be consistently disseminated simultaneously over many warning systems to many applications. CAP increases warning effectiveness and simplifies the task of activating a warning for responsible officials.

Individuals can receive standardized alerts from many sources and configure their applications to process and respond to the alerts as desired. Alerts from the United States Geological Survey, the Department of Homeland Security, NOAA and the California Office of Emergency Services can all be received in the same format, by the same application. That application can, for example, sound different alarms based on the information received.

By normalizing alert data across threats, jurisdictions and warning systems, CAP also can be used to detect trends and patterns in warning activity, such as trends that might indicate an undetected hazard or hostile act. From a procedural perspective, CAP reinforces a research-based template for effective warning message content and structure.

The CAP data structure is backward-compatible with existing alert formats including the Specific Area Message Encoding (SAME) used in Weatheradio and the broadcast Emergency Alert System as well as new technology such as the Commercial Mobile Alert System (CMAS), while adding capabilities including:

- Flexible geographic targeting using latitude/longitude "boxes" and other geospatial representations in three dimensions;
- Multilingual and multi-audience messaging;
- Phased and delayed effective times and expirations;
- Enhanced message update and cancellation features;
- Template support for framing complete and effective warning messages;
- Digital encryption and signature capability; and,
- Facility for digital images, audio and video.

Background

The National Science and Technology Council (NSTC) report on "Effective Disaster Warnings" PDF (November, 2000) recommended that "a standard method should be developed to collect and relay instantaneously and automatically all types of hazard warnings and reports locally, regionally and nationally for input into a wide variety of dissemination systems."

In 2001 an international, independent group of over 120 emergency managers began specifying and prototyping the Common Alerting Protocol data structure based on the recommendations of the NSTC report. The project was embraced by the non-profit Partnership for Public Warning and a number of international warning system vendors. A series of field trials and long-term demonstration projects during 2002-03 led to the submission of a draft CAP specification to the OASIS standards process for formalization.

The CAP 1.0 specification was approved by OASIS in April, 2004. Based on experience with CAP 1.0, the OASIS Emergency Management Technical Committee adopted an updated CAP 1.1 specification in October 2005. At a meeting in Geneva in October, 2006 the CAP 1.1 specification was taken under consideration by the International Telecommunications Union for adoption as an ITU recommendation.

Current Implementations

According to a CAP 1.0 Fact Sheet, CAP implementations have been demonstrated by agencies and companies including: United States Department of Homeland Security; National Weather Service; United States Geological Survey; California Office of Emergency Services; Virginia Department of Transportation; GeoDecisions, Inc.; Blue292; Warning Systems, Inc.; Comlabs, Inc.; mobileFoundations; Ship Analytics; MyStateUSA; IEM, Inc.; Hormann America, Inc.; Oregon RAINS; and others.

It is also mentioned by the Internet Society in its 2005 "Public Warning Network Challenge".

During early 2005 the U.S. Department of Homeland Security (DHS), in partnership with the Association of Public Television Stations, demonstrated CAP-based "digital EAS" broadcasts over public television digital TV transmitters and satellite links in the Washington, D.C. area and nationwide.

CAP is the foundation technology for the planned "Integrated Public Alert and Warning System," an all-hazard, all-media national warning architecture being developed by DHS, the National Weather Service and the Federal Communications Commission.

In Canada, a working group composed of public alerting practitioners and government agencies has developed a CAP Canadian Profile (CAP-CP) based on CAP but specialized to address the needs of Canadian public alerting stakeholders, such as bilingualism, geocoding for Canada, managed lists of locations and events, etc. The Canadian government has adopted CAP-CP for its National Public Alerting System (NPAS) project. The CAP-CP working group, along with stakeholders and projects such as the Canadian Association for Public Alerting and Notification (CAPAN) and Netalerts' Sarnia Lambton trial, are now working with and refining CAP-CP for national application in Canada.

CAP has been implemented for a small-scale, grassroots hazard information system in Sri Lanka following the 2004 Indian Ocean Tsunami. This implementation was part of the "HazInfo Project" funded by Canada's International Development Research Centre.

In 2007, the International Telecommunication Union, Telecommunication Standardization Sector (ITU-T) adopted the

Common Alerting Protocol as Recommendation X.1303. The recommendation annex contains an authoritative ASN.1 module translation of the CAP XML schema that may be useful for some implementations. Rec. X.1303 is within the remit of ITU-T Study Group 17 (Security), Rapporteur Group on Cybersecurity (Q.4/17) for purposes of further evolution of the standard.

Contingency Plan

A contingency plan is a plan devised for a specific situation when things could go wrong. Contingency plans are often devised by governments or businesses who want to be prepared for anything that could happen.

Business and government contingency plans need to include planning for marketing to gain stakeholder support and understanding. Stakeholders need to be kept informed of the reasons for any changes, the vision of the end result and the proposed plan for getting there. The level of stakeholders' importance and influence should be considered when determining the amount of marketing required, the timescales for implementation and completion, and the overall effectiveness of the plan. If time permits, input and consultation from the most influential stakeholders should be incorporated into the building of any contingency plan as without acceptance from these people any plan will at best encounter limited success.

During times of crisis, contingency plans are often developed to explore and prepare for any eventuality. During the Cold war, many governments made contingency plans to protect themselves and their citizens from nuclear attack. Examples of contingency plans designed to inform citizens of how to survive a nuclear attack are the booklets *Survival Under Atomic Attack, Protect and Survive,* and *Fallout Protection,* which were issued by the British and American governments. Today there are still contingency plans in place to deal with terrorist attacks or other catastrophes. The National Institute of Standards and Technology has published a contingency planning guide for Information Technology Systems (2002).

In the United States

In the United States, the Contingency Plans are industrial

regulatory requirements for all HAZMAT operations. The United States Environmental Protection Agency through RCRA and EPCRA has defined specific formats for Local Emergency Planning and the National Contingency Plan.

Crisis

A crisis (plural: "crises"; adjectival form: "critical") is any event that is, or expected to lead to, an unstable and dangerous situation affecting an individual, group, community or whole society. Crises are deemed to be negative changes in the security, economic, political, societal or environmental affairs, especially when they occur abruptly, with little or no warning. More loosely, it is a term meaning 'a testing time' or an 'emergency event'.

Definition of a Crisis

Crisis has several defining characteristics. Seeger, Sellnow and Ulmer say that crises have four defining characteristics that are "specific, unexpected, and non-routine events or series of events that [create] high levels of uncertainty and threat or perceived threat to an organization's high priority goals." Thus the first three characteristics are that the event is

1. unexpected (i.e., a surprise)
2. creates uncertainty
3. is seen as a threat to important goals.

Venette argues that "crisis is a process of transformation where the old system can no longer be maintained." Therefore the fourth defining quality is the need for change. If change is not needed, the event could more accurately be described as a failure.

Apart from natural crises that are inherently unpredictable (volcanic eruptions, tsunami etc.) most of the crises that we face are created by man. Hence the requirements of their being 'unexpected' depends upon man failing to note the onset of crisis conditions. Some of our inability to recognise crises before they become dangerous is due to denial and other psychological responses that provide succour and protection for our emotions.

A different set of reasons for failing to notice the onset of crises is that we allow ourselves to be 'tricked' into believing that we are doing something for reasons that are false. In other words, we are doing the wrong things for the right reasons. For example, we might believe that we are solving the threats of climate change by engaging in economic trading activity that has no real impact on the climate. Mitroff and Silvers posit two reasons for these mistakes, which they classify as Type 3 (inadvertent) and Type 4 (deliberate) errors.

The effect of our inability to attend to the likely results of our actions can result in crisis.

From this perspective we might usefully learn that failing to understand the real causes of our difficulties is likely to lead to repeated downstream 'blowback' that will eventually be our undoing.

Where states are concerned, Michael Brecher, based on case studies of the International Crisis Behaviour (ICB) project, suggested a different way of defining crisis as conditions are perceptions held by the highest level decision-makers of the actor concerned:

1. threat to basic values, with a simultaneous or subsequent
2. high probability of involvement in military hostilities, and the awareness of
3. finite time for response to the external value threat.

Poverty-related Crisis

- Soup kitchen

Unemployment and Underemployment

Not paying rent may lead to homelessness through foreclosure or eviction. Being unemployed, and the financial difficulties and loss of health insurance benefits that come with it, may cause malnutrition and illness, and are major sources of self-esteem which may lead to depression, which may have a further negative impact on health. Lacking a job often means lacking social contact with fellow employees, a purpose for many hours of the day, lack of self-esteem, and mental stress.

Economic Crisis

An *economic crisis* is a sharp transition to a recession. See for example 1994 economic crisis in Mexico, Argentine economic crisis

(1999-2002), South American economic crisis of 2002, Economic crisis of Cameroon.

A financial crisis may be a banking crisis or currency crisis.

Environmental Crisis

Crises pertaining to the environment include:

Environmental Disaster

An environmental disaster is a disaster that is due to human activity and should not be confused with natural disasters. In this case, the impact of humans' alteration of the ecosystem has led to widespread and/or long-lasting consequences. It can include the deaths of animals (including humans) and plant systems, or severe disruption of human life, possibly requiring migration.

Natural Disaster

A *natural disaster* is the consequence of a natural hazard (e.g. volcanic eruption, earthquake, landslide) which moves from potential in to an active phase, and as a result affects human activities. Human vulnerability, exacerbated by the lack of planning or lack of appropriate emergency management, leads to financial, structural, and human losses. The resulting loss depends on the capacity of the population to support or resist the disaster, their resilience. This understanding is concentrated in the formulation: "disasters occur when hazards meet vulnerability". A natural hazard will hence never result in a natural disaster in areas without vulnerability, e.g. strong earthquakes in uninhabited areas.

Endangered Species

An *endangered species* is a population of an organism which is at risk of becoming extinct because it is either few in number, or threatened by changing environmental or predation parameters. An endangered species is usually a taxonomic species, but may be another evolutionary significant unit. The World Conservation Union (IUCN) has classified 38 percent of the 44,837 species assessed by 2008 as threatened.

International Crisis

For information about crises in the field of study in international relations, see crisis management and international crisis. In this context, a crisis can be loosely defined as a situation where there is a perception of threat, heightened anxiety, expectation of possible violence and the belief that any actions will have far-reaching consequences (Lebow, 7-10).

Personal Crisis

A personal crisis can occur when events of an extraordinary nature trigger extreme tension and stress within an individual which require major decisions or actions to resolve. A crisis situation can revolve around a dangerous situation such as extreme weather conditions or a medical emergency or long-term illness. A crisis can also be related to a change in events that comprise the day-to-day life of a person and those in their close circle. Such situations may be loss of a job; extreme financial hardship; alcoholism or addiction and other situations that are life altering and require action that is outside the "normal" daily routine.

Emergency Service

Emergency services are organizations which ensure public safety and health by addressing different emergencies. Some agencies exist solely for addressing certain types of emergencies whilst others deal with ad hoc emergencies as part of their normal responsibilities. Many agencies will engage in community awareness and prevention programs to help the public avoid, detect, and report emergencies effectively.

The availability of emergency services depends very heavily on location, and may in some cases also rely on the recipient giving payment or holding suitable insurance or other surety for receiving the service.

Main Emergency Service Functions

There are three main emergency service functions:

- Police – providing community safety and acting to reduce crime against persons and property
- Fire and Rescue Service – providing firefighters to deal with fire and rescue operations, and may also deal with some secondary emergency service duties
- Emergency medical service – providing ambulances and staff to deal with medical emergencies.

In some countries (e.g. the UK) these three functions are performed by three separate organisations in a given area. However there are also many countries where fire, rescue and ambulance functions are all performed by a single organisation. Emergency services have one or more dedicated emergency telephone numbers reserved for critical emergency calls. In some countries, one number is used for all the emergency services (e.g. 911 in the USA, 999 in the UK). In some countries, each emergency service has its own emergency number.

Other Emergency Services

These services can be provided by one of the core services or by a separate government or private body.

- Military — to provide specialist services, such as bomb disposal or to supplement emergency services at times of major disaster, civil dispute or high demand.
- Coastguard — Provide coastal patrols with a security function at sea, as well as involvement in search and rescue operations
- Lifeboat — Dedicated providers of rescue lifeboat services, usually at sea (such as by the RNLI in the United Kingdom).
- Mountain rescue — to provide search and rescue in mountainous areas, and sometimes in other wilderness environments.
- Cave rescue — to rescue people injured, trapped, or lost during caving explorations.
- Mine rescue — specially trained and equipped to rescue miners trapped by fires, explosions, cave-ins, toxic gas, flooding, etc.
- Technical rescue — other types of technical or heavy rescue, but usually specific to a discipline (such as swift water).
- Search and rescue — can be discipline-specific, such as urban, wildland, maritime, etc.
- Wildland fire suppression — to suppress, detect and control fires in forests and other wildland areas.
- Bomb disposal — to render safe hazardous explosive ordnance, such as terrorist devices or unexploded wartime bombs.

- Blood/organ transplant supply — to provide organs or blood on an emergency basis, such as the National Blood Service of the United Kingdom.
- Emergency management — to provide and coordinate resources during large-scale emergencies.
- Amateur radio emergency communications — to provide communications support to other emergency services.
- Hazmat — removal of hazardous materials
- Air search providing aerial spotting for the emergency services, such as conducted by the Civil Air Patrol in the US, or Sky Watch in the UK.

Civil Emergency Services

These groups and organisations respond to emergencies and provide other safety-related services either as a part of their on-the-job duties, as part of the main mission of their business or concern, or as part of their hobbies.

- Public utilities — safeguarding gas, electricity and water, which are all potentially hazardous if infrastructure fails
- Emergency road service — provide repair or recovery for disabled or crashed vehicles
- Civilian Traffic Officers — such as operated by the Highways Agency in the UK to facilitiate clearup and traffic flow at road traffic collisions
- Emergency social services
- Community emergency response teams — help organize facilities such as rest centres during large emergencies
- Disaster relief — such as services provided by the Red Cross and Salvation Army
- Famine relief teams
- Amateur radio communications groups — provide communications support during emergencies
- Poison Control — providing specialist support for poisoning
- Animal control — can assist or lead response to emergencies involving animals

- Forest Service
- St. John Ambulance/Red Cross/Order of Malta Ambulance Corps — Medical & First Aid Support.

Location-specific Emergency Services

Some locations have emergency services dedicated to them, and whilst this does not necessarily preclude employees using their skills outside this area (or be used to support other emergency services outside their area), they are primarily focused on the safety or security of a given geographical place.

- Park rangers — looking after many emergencies within their given area, including fire, medical and security issues
- Lifeguards — charged with reacting to emergencies within their own given remit area, usually a pool, beach or open water area.

Working Together

Effective emergency service management requires agencies from many different services to work closely together and to have open lines of communication. Most services do, or should, have procedures and liaisons in place to ensure this, although absence of these can be severely detrimental to good working. There can sometimes be tension between services for a number of other reasons, including professional versus voluntary crew members, or simply based on area or division.

To aid effective communications, different services may share common practices and protocol for certain large-scale emergencies. In the UK, commonly used shared protocols include CHALET and ETHANE while in the US, the Department of Homeland Security has called for nationwide implementation of the National Incident Management System (NIMS), of which the Incident Command System (ICS) is a part.

3

Emergency Management

Emergency management is the generic name of an interdisciplinary field dealing with the strategic organizational management processes used to protect critical assets of an organization from hazard risks that can cause disasters or catastrophes, and to ensure the continuance of the organization within their planned lifetime. Assets are categorized as either living things, non-living things, cultural or economic. Hazards are categorized by their cause, either natural or human-made. The entire strategic management process is divided into four fields to aid in identification of the processes.

The four fields normally deal with risk reduction, preparing resources to respond to the hazard, responding to the actual damage caused by the hazard and limiting further damage (e.g., emergency evacuation, quarantine, mass decontamination, etc.), and returning as close as possible to the state before the hazard incident. The field occurs in both the public and private sector, sharing the same processes, but with different focuses.

Emergency Management is a strategic process, and not a tactical process, thus it usually resides at the Executive level in an organization. It normally has no direct power, but serves as an advisory or coordinating function to ensure that all parts of an organization are focused on the common goal. Effective Emergency Management relies on a thorough integration of emergency plans at all levels of the organization, and an understanding that the lowest levels of the organization are responsible for managing the emergency and getting additional resources and assistance from the upper levels.

The most senior person in the organization administering the program is normally called an Emergency Manager, or a derived form based upon the term used in the field (e.g. Business Continuity Manager).

Fields that are under this definition include:

- *Civil Defence* (used in the United States during the Cold War, focusing on protection from nuclear attack)
- *Civil Protection* (widely used with the European Union)
- Crisis Management (emphasizes the political and security dimension rather than measure to satisfy the immediate needs of the civilian population.)
- Disaster Risk Reduction (focus on the mitigation and preparedness aspects of the emergency cycle.)
- Homeland Security (used in the United States, focusing on preventing terrorism.)
- Business Continuity and Business Continuity Planning (Focused on ensuring a continuous upward trend of income.)
- Continuity of Government.

Phases and Professional Activities

The nature of management depends on local economic and social conditions. Some disaster relief experts such as Fred Cuny have noted that in a sense the only real disasters are economic. Experts, such as Cuny, have long noted that the cycle of Emergency Management must include long-term work on infrastructure, public awareness, and even human justice issues. The process of Emergency Management involves four phases: mitigation, preparedness, response, and recovery.

Recently the Department of Homeland Security and FEMA have adopted the terms "resilience" and "prevention" as part of the paradigm of EM. The latter term was mandated by PKEMA 2006 as statute enacted in October 2006 and made effective March 31, 2007. The two terms definitions do not fit easily as separate phases. Prevention is 100% mitigation, by definition. Resilience describes the goal of the four phases: an ability to recover from or adjust easily to misfortune or change.

Mitigation

Mitigation efforts are attempts to prevent hazards from developing into disasters altogether or to reduce the effects of disasters. The mitigation phase differs from the other phases in that it focuses on long-term measures for reducing or eliminating risk. The implementation of mitigation strategies is a part of the recovery process if applied after a disaster occurs. Mitigation measures can be structural or non-structural. Structural measures use technological solutions like flood levees. Non-structural measures include legislation, land-use planning (e.g. the designation of nonessential land like parks to be used as flood zones), and insurance. Mitigation is the most cost-efficient method for reducing the effect of hazards although not always the most suitable. Mitigation includes providing regulations regarding evacuation, sanctions against those who refuse to obey the regulations (such as mandatory evacuations), and communication of risks to the public. Some structural mitigation measures may harm the ecosystem.

A precursor to mitigation is the identification of risks. Physical risk assessment refers to identifying and evaluating hazards. The hazard-specific risk (R_h) combines a hazard's probability and effects. The equation below states that the hazard multiplied by the populations' vulnerability to that hazard produces a risk Catastrophe modeling. The higher the risk, the more urgent that the vulnerabilities to the hazard are targeted by mitigation and preparedness. If, however, there is no vulnerability then there will be no risk, e.g. an earthquake occurring in a desert where nobody lives.

$$R_h = H \times V_h$$

Preparedness

Preparedness is a continuous cycle of planning, manageging, organizing, training, equipping, exercising, creatining, monitoring, evaluation and improvement activities to ensure effective coordination and the enhancement of capabilities of concerened organizations to prevent, protect against, respond to, recover from, create resources and mitigate the effects of natural disasters, acts of terrorism, and other man-made disasters. In the preparedness phase, emergency managers develop plans of action carfully to manage and counter their risks and take action to build the necessary capabilities needed to implement such plans. Common preparedness measures include:

- communication plans with easily understandable terminology and methods.
- proper maintenance and training of emergency services, including mass human resources such as community emergency response teams.
- development and exercise of emergency population warning methods combined with emergency shelters and evacuation plans.
- stockpiling, inventory, streamline foods supplies, and maintain other disaster supplies and equipment
- develop organizations of trained volunteers among civilian populations. Professional emergency workers are rapidly overwhelmed in mass emergencies so trained, organized, responsible volunteers are extremely valuable. Organizations like Community Emergency Response Teams and the Red Cross are ready sources of trained volunteers. The latter's emergency management system has gotten high ratings from both California, and the Federal Emergency Management Agency (FEMA).

Another aspect of preparedness is casualty prediction, the study of how many deaths or injuries to expect for a given kind of event. This gives planners an idea of what resources need to be in place to respond to a particular kind of event.

Emergency Managers in the planning phase should be flexible, and all encompassing-carefully recognizing the risks and exposures of their respective regions and employing unconventional, and atypical means of support. Depending on the region-municipal, or private sector emergency services can rapidly be depleted and heavily taxed. Non-governmental organizations that offer desired resources, i.e., transportation of displaced homeowners to be conducted by local school district buses, evacuation of flood victims to be performed by mutual aide agreements between fire departments and rescue squads, should be identified early in planning stages, and practiced with regularity.

Response

The response phase includes the mobilization of the necessary emergency services and first responders in the disaster area. This is likely to include a first wave of core emergency services, such as firefighters, police and ambulance crews. When conducted as a military operation, it is termed Disaster Relief Operation (DRO) and can be a follow-up to a Non-combatant evacuation operation (NEO). They may be supported by a number of secondary emergency services, such as specialist rescue teams.

A well rehearsed emergency plan developed as part of the preparedness phase enables efficient coordination of rescue. Where required, search and rescue efforts commence at an early stage. Depending on injuries sustained by the victim, outside temperature, and victim access to air and water, the vast majority of those affected by a disaster will die within 72 hours after impact.

Organizational response to any significant disaster-natural or terrorist-borne-is based on existing emergency management organizational systems and processes: the Federal Response Plan (FRP) and the Incident Command System (ICS). These systems are solidified through the principles of Unified Command (UC) and Mutual Aid (MA)

There is a need for both discipline (structure, doctrine, process) and agility (creativity, improvisation, adaptability) in responding to a disaster. Combining that with the need to onboard and build a high functioning leadership team quickly to coordinate and manage efforts as they grow beyond first responders indicates the need for a leader and his or her team to craft and implement a disciplined, iterative set of response plans. This allows the team to move forward with coordinated, disciplined responses that are vaguely right and adapt to new information and changing circumstances along the way.

Recovery

The aim of the recovery phase is to restore the affected area to its previous state. It differs from the response phase in its focus; recovery efforts are concerned with issues and decisions that must be made after immediate needs are addressed. Recovery efforts are primarily concerned with actions that involve rebuilding destroyed property, re-employment, and the repair of other essential infrastructure. Efforts should be made to "build back better", aiming to reduce the pre-disaster risks inherent in the community and infrastructure. An important aspect of effective recovery efforts is taking advantage of a 'window of opportunity' for the implementation of mitigative measures that might otherwise be unpopular. Citizens of the affected area are more likely to accept more mitigative changes when a recent disaster is in fresh memory.

In the United States, the National Response Plan dictates how the resources provided by the Homeland Security Act of 2002 will be used in recovery efforts. It is the Federal government that often provides the most technical and financial assistance for recovery efforts in the United States.

Phases and Personal Activities

Mitigation

"it can be right or may be wrong".

Personal mitigation is mainly about knowing and avoiding unnecessary risks. This includes an assessment of possible risks to personal/family health and to personal property.

One example of mitigation would be to avoid buying property that is exposed to hazards, e.g., in a flood plain, in areas of subsidence or landslides. Home owners may not be aware of a property being exposed to a hazard until it strikes. However, specialists can be hired to conduct risk identification and assessment surveys. Purchase of insurance covering the most prominent identified risks is a common measure.

Personal structural mitigation in earthquake prone areas includes installation of an Earthquake Valve to instantly shut off the natural gas supply to a property, seismic retrofits of property and the securing of items inside a building to enhance household seismic safety. The latter may include the mounting of furniture, refrigerators, water heaters and breakables to the walls, and the addition of cabinet latches. In flood prone areas houses can be built on poles/stilts, as in much of southern Asia. In areas prone to prolonged electricity black-outs installation of a generator would be an example of an optimal structural mitigation measure. The construction of storm cellars and fallout shelters are further examples of personal mitigative actions.

Mitigation involves Structural and Non-structural measures taken to limit the impact of disasters.

Structural Mitigation:- This involves proper layout of building, particularly to make it resistant to disasters.

Non Structural Mitigation:- This involves measures taken other than improving the structure of building.

Preparedness

Personal preparedness focuses on preparing equipment and procedures for use *when* a disaster occurs, i.e., planning. Preparedness measures can take many forms including the construction of shelters, installation of warning devices, creation of back-up life-line services (e.g., power, water, sewage), and rehearsing evacuation plans. Two simple measures can help prepare the individual for sitting out the event or evacuating, as necessary. For evacuation, a disaster supplies kit may be prepared and for sheltering purposes a stockpile of supplies may be created. The preparation of a survival kit such as a "72-hour kit", is often advocated by authorities. These kits may include food, medicine, flashlights, candles and money. Also, putting valuable items in safe area is also recommended.

Response

The response phase of an emergency may commence with search and rescue but in all cases the focus will quickly turn to fulfilling the basic humanitarian needs of the affected population. This assistance may be provided by national or international agencies and organisations. Effective coordination of disaster assistance is often crucial, particularly when many organizations respond and local emergency management agency (LEMA) capacity has been exceeded by the demand or diminished by the disaster itself.

On a personal level the response can take the shape either of a *shelter in place* or an *evacuation*. In a shelter-in-place scenario, a family would be prepared to fend for themselves in their home for many days without any form of outside support. In an *evacuation*, a family leaves the area by automobile or other mode of transportation, taking with them the maximum amount of supplies they can carry, possibly including a tent for shelter. If mechanical transportation is not available, evacuation on foot would ideally include carrying at least three days of supplies and rain-tight bedding, a tarpaulin and a bedroll of blankets being the minimum.

Recovery

The recovery phase starts after the immediate threat to human life has subsided. During reconstruction it is recommended to consider the location or construction material of the property.

The most extreme home confinement scenarios include war, famine and severe epidemics and may last a year or more. Then recovery will take place inside the home. Planners for these events usually buy bulk foods and appropriate storage and preparation equipment, and eat the food as part of normal life. A simple balanced diet can be constructed from vitamin pills, whole-meal wheat, beans, dried milk, corn, and cooking oil. One should add vegetables, fruits, spices and meats, both prepared and fresh-gardened, when possible.

As a Profession

Emergency managers are trained in a wide variety of disciplines that support them throughout the emergency life-cycle. Professional emergency managers can focus on government and community preparedness (Continuity of Operations/Continuity of Government Planning), or private business preparedness (Business Continuity Management Planning). Training is provided by local, state, federal and private organizations and ranges from public information and media relations to high-level incident command and tactical skills such as studying a terrorist bombing site or controlling an emergency scene.

In the past, the field of emergency management has been populated mostly by people with a military or first responder background. Currently, the population in the field has become more diverse, with many experts coming from a variety of backgrounds without military or first responder history. Educational opportunities are increasing for those seeking undergraduate and graduate degrees in emergency management or a related field. There are over 180 schools in the US with emergency management-related programs, but only one doctoral program specifically in emergency management.

Professional certifications such as Certified Emergency Manager (CEM) and Certified Business Continuity Professional (CBCP) are becoming more common as the need for high professional standards is recognized by the emergency management community, especially in the United States.

Principles of Emergency Management

In 2007, Dr. Wayne Blanchard of FEMA's Emergency Management Higher Education Project, at the direction of Dr. Cortez Lawrence, Superintendent of FEMA's Emergency Management Institute, convened a working group of emergency management practitioners and academics to consider principles of emergency management. This project was prompted by the realization that while numerous books, articles and papers referred to "principles of emergency management," nowhere in the vast array of literature on the subject was there an agreed-upon definition of what these principles were. The group agreed on eight principles that will be used to guide the development of a doctrine of emergency management. The summary provided below lists these eight principles and provides a brief description of each.

Principles: Emergency management must be:

1. Comprehensive – emergency managers consider and take into account all hazards, all phases, all stakeholders and all impacts relevant to disasters.
2. Progressive – emergency managers anticipate future disasters and take preventive and preparatory measures to build disaster-resistant and disaster-resilient communities.
3. Risk-driven – emergency managers use sound risk management principles (hazard identification, risk analysis, and impact analysis) in assigning priorities and resources.
4. Integrated – emergency managers ensure unity of effort among all levels of government and all elements of a community.

5. Collaborative – emergency managers create and sustain broad and sincere relationships among individuals and organizations to encourage trust, advocate a team atmosphere, build consensus, and facilitate communication.
6. Coordinated – emergency managers synchronize the activities of all relevant stakeholders to achieve a common purpose.
7. Flexible – emergency managers use creative and innovative approaches in solving disaster challenges.
8. Professional – emergency managers value a science and knowledge-based approach; based on education, training, experience, ethical practice, public stewardship and continuous improvement.

A fuller description of these principles can be found at Principles of Emergency Management

Tools

In recent years the continuity feature of emergency management has resulted in a new concept, Emergency Management Information Systems (EMIS). For continuity and interoperability between emergency management stakeholders, EMIS supports the emergency management process by providing an infrastructure that integrates emergency plans at all levels of government and non-government involvement and by utilizing the management of all related resources (including human and other resources) for all four phases of emergencies. In the healthcare field, hospitals utilize HICS (Hospital Incident Command System) which provides structure and organization in a clearly defined chain of command with set responsibilities for each division.

Within other Professions

Practitioners in emergency management (disaster preparedness) come from an increasing variety of backgrounds as the field matures. Professionals from memory institutions (e.g., museums, historical societies, libraries, and archives) are dedicated to preserving cultural heritage—objects and records contained in their collections. This has been an increasingly major component within these field as a result of the heightened awareness following the September 11 attacks in 2001, the hurricanes in 2005, and the collapse of the Cologne Archives.

To increase the opportunity for a successful recovery of valuable records, a well-established and thoroughly tested plan must be developed. This plan must not be overly complex, but rather emphasize simplicity in order to aid in response and recovery. As an example of the simplicity, employees should perform similar tasks in the response and recovery phase that they perform under normal conditions. It should also include mitigation strategies such as the installation of sprinklers within the institution. This task requires the cooperation of a well-organized committee led by an experienced chairperson. Professional associations schedule regular workshops and hold focus sessions at annual conferences to keep individuals up to date with tools and resources in practice in order to minimize risk and maximize recovery.

Tools

The joint efforts of professional associations and cultural heritage institutions have resulted in the development of a variety of different tools to assist professionals in preparing disaster and recovery plans. In many cases, these tools are made available to external users. Also frequently available on websites are plan templates created by existing organizations, which may be helpful to any committee or group preparing a disaster plan or updating an existing plan. While each organization will need to formulate plans and tools which meet their own specific needs, there are some examples of such tools that might represent useful starting points in the planning process. These have been included in the External Links section.

In 2009, the US Agency for International Development created a web-based tool for estimating populations impacted by disasters. Called Population Explorer the tool uses Landscan population data, developed by Oak Ridge National Laboratory, to distribute population at a resolution 1 km^2 for all countries in the world. Used by USAID's FEWS NET Project to estimate populations vulnerable and or impacted by food insecurity, Population Explorer is gaining wide use in a range of emergency analysis and response actions, including estimating populations impacted by floods in Central America and a Pacific Ocean Tsunami event in 2009.

In 2007, a checklist for veterinarians pondering participation in emergency response was published in the Journal of the American Veterinary Medical Association, it had two sections of questions for a professional to ask them self before assisting with an emergency: Absolute requirements for participation: Have I chosen to participate?, Have I taken ICS training?, Have I taken other required background courses?, Have I made arrangements with my practice to deploy?,Have I made arrangements with my family?

Incident Participation: Have I been invited to participate?, Are my skill sets a match for the mission?, Can I access just-in-time training to refresh skills or acquire needed new skills?, Is this a self-support mission?, Do I have supplies needed for three to five days of self support?

While written for veterinarians, this checklist is applicable for any professional to consider before assisting with an emergency.

International Organizations

International Association of Emergency Managers

The International Association of Emergency Managers (IAEM) is a non-profit educational organization dedicated to promoting the goals of saving lives and protecting property during emergencies and disasters. The mission of IAEM is to serve its members by providing information, networking and professional opportunities, and to advance the emergency management profession.

It currently has seven Councils around the World: Asia, Canada, Europa, International, Oceania, Student and USA

IAEM also administrates the following programs on behalf of the profession: Certified Emergency Manager(CEM) Scholarship Program

The Air Force Emergency Management Association, affiliated by membership with the IAEM, provides emergency management information and networking for US Air Force Emergency Managers.

Red Cross/Red Crescent

National Red Cross/Red Crescent societies often have pivotal roles in responding to emergencies. Additionally, the International Federation of Red Cross and Red Crescent Societies (IFRC, or "The Federation") may deploy assessment teams, e.g. Field Assessment and Coordination Team-(FACT) to the affected country if requested by the national Red Cross or Red Crescent Society. After having assessed the needs Emergency Response Units (ERUs) may be deployed to the affected country or region. They are specialized in the response component of the emergency management framework.

United Nations

Within the United Nations system responsibility for emergency response rests with the Resident Coordinator within the affected country. However, in practice international response will be coordinated, if requested by the affected country's government, by the UN Office for the Coordination of Humanitarian Affairs (UN-OCHA), by deploying a UN Disaster Assessment and Coordination (UNDAC) team.

World Bank

Since 1980, the World Bank has approved more than 500 operations related to disaster management, amounting to more than US$40 billion. These include post-disaster reconstruction projects, as well as projects with components aimed at preventing and mitigating disaster impacts, in countries such as Argentina, Bangladesh, Colombia, Haiti, India, Mexico, Turkey and Vietnam to name only a few.

Common areas of focus for prevention and mitigation projects include forest fire prevention measures, such as early warning measures and education campaigns to discourage farmers from slash and burn agriculture that ignites forest fires; early-warning systems for hurricanes; flood prevention mechanisms, ranging from shore protection and terracing in rural areas to adaptation of production; and earthquake-prone construction.

In a joint venture with Columbia University under the umbrella of the ProVention Consortium the World Bank has established a Global Risk Analysis of Natural Disaster Hotspots.

In June 2006, the World Bank established the Global Facility for Disaster Reduction and Recovery (GFDRR), a longer term partnership with other aid donors to reduce disaster losses by mainstreaming disaster risk reduction in development, in support of the Hyogo Framework of Action. The facility helps developing countries fund development projects and programs that enhance local capacities for disaster prevention and emergency preparedness.

European Union

Since 2001, the EU adopted Community Mechanism for Civil Protection which started to play a significant role on the global scene. Mechanism's main role is to facilitate co-operation in civil protection assistance interventions in the event of major emergencies which may require urgent response actions. This applies also to situations where there may be an imminent threat of such major emergencies.

The heart of the Mechanism is the Monitoring and Information Centre. It is part of Directorate-General for Humanitarian Aid & Civil Protection of the European Commission and accessible 24 hours a day. It gives countries access to a platform, to a one-stop-shop of civil protection means available amongst the all the participating states. Any country inside or outside the Union affected by a major disaster can make an appeal for assistance through the MIC. It acts as a communication hub at headquarters level between participating states, the affected country and despatched field experts. It also provides useful and updated information on the actual status of an ongoing emergency.

International Recovery Platform

The International Recovery Platform (IRP) was conceived at the World Conference on Disaster Reduction (WCDR) in Kobe, Hyogo, Japan in January 2005. As a thematic platform of the International Strategy for Disaster Reduction (ISDR) system, IRP is a key pillar for the implementation of the Hyogo Framework for Action (HFA) 2005–2015: Building the Resilience of Nations and Communities to Disasters, a global plan for disaster risk reduction for the decade adopted by 168 governments at the WCDR.

The key role of IRP is to identify gaps and constraints experienced in post disaster recovery and to serve as a catalyst for the development of tools, resources, and capacity for resilient recovery. IRP aims to be an international source of knowledge on good recovery practice.

National Organizations

Australia

The key federal coordinating and advisory body for emergency management in Australia is Emergency Management Australia (EMA). The five states and two territories each has its own State Emergency Service. The Emergency Call Service provides a national 000 emergency telephone number to contact state Police, Fire and Ambulance services. Arrangements are in place for state and federal cooperation.

Canada

Public Safety Canada is Canada's national emergency management agency. Each province is required to have legislation in place for dealing with emergencies, as well as establish their own emergency management agencies, typically called an "Emergency Measures Organization" (EMO), which functions as the primary liaison with the municipal and federal level.

Public Safety Canada coordinates and supports the efforts of federal organizations ensuring national security and the safety of Canadians. They also work with other levels of government, first responders, community groups, the private sector (operators of critical infrastructure) and other nations.

Public Safety Canada's work is based on a wide range of policies and legislation through the Public Safety and Emergency Preparedness Act which defines the powers, duties and functions of PS are outlined. Other acts are specific to fields such as corrections, emergency management, law enforcement, and national security.

Germany

In Germany the Federal Government controls the German *Katastrophenschutz* (disaster relief) and *Zivilschutz* (civil protection) programs. The local units of German fire department and the Technisches Hilfswerk (*Federal Agency for Technical Relief*, THW) are part of these programs. The German Armed Forces (Bundeswehr), the German Federal Police and the 16 state police forces (Länderpolizei) all have been deployed for disaster relief operations. Besides the German Red Cross, humanitarian help is dispensed by the Johanniter-Unfallhilfe, the German equivalent of the St. John Ambulance, the Malteser-Hilfsdienst, the Arbeiter-Samariter-Bund, and other private Organization, to cite the largest relief organisation that are equipped for large-scale emergencies. As of 2006, there is a joint course at the University of Bonn leading to the degree "Master in Disaster Prevention and Risk Governance"

India

The role of emergency management in India falls to National Disaster Management Authority of India, a government agency subordinate to the Ministry of Home Affairs. In recent years there has been a shift in emphasis from response and recovery to strategic risk management and reduction, and from a government-centered approach to decentralized community participation. The Ministry of Science and Technology supports an internal agency that facilitates research by bringing the academic knowledge and expertise of earth scientists to emergency management.

A group representing a public/private partnership has recently been formed by the Government of India. It is funded primarily by a large India-based computer company and aimed at improving the general response of communities to emergencies, in addition to those incidents which might be described as disasters. Some of the groups' early efforts involve the provision of emergency management training for first responders (a first in India), the creation of a single emergency telephone number, and the establishment of standards for EMS staff, equipment, and training. It operates in three states, though efforts are being made in making this a nation-wide effective group.

The Netherlands

In the Netherlands the Ministry of the Interior and Kingdom Relations is responsible for emergency preparedness en emergency management on national level and operates a national crisis centre (NCC). The country is divided in 25 safety regions (veiligheidsregio). Each safety region is covered by three services: police, fire and ambulance. All regions operate according to the Coordinated Regional Incident Management system. Other services such as the Ministry of Defence, waterboard(s), Rijkswaterstaat etc. can have an active role in the emergency management process.

New Zealand

In New Zealand, responsibility for emergency management moves from local to national depending on the nature of the emergency or risk reduction programme. A severe storm may be manageable within a particular area, whereas a national public education campaign will be directed by central government. Within each region, local governments are unified into 16 Civil Defence Emergency Management Groups (CDEMGs). Every CDEMG is responsible for ensuring that local emergency management is robust as possible. As local arrangements are overwhelmed by an emergency, pre-existing mutual-support arrangements are activated. As warranted, central government has the authority to coordinate the response through the National Crisis Management Centre (NCMC), operated by the Ministry of Civil Defence & Emergency Management (MCDEM). These structures are defined by regulation, and best explained in *The Guide to the National Civil Defence Emergency Management Plan 2006*, roughly equivalent to the U.S. Federal Emergency Management Agency's National Response Framework.

Terminology

New Zealand uses unique terminology for emergency management to the rest of the English-speaking world.

4Rs is a term used to describe the emergency management cycle locally. In New Zealand the four phases are known as:

- Reduction = Mitigation
- Readiness = Preparedness
- Response
- Recovery.

Emergency management is rarely used locally; many government publications retain usage of the term civil defence. For example, the Minister of Civil Defence is responsible for central government's emergency management agency, MCDEM.

Civil Defence Emergency Management is a term in its own right. Often abbreviated as CDEM, it is defined by statute as the application of knowledge to prevent harm from disasters. Disaster very rarely appears in official publications. In a New Zealand context, the terms emergency and incident usually appear when speaking about disasters in general. When describing an emergency that has had a response from the authorities, the term event is also used. For example, publications refer to the "Canterbury Snow Event 2002"

Russia

In Russia the Ministry of Emergency Situations (EMERCOM) is engaged in fire fighting, Civil Defence, Search and Rescue, including rescue services after natural and human-made disasters.

United Kingdom

The United Kingdom adjusted its focus on emergency management following the 2000 UK fuel protests, severe flooding in the same year and the 2001 United Kingdom foot-and-mouth crisis. This resulted in the creation of the Civil Contingencies Act 2004 (CCA) which defined some organisations as Category 1 and 2 Responders. These responders have responsibilities under the legislation regarding emergency preparedness and response. The CCA is managed by the Civil Contingencies Secretariat through Regional Resilience Forums and at the local authority level.

Disaster Management training is generally conducted at the local level by the organisations involved in any response. This is consolidated through professional courses that can be undertaken at the Emergency Planning College. Furthemore diplomas, undergraduate and postgraduate qualifications can be gained throughout the country-the first course of this type was carried out by Coventry University in 1994. The Institute of Emergency Management is a charity, established in 1996, providing consulting services for the government, media and commercial sectors.

The Professional Society for Emergency Planners is the Emergency Planning Society. One of the largest emergency exercises in the UK was carried out on 20 May 2007 near Belfast, Northern Ireland, and involved the scenario of a plane crash landing at Belfast International Airport. Staff from five hospitals and three airports participated in the drill, and almost 150 international observers assessed its effectiveness.

United States

Under the Department of Homeland Security (DHS), the Federal Emergency Management Agency (FEMA) is lead agency for emergency management. The HAZUS software package developed by FEMA is central in the risk assessment process in the country. The United States and its territories are covered by one of ten regions for FEMA's emergency management purposes. Tribal, state, county and local governments develop emergency management programs/departments and operate hierarchically within each region. Emergencies are managed at the most-local level possible, utilizing mutual aid agreements with adjacent jurisdictions. If the emergency is terrorist related or if declared an "Incident of National Significance", the Secretary of Homeland Security will initiate the National Response Framework (NRF). Under this plan the involvement of federal resources will be made possible, integrating in with the local, county, state, or tribal entities. Management will continue to be handled at the lowest possible level utilizing the National Incident Management System (NIMS).

The Citizen Corps is an organization of volunteer service programs, administered locally and coordinated nationally by DHS, which seek to mitigate disaster and prepare the population for emergency response through public education, training, and outreach. Community Emergency Response Teams are a Citizen Corps program focused on disaster preparedness and teaching basic disaster response skills. These volunteer teams are utilized to provide emergency support when disaster overwhelms the conventional emergency services.

The US Congress established the Center for Excellence in Disaster Management and Humanitarian Assistance (COE) as the principal agency to promote disaster preparedness and societal resiliency in the Asia-Pacific region. As part of its mandate, COE facilitates education and training in disaster preparedness, consequence management and health security to develop domestic, foreign and international capability and capacity.

Social Responsibility

Social responsibility is an ethical ideology or theory that an entity, be it an organization or individual, has an obligation to act to benefit society at large. This responsibility can be passive, by avoiding engaging in socially harmful acts, or active, by performing activities that directly advance social goals. Businesses can use ethical decision making to secure their businesses by making decisions that allow for government agencies to minimize their involvement with the corporation. (Kaliski, 2001) For instance if a company is proactive and follows the United States Environmental Protection Agencyý (EPA) guidelines for emissions on dangerous pollutants and even goes an extra step to get involved in the community and address those concerns that the public might have; they would be less likely to have the EPA investigate them for environmental concerns. "A significant element of current thinking about privacy, however, stresses "self-regulation" rather than market or government mechanisms for protecting personal information" (Swire, 1997) Most rules and regulations are formed due to public outcry, if there is not outcry there often will be limited regulation.

Critics argue that Corporate social responsibility (CSR) distracts from the fundamental economic role of businesses; others argue that it is nothing more than superficial window-dressing; others argue that it is an attempt to pre-empt the role of governments as a watchdog over powerful multinational corporations though there is no systematic evidence to support these criticisms. A significant number of studies have shown no negative influence on shareholder results from CSR but rather, a slightly positive correlation with improved shareholder returns.

Emerging Normative Status of Social Responsibility

Social responsibility as a non-binding, or soft law principle has received some normative status in relation to private and public corporations in the United Nations Educational, Social and Cultural Organization (UNESCO) *Universal Declaration on Bioethics and Human Rights* developed by the UNESCO International Bioethics Committee particularly in relation to child and maternal welfare.(Faunce and Nasu 2009) The International Organization for Standardization (ISO) is developing an international standard to provide guidelines for adopting and disseminating social responsibility: ISO 26000-Social Responsibility. Due for publication in 2010, this standard will "encourage voluntary commitment to social responsibility and will lead to common guidance on concepts, definitions and methods of evaluation." (ISO, 2009) The standard describes itself as a guide for dialogue and language, not a constraining or certifiable management standard.

Crisis Theory

Crisis theory is generally associated with Marxian economics. In this context crisis refers to what is called, even currently and outside Marxian theory in many European countries a "conjuncture" or especially sharp bust cycle of the regular boom and bust pattern of what Marxists term "chaotic" capitalist development, which, if no countervailing action is taken, develops into a recession or depression-see, for example, 1994 economic crisis in Mexico, Argentine economic crisis (1999-2002), South American economic crisis of 2002, Economic crisis of Cameroon, Financial crisis of 2007–2010, Great Depression, etc. In terms of historical materialism, such crises repeat until objective and subjective factors combine to precipitate the transition to the new mode of production.

Causes of Crisises

In Marxist terms, the economic crises are crises of overproduction and immiseration of the workers who, were it not for the capitalist control of the society, would be the determiners of both demand and production in the first place. Karl Marx in his many works (published and unpublished) suggested several different theories, none of them free from controversy to explain how this worked out in particular circumstances. In his mature work his theory of crisis is framed as a *Law of Tendency for the Rate of Profit to Fall* combined with a discussion of various counter tendencies, which may slow or modify it's impact. A key characteristic of these theoretical factors is that none of them are natural or accidental in origin but instead arise from systemic elements of capitalism as a mode of production and basic social order. In Marx's words, "The *real barrier* of capitalist production is *capital itself.*

These systemic factors include the classical :

- *Full employment profit squeeze.* Capital accumulation can pull up the demand for labor power, raising wages. If wages rise "too high," it hurts the rate of profit, causing a recession.

- *The tendency of the rate of profit to fall.* The accumulation of capital, the general advancement of techniques and scale of production, and the inexorable trend to oligopoly by the victors of capitalist market competition, all involve a general tendency for the degree of capital intensity, i.e., the "organic composition of capital" of production to rise. All else constant, this leads to a fall in the rate of profit, which leads to a slow-down of accumulation and attempts to remedy this either within the circuit of production or by non-production means such as the financialization based booms of the 1920s or 1990s and early 2000s. Since only real production can be the basis of sustained accumulation at the macroeconomic and international scale, the failure of such remedies can result in panic and systemic crisis.
- *Underconsumption.* If the capitalists win the class struggle to push wages down and labor effort up, raising the rate of surplus value, then a capitalist economy faces regular problems of inadequate consumer demand and thus inadequate aggregate demand.

However, as stated above, all such factors resolve to the synthetic viewpoint that all such crises are crises of over and/or misappropriated production relative to the ability and/or willingness of the workers who generate the bulk of demand to consume.

Application

It is a tenet of many Marxists groupings that crises are inevitable and will be increasingly severe until the contradictions inherent in the mismatch between the mode of production and the development of productive forces reach the final point of failure, determined by the quality of their leadership, the development of the consciousness of the various social classes, and other "subjective factors".

Thus the degree of "tuning" necessary for intervention in otherwise "perfect" market mechanisms becomes more and more extreme as the time in which the capitalist order is a progressive factor in the development of productive forces recedes further and further into the past. But the subjective factors are the explanation for why purely objective factors such as the severity of a crisis, the rate of exploitation, etc. do not alone determine the revolutionary upsurge. A common example is the contrast of the oppression of the working classes in France in centuries prior to 1789 which although greater did not lead to social revolution as it did once the complete correlation of forces appeared.

Influence

The place of crisis theory within Marx's theory is central and recurs throughout his writings and correspondence. This is one of the abiding and most revolutionary aspects of Marx's work. Alongside Lenin's complementary study of the "barbarous dynamic" of capitalism, this theory underpins marxists' understanding of the enduring necessity for systemic change. Its contested treatment is therefore unsurprising, and as Roman Rosdolsky explains ... "The assertion that Marx did not propose a 'breakdown theory' is primarily attributable to the revisionist interpretation of Marx before and after the First World War. Rosa Luxemburg and Henryk Grossman both rendered inestimable theoretical services by insisting, as against the revisionists, on the breakdown theory." More recently David Yaffe 1972,1978 and Tony Allen et al 1978,1981 in using the theory to explain the conditions of the 1970's and 80's re-introduced the theory to a new generation and gained new readers for Grossman's presentation of Marx's crisis theory.

An attempt was made to re-present aspects of the working out of the theory in a mathematical form in the work of Henryk Grossman. Central to the argument is the claim that, within a given business cycle, the accumulation of surplus from year to year leads to a kind of top-heaviness, in which a relatively fixed number of workers have to add profit to an ever-larger lump of investment capital.

This observation leads to what is known as Marx's law of the tendency of the rate of profit to fall. Unless certain countervailing possibilities are available, the exponential growth of capital outpaces the growth in labor productivity, so the profits of economic activity have to be shared out more thinly among capitals, i.e., at a lower profit rate. When countervailing tendencies are unavailable or exhausted, the system requires the destruction of capital values in order to return to profitability.

Paul Mattick's *Economic Crisis and Crisis Theory* published by Merlin Press in 1981 is an accessible introduction and discussion derived from Grossman's work. François Chesnais's [1984] chapter *Marx's Crisis Theory Today* in Christopher Freeman ed. *Design, Innovation and Long Cycles in Economic Development* Frances Pinter, London, discussed the continuing relevance of the theory.

Difference between Marxists and Keynesians

Keynesian Economics which attempts a "middle way" between laissez-faire, unadulterated capitalism and state guidance and partial control of economic activity, such as in the French dirigisme or the policies of the Golden Age of Capitalism attempts to address such crises with the policy of having the state actively supplying the deficiencies of unaltered markets. Marxists and Keynesians approach and apply the concept of economic crisis in distinct and opposite ways. The Keynesian approach attempts to stay strictly within the economic sphere and describes 'boom' and 'bust' cycles that balance out. Marxists, on the other hand, see economic crisis as part of the larger crisis of the social order they wish to supplant. There is also a Post-Keynesian economics debt-crisis theory of Hyman Minsky.

International Crisis

An international crisis is a crisis between states. There are many definitions of an international crisis. Snyder "...a sequence of interactions between the governments of two or more sovereign states in severe conflict, short of actual war, but involving the perception of a dangerously high probability of war".

Types

Lebow gives a breakdown of three types of international crises:

- Justification of Hostilities. One of the nations decides, before the crisis starts, to go to war and constructs a crisis to justify it. The pattern of justificaion is almost always the same: Rouse public opinion, make impossible demands, try to legitimize the demands, deny your real intentions then employ the rejection of the demands as a reason for war. A recent example, commonly employed by critics of George W. Bush, is the Iraq disarmament crisis, which precipitated the Iraq War.

- Spinoff Crisis. The nations are involved in a war or crisis with another nation or nations and this precipitates another crisis, e.g. the Lusitania incident in 1915.
- Brinkmanship. Intentionally forcing a crisis to get the other side to back down. The Cuban Missile Crisis of 1962 is a well-known example of brinkmanship.

With the exception of a justification of hostilities, the study of international crises assumes that neither side actually wants to go to war, but must be visibly prepared to do so. In the words of Groucho Marx, "Always be sincere, even if you don't mean it".

Strategies

George's book presents an overview of the process and conflicting goals of crisis management as well as many examples. He discusses a number of strategies, including:

Offensive Strategies

- blackmail
- limited and reversible response
- controlled pressure
- attrition
- fait accompli.

Defensive Strategies

- coercion
- limited escalation
- tit-for-tat
- test of capabilities
- "drawing a line"
- Buying time strategy
- Conveying commitment and resolve to avoid miscalculation by the adversary.

List of Defused Crises

International crises tend to result in war, almost by definition; they are then remembered best not as crises but as causes of wars. For information on international crises that resulted immediately in war. Given the above, some of the crises that are best-known *as crises* were defused. The following crises did not immediately provoke large-scale violence, but set of anger in countries:

- Anglo-Portuguese Crisis (1889-1890)
- Fashoda Incident (1898-1899)
- First Moroccan Crisis (1904-1906)
- Bosnian crisis (1908-1909)
- Agadir Crisis (1911)
- Åland crisis (1916-1920)
- Remilitarization of the Rhineland (1936)
- Anschluss (1938)
- Sudetenland Crisis (1938)
- Iran crisis (1946-1947)
- Berlin Blockade (1948-1949)
- Cuban Missile Crisis (1962)
- *Pueblo* incident (1968)
- Damansky Island Crisis (1969)
- Axe Murder Incident (1976)
- Beagle conflict (1978)
- Iran hostage crisis (1979)
- Able Archer 83 (1983)
- 2001 Indian Parliament attack (2001)
- November 2008 Mumbai attacks (2008).

Pre-crisis and Emergency Risk Communication in the Hotel Industry, in Partnership with Non-governmental Organizations

The first disaster hit on the hotel industry in the 21st century is undoubtedly the 2004 tsunami in Phucket, Thaïland on December 26th, which resulted in 230 000 deaths. The Sofitel Magic Lagoon Resort 'Khao Lak' suffered perhaps the most extensive losses in the area with 200 deaths. In September 2005, a dozen families of the French victims filed a lawsuit accusing Accor of not having taken into account the risk of danger at its Sofitel, located on a beach in a region affected by tsunamis. It accused hotel management of alerting guests too late and not handling the situation properly, said hotel staff were not trained to cope with a tsunami, and said nearby hotels suffered fewer casualties. The complaint also accused Thai weather authorities of a delayed reaction in spreading a warning (Von Derschau, 2007).

The negative impact of a disaster on the image of a tourist destination or hotel can be both serious and long lasting. The corporate or business interests of the hotel industry actually provide an entry point to a broader approach incorporating corporate social responsibility (CSR) to address disaster mitigation.

This paper presents a plan integrating CSR and disaster preparedness for the hospitality industry by proposing collaboration with humanitarian organization, particularly the International Federation of Red Cross and Societies (IFRCS). How can the hospitality industry be encouraged to address issues of crisis management that are at the heart of IFRCS work around the world and benefit from the Red Cross's disaster preparedness, disaster recovery and risk reduction know-how as a competitive advantage?

The focus in this presentation is on pre-crisis communication, to help increase preparedness from hoteliers and the public in general and to communicate effectively on disaster preparedness. It is our belief that the first hoteliers to implement this solution will gain considerable credibility and trust from the public, both usually considered as serious competitive advantages.

It is our belief that communication on disaster preparedness is a growing demand of the public that would not have significant adverse effect as anticipated by the hotel industry, namely focus customers on disasters or divert them from destinations with higher risks.

Recent events in Japan following March 11th, 2011 earthquake and tsunami have led disaster management experts to call for a new level of crisis management (Paraskevas, 2011) including plans for people, facility and processes recovery. The hotel industry needs 'champions' and 'best practices' in this field, that can only emerge if a communication on crisis management plans (CMP) is made possible.

Crisis and Emergency Risk Communication and (CSR) Corporate Social Responsibility

The emerging perspective on CSR focuses on responsibility towards stakeholders (shareholders, employees, management, consumers and community) rather than on maximization of profit for shareholders. The leading companies have discovered that working together with non-profit and government organizations to solve problems can give them new insights and approaches to creating business opportunities as well (Subbalakshmi, 2007).

According to surveys on consumer attitude and global public opinion, people around the world focus on corporate social citizenship ahead of either brand reputation or financial factors; two in three people want companies to go beyond their historical role of making a profit, paying taxes, employing people and obeying laws; they also want companies to contribute to broader societal goals.

Half the population on the surveys had paid attention to the social behaviour of companies. Because of the change of consumer attitude, the conclusion is that this pressure on companies will likely increase more and more (World Travel and Tourism Council, 2002). While the benefits of CSR activities to corporations may vary depending on the nature of the company and are often hard to gauge, there is a wide range of articles and websites that argue for the business case of CSR (Nord, 2006). Commonly cited reasons to engage in CSR activities include enhanced reputation, employee satisfaction, risk management and financial performance.

Present CSR Practices in the Hotel Industry

Holcomb et al. (2007) conducted a study of the major hotel chains CSR communication on their website and found out that "eight out of the ten top hotel companies (80%) reported giving charitable donations, 60% reported having diversity policies, and 40% mentioned social responsibility as part of their company mission statements. Community, environment, marketplace, vision and values, and workforce were the categories the top ten hotel companies' available information was entered into. Hilton Corporation was found to have the most comprehensive CSR reporting. Marriot came in as second and the Accor hotel group was third.

According to this reference, most hotel companies should improve their CSR reporting and live up to their reputation of being 'hospitable' not only to their guests but also to society". Some initiatives are worth mentioning:

Cash Donations

Cash is still the most important, and often the most appropriate, donation for humanitarian relief and recovery efforts. For instance, Marriott International converts donated points to cash for a contribution to the IFRC Disaster Relief Emergency Fund (Marriott, 2010). Bali Hotels association raises funds for Mount Merapi volcanic disaster which occurred just recently. Rhode Island Hotels has shown Charity to Flood Victims. In Pakistan, during the heavy flood that impaired a large portion of the country, Serena Hotels through its Corporate Social Responsibility Program-SEED (Environmental and Educational Development) has embarked upon a comprehensive fund raising effort throughout Pakistan. In 2007, IHG donated £626,000 in support of community initiatives and charitable causes at corporate level (IHG, 2010).

Work Force Initiative

Hyatt's F.O.R.C.E (Hyatt, 2010) is a volunteer program that allows Hyatt associates worldwide to participate in local community outreach and volunteer efforts on paid company time. "Business is often willing to provide in-kind support facilities, technical expertise and volunteer labour rather than money. This can be used to good effect. A growing number of employees wish to make a greater contribution to society through volunteering, and companies are increasingly recognizing that volunteering improves staff skills and motivation".

Partnership with NGOs

In Bali, Indonesia, the Red Cross has an outstanding way of collecting blood for utilizing in emergency condition which involves hotels. They put signs in hotels and visit to collect blood, but only if its rhesus is negative, as rhesus negative blood is scarce in Indonesia. Hotels are flooded by millions of people from different parts of the world each year with tourists having rhesus negative blood. Hence the Indonesian Red Cross capitalizes on this opportunity.

Shelter and Evacuation

In the Bahamas, for example, some hotels have secure locations to save the senior managers when a hurricane hits the island. Hotels sometimes have planes for the senior managers to transfer to a secure location. If hotels had extra secure locations and planes for guests and local employees, this could be something to communicate on, to show the world they are willing to help (Suarez, 2010).

Crisis Management Plan

Disaster preparedness and mitigation plans have become a major issue for all businesses, including the hotel industry, even more as hotels have a responsibility towards their customers, considered as guests. Crisis Management has become a part of the responsibility of hotels towards their guest, i.e. a part of their Corporate Social Responsibility.

The historical record is full of cases in which the tourism industry has been affected by a range of disasters (Garraway, 2008). Tourism destinations are often remote and exposed to both natural and man-made threats such as terrorist attacks. Whenever a natural disaster strikes a particular region, the tourism industry is also badly affected. The Indian Ocean tsunami of 26 December 2004 has shown the tragic consequences on international tourists in a natural disaster: thousands of western tourists were the victims of the tsunami. One estimate puts the overall death toll as surpassing 280,000 and the number of tourist casualties at more than 3,500. In 2005, Hurricane Katrina left more than 80 per cent of New Orleans underwater and blew away the state's largest source of revenue-tourism-which in 2004 drew more than 10 million visitors and created 80,000 tourism-related jobs (Reuters, 2005). Terrorism has also become a global concern, afflicting the hospitality industry directly and indirectly: 56 persons were killed and 265 injured at the attack on the Marriot hotel in Islamabad on 20 September 2008, among the casualties, 30 were hotel associates (Gunaratna, 2008); In the same year, 165 persons were killed, including 26 foreigners, at the Taj Hotel in Mumbai (Kronstadt, 2008); Again in the coordinated terrorist attack on the Ritz Carlton and JW Marriott hotels on 17 July 2009 in Jakarta, Indonesia, nine people were Killed and 25 injured, further emphasizing that hotels have become a target for many terrorist groups (Solomon, 2009). In the Great Hanshin Earthquake in Kobe, Japan in January 1995, which was measured at a magnitude of 7.3, 249 180 buildings collapsed, 6 436 people lost their lives and 43 792 were injured. However, in the midst of this destruction, for the tourism industry, precautions such as earthqua2e proof architecture, fire proof equipment and the value of frequent fire and evacuation drills had paid off. In addition, although in many cases, guests had to stay in hotel lobbies for 2 to 3 days, they were given frequent situation reports in order to prevent panic and employee morale was kept high.

Four points have come out of that disaster (Garraway, 2008):

1. The basic rule of prioritizing human life prevailed – each employee must act for guest safety soon after an emergency event. This was evident by the fact that most guests were evacuated from their rooms on hour after the event;
2. The importance of having a unified information flow that prevents the spread of rumours that may lead to panic and confusion;
3. Moving down decision making power to the front lines in emergencies;
4. Maintaining a good relationship with the local community so that there is rapid cooperation during disasters.

Research on crisis management and complexity thinking have shown that a CMP should not aim at specific agent behaviours and actions but at the collective robustness and resilience of the organisation. It should set the rules of interaction between its various agents but not dictate their actions. Such CMP can only work in an environment where hotel managers are fully, understand regularly, trained on crisis management. As stressed by Reynolds and Seeger (2005), crisis management plans (CMP) should be designed with the help of outside experts; the American Red Cross, for example, with its emphasis on disaster relief, has been a traditional proponent of emergency preparation.

Crisis and Emergency Risk Communication

Crisis and Emergency Risk Communication (CERC) was first introduced in 2002 as a merged approach of crisis communication and risk communication. One of the main contributions of this merged approach is the recognition that communication is part of the preparation process, and that effective communication must be an integrated and ongoing process (Seeger, 2006). Pre-crisis communication includes the public preparation for the possibility of an adverse event and alliances, cooperation and the development of consensual recommendations by experts.

If disaster preparedness is a growing concern in the hotel industry, there is surprisingly few communication on this point, not on any hotel chain website anyway. And though the hotel industry has been introducing Corporate Social Responsibility initiatives since the 1990s (Holcomb, 2007), disaster management, such as needed after the 2004 Indian Ocean tsunami, is not generally listed on any of the CSR checklists commonly agreed upon in the literature (Lynn, 2009). Best Western, Hilton group, Accor, Intercontinental, and Six Senses did commit over $2.5 million for the 2004 tsunami relief, and other chains also provided aid ((Henderson, 2007) quoted in, but their communication is centred on charity and completely excludes any initiatives taken to prepare their hotels and resorts for inevitable future disasters.

Best practices in crisis communication (Seeger, 2006) include pre-event planning; partnership with the public; credibility building and strategic partnership with experts before a crisis occurs. Hoteliers can generalise Crisis Management Plans but if Kept secret, their efficiency is proved to be hindered as communication is a part of the process, and best practices in crisis communication can not be applied as long as pre-crisis communication is avoided. As the public is not aware of the risks, plans and basic safety procedures, CMP will be deficient.

As the hotel industry is not communicating on crisis management, it is weakening its own and the public disaster preparedness, putting their customers at risk. All CSR efforts are also plundered by the silence around disaster preparedness and every new disaster comforts the negative image of hotels that are not responsible of their guests safety and can not help during disasters.

Partnership Concept

It is not easy to conduct pre-crisis communication initiated solely by hotels, as the hospitality industry cannot communicate easily on disaster mitigation for its own business interests. The hotel industry needs to function through an "integrated triangle model" where three actors (hotel, IFRCS and the public) take part. The trade-off is a "handshake": if the hospitality industry renders cooperation and financial support to the IFRCS, the latter will act as an intermediary between the hotel and the public to implement the hotel's CSR program, including disaster preparedness.

The hotel will benefit from the IFRCS' expertise and thus, ensure the safety and security of guests, employees and property while enhancing its brand reputation and image by using the trade-off as a marketing tool. Further, it will increase staff morale and motivation, and help employees to acquire new skills and experience, all leading to a more committed and productive workforce. It will also strengthen relationships with visitors or guests and local and national authorities.

Roles of Hotels

Assess Vulnerability

A list of questions can serve as a checklist regarding vulnerability to different kinds of disasters: "natural disasters" (tsunamis, earthquakes and wild fires), industrial accidents (spills, explosions and product defects including food poisoning) and intentional events (product tampering and terrorist attacks (Seeger at al, 2003). Self-assessment includes questions on potential risks, evacuation questions, staff responsibility and training, guest preparedness, business recovery and post-disaster management (Udu-gama, 2008).

Prepare Staff

In November 2010, the authors interviewed Pablo Suarez, Phd, Technical advisor for Red Cross/Red Crescent Climate Centre. He stressed that employees should be trained on a regular basis, instilling them with the aptitude to adjust with any disaster and thereby ensuring safety and security of the hotel and the guests. Hotels should also contribute to the response and recovery process by supporting the families of hotel staff.

Command Post & Logistic Support

Hotels can allocate space and accommodation to the IFRC,

based on availability, to establish a temporary command post during disaster and post disaster recovery, to enable them to conduct their operations smoothly. Hotels could also provide logistic support. The various hotel departments could lend the following services: housekeeping can distribute relief items (blankets, water, food, health, etc.); food & Beverage (F&B) department can arrange sustenance for IFRC personnel; front desk can organize accommodation for IFRC staff when available, ultimately grouping customers to free rooms; the Administration & HR departments can allocate employees to work closely with IFRC personnel during immediate post disaster response (Suarez, 2010).

Roles of IFRC

Make Communication Happen

The partnership makes it possible to communicate on disaster for the hotel industry as the primary message "This hotel is prepared, as much as possible, to handle disasters" is converted to "This hotel partners with International Red Cross to protect guests and help during disasters". It can even be positive for any hotel to use the name and resources of an internationally recognised humanitarian organization, such as Red Cross.

Training

Hotel employees are not essentially trained to act in case of a disaster. Untrained employees may intricate the situation more. Hotels could benefit from training by the IFRC to have their employees react in an appropriate manner in times of need, including during normal operations. Training includes first aid and community or businesses disaster preparedness through short guides like "Preparing your business for the unthinkable".

Technology

Communication and sharing of information is essential during a disaster and when disaster strikes, usual means of communication are often disrupted. Red Cross uses innovative technology like Global Relief Technologies Trimble Nomad handhelds for data collection. The device is generally connected via GPRS technology (General Packet Radio Service) that is built in. In the event that GPRS is not available, because of the location or adverse weather conditions, the Trimble Nomad handhelds can also interface via Bluetooth with a BGAN Satellite terminal to send data. BGAN (Broadband Global Area Network) is a mobile communications system created to transmit broadband wireless voice and data communications almost anywhere on the earth's surface.

Certification

An external expert, such as IFRC, may certify the preparedness, ability and concern of a hotel, reassuring clients that the hotel is prepared to handle any kind of problem in an efficient and effective way. As an existing starting point, "the American Red Cross *Ready Rating program* is a free, self-guided program designed to help businesses, organizations and schools become better prepared for emergencies. Members complete a 123-point self assessment of their level of preparedness, gain access to tips and best practices, and commit to improving their score each year to maintain membership. The 123 Assessment has been aligned with the federal government's private sector preparedness standards (PS-Prep)."

Current Ready Rating member listing on the American Red Cross website includes hotels from major hotel chains: Courtyard by Marriott, Newport News; Element hotel, Hanover (Starwood); Hilton Garden Inn, Hampton and Hilton Garden Inn, Frederick; Holiday Inn Express Williamsburg; Hyatt Place, Richmond Airport and Hyatt Regency, Long Beach. It is striking that lone properties are part of the program and nothing is done at the chain level; it is also striking that no hotel chain or property page mentions their Ready Rating membership.

Partnership Communication Strategy

The overall objective of the proposed partnership campaign is to raise public awareness and to increase will and resource allocation among the hotels, public, NGO's, and humanitarian organization for preventing and responding to all forms of natural and man-made calamities in a collaborative manner with the primary aim of enhancing work among the mentioned entities. The campaign will focus on global encouragement, strengthened efforts and partnerships at national levels and regional levels.

The collaboration plan will only happen with the active commitment of partners to prevent and response to all forms of natural and man-made calamities in order to achieve sustainable and responsible tourism practices by ensuring safe and secure environment to the visitors, employees and neighbouring community.

Aims

The purpose of this communication strategy is to enable the hotel industry to communicate on their crisis management efforts and preparedness of staff and hotel properties. By communicating, hotels will raise the public awareness thus helping management during crisis; and also raise their staff demand for training and preparation. It can also help the industry to develop its Corporate Social Responsibility and protect its global image during future disasters. The hospitality industry has an immediate opportunity – and an obligation – to enhance its image in disaster preparedness and mitigation. It might bring the ultimate competitive advantage for the first hotels to implement the concept.

Key Message

The key message for all audiences is a two-way partnership between the hotel industry and NGOs where the hotel industry supports NGOs by providing support to their operations throughout the world, when disaster happens; and that NGOs in return share their experience and knowledge with the hotel industry to prepare them to protect staff and guests in case of an emergency.

Communications Tools

The following tools can be developed:

- A basic website can be created in different languages for the launch of the campaign. It can be updated and expanded to include feature highlighting news and activities carried out in conjunction with the campaign.
- A coordinated database on disaster risk mitigation and sustainable tourism destination can be established as a way of monitoring progress under the campaign.
- A logo has to be developed and has to be made available, with guidelines for its use, on the campaign website.
- Online outreach tools can be explored, such as social networking sites and blogs, as an effective way to reach

large audiences, raise awareness and build constituencies that can be further engaged.

- A brochure and fact sheets about the campaign can be developed, first on-line and then in print form.
- Guidelines for safety procedures can be developed and distributed to the media.

Conclusion

The proposed partnership between NGOs and the hotel industry can help mitigate natural or man-made disasters and reduce the impact on destinations. Also, by allowing early adopters to communicate on crisis management and disaster preparedness, the partnership will raise public expectations, thus participating in the spread of crisis management practices. As the hotel industry can not communicate effectively on disaster preparedness and all efforts are kept secret, required investments and budgets are not fully allocated and the public is not prepared, resulting in additional casualties during disasters. The virtuous circle led in motion by the partnership will move the whole industry and should benefit particularly to the first partners. Before any implementation of the partnership, future research is required on the expected negative impact of communication on disaster preparedness, as anticipated by the hotel industry, and means to soften the effects, with samples of reactions and customer survey. Additional research should also identify best practices in disaster management and their impact on the public when used in communication.

4

Responsible Crisis Management and Risk Mitigation

Safety and security are of great importance when visitors consider destinations for their annual holidays. Media coverage of terrorism, national public/political strikes and extreme climate events can have a negative impact on a country/region's appeal. How tourists were warned, looked after and helped evacuate, have impacts on a destination's brand image – broadcast by the ever present social networks. In Australia staff and guest safety, and implemented Climate Change Adaptation plans should be acknowledged as tourism businesses 'licence to operate'. They must plug into a wider destination crisis management plan. A 'whole of tourism' approach in destinations that managing risk as a foundation for sustainable development. There is also the moral responsibility, that should be put above commercial factors, where the hospitality sector and destination managers acknowledge their responsibility to look after the guests they invite and act to minimise their negative environmental impacts.

Practical Steps to a more Responsible Crisis Management and Risk Mitigation for Tourism

Risk Mitigation

There exists a very comprehensive Federal Government Climate Change Mitigation and Adaptation Risk Management program with a practical methodology and workshop procedure guide. Destinations across Australia need to conduct workshops and prepare Crisis Management Plans. Such plans need to be dovetailed with the emergency services reporting structures and communications. Tourism Australia and the state agencies could endorse accreditation programmes which emphasise Climate Change Adaptation and promote operators whose accreditation policies integrate with the destination's responsible risk management plan. Operators who comply could be highlighted on new online serach facilities within the Australian Tourism Data Warehouse.

Implementation of Local Agenda 21. There was an Australian Government commitment to LA21. The previous government gave an APEC commitment to double participation by 2003, although a dormant program now, it represents a single clear plan to create more sustainable development in local government areas, many are tourist destinations. Government agencies and peak bodies need to work more closely with local government and establish Responsible Tourism Partnerships that implement many of the guiding principles within LA21. This way we can progress to a more sustainable tourism sector. Local Government planning along coastal areas also needs to consider the lastest international thinking on building design.

Peak industry bodies can organise special sector insurance programmes. Initially with third party insurers but there is scope to develop their own programmes to support their members. There are already examples in tourism transport.

Explore the scope for Volunteer Tourism, by involving conservation NGOs who might assist in the repair of natural habitat and injured wildlife. A partnership plan involving nature tourism businesses, national parks and the NGOs could be prepared for future implementation.

The tourism sector must take responsibility for the negative environmental impacts that result from bringing visitors to destinations. 75% of tourisms overall GHG footprint is generated from transport (UNEP 2008). Low carbon transport options could be imbedded into the destination's travel planning communications. This supports a moral argument to visit after extreme climatic events.

Tourism also needs to be seen to act Responsibly to protect the natural heritage assets it consumes. Both tourism businesses and visitors therefore need to contribute to the repair and conservation of protected land and The Commons. Such programmes can become a keystone in a destination's Local Distinctiveness.

Crisis Management

Tourism Australia and state agencies, should create a national tourism crisis management plan to implement:

a) world class visitor communications in the destination and to the outside world before/during/after events

b) sponsor tourism destination crisis management training and develop a Destination Crisis Management Communication Plan. This should interlink with regional and state plans (and the emergency services-we need to speak with one voice and responsibly advise would be visitors).

c) establish destination teams responsible for planning and implementing media communications including flexible website solutions which permit immediate updates, VIC staff scripts, local radio contacts and briefings, maintaining comprehensive operator contact lists (mobile phones) and designated roles and responsibilities.

d) appointing a local Tourism Recovery team that plan and speak on behalf of the destination to assist its economic recovery. This permits the media to concentrate on key approved spokespeople and focuses the message(s).

For recovery, Australian's need to be presented with the moral argument of helping their countrymen and holiday at home at this time rather than taking breaks overseas. Many regions are safe and suitable for visitors but are suffering from consumer fear. Endorsement advertising using key opinion formers who are well respected by the public could be considered and be ready to action 'at the push of a button'. This means developing concepts, testing them and contractually agreeing with personalities now for future implementation.

So many lives and livelihoods are intertwined directly and indirectly with tourism. As recent events demonstrate tourism is vulnerable to climate. We cannot afford to ignore the need for national support, local plans, peak body services and the method to build the capacity of tourism businesses' participation. Tourism is the economic lifeblood of many rural economies operated by micro and small businesses. A responsible plan is required if we are to maintain communities after future natural disasters which Australian scientists predict will occure more frequently.

Hospitality Industry Risks: Hotel And Restaurant Owners And Management must have Emergency Plans and Insurance In Place to Manage Crisis

Hotel owners and management must be able to deal with catastrophic events and know the answers to the following:

1. How quickly could you restart?
2. Would insurance provide money for next week's rent and wages?
3. What would the bank say?

Massive floods are one thing, but what if a neighbouring building caught fire or your kitchen burst into flames? Start your managers and staff thinking through the issues, while they're still in the headlines...

- Check Data Backup Systems: are they all onsite or are copies of data, systems and staff records kept elsewhere? Is the safe fireproof or just a box with a key? Online backup systems like Carbonite work well, and data storage is very cheap – but you need to start it happening!
- Is the Insurance cover complete? Would it cover a situation like the current floods? Does it cover intangible items as well as equipment? What about loss of profits and staff wages while rebuilding happens?
- Are Staff trained for fire and first-aid emergencies? This is the type of training that's usually regarded as 'nice to have' rather than essential. Do they know how to handle a fat or an electrical fire? What about an elderly customer who faints or collapses? Or flood waters coming near electrical connections?
- How will you keep Customers & Staff informed? It's more effective if your email newsletter or SMS alerts are already

part of their world, then you can really keep their loyalty active. Your Facebook Page and Twitter updates will also reach many others...

- Have a Crisis Management Plan, designed to cover the many risky situations where you depend on only one alternative: eg only one staff member who's qualified with first aid, one chef who knows how to cook the favourite dessert, one key for the liquor store, or one computer with all the staff records.
- Crisis Management Downloads: ready to use (and edit) Safety Manual and Rules, Maintenance Logbook, Cleaning Rosters (greasy dirt is a big cause of kitchen fires) and a raft of other systems designed to keep your business organised and safe.

Tourism and Crisis-Management Issues (4)

One of the factors that shape tourists' risk perception, and thus their subsequent travel behaviour, is the availability of security oriented information and the type of information source. In a article on the role of security information in tourism crisis management Yoel Mansfeld analyzes the importance of crisis communications and of generating balanced, comprehensive, and up-to-date security information, to control the security image of potential and actual tourists. His main conclusions are that:-

- The proactive provision of security and risk related information by the host destinations is imperative in order to balance the biased information provided by the media and governments in the generating markets.
- The provision of comprehensive and accurate security related information should not target would-be travellers but be directed toward those who have already made a commitment to travel to affected destinations; tourists who are visiting affected destinations; and tourists who have already returned from a visit to affected destinations.
- Information on current security situations in affected destinations should not be based only on facts, but also on their interpretation in order to assist tourists to make a more balanced evaluation of the risk involved.

- The provision of security information by affected destinations should be both proactive and dynamic to increase the confidence of tourists in this type of information source.

On a more narrow perspective of tourism crisis management, Greg Stafford, Larry Yu, and Alex Kobina Armoo look at how Washington, DC, hotels responded to the September 11, 2001, terrorist attack on the Pentagon. Following an in-depth analysis of the human and financial implications of this crisis on the local hospitality sector, their main conclusions are that:

- A well-coordinated effort from the early stages of the tourism crisis, accompanied by proper objectives, helped hospitality businesses in the Washington, DC, area regain their pre-September 11 business levels.
- This success was attributed to the well-coordinated and centralized industry response which provided a single and reliable information source about the industry status.
- The lesson as to how the DC hospitality sector dealt with the crisis is that contingency plans must be built on solid knowledge of crisis-management skills and refined through workplace practices.
- When emergency conditions have subsided, management must make the transition quickly to the process of recovery.
- Familiarity with crisis characteristics will better enable hotel managers to handle future security oriented crises.

On a similar topic but more related to crisis-management strategies among hotel managers, Aviad Israeli and Arie Reichel discuss how the Israeli hospitality sector tried to mitigate the ramifications of the second period of Palestinian uprising (the Intifada). Their main conclusions are that:

- When assessing the performance of hotel managers in times of security induced tourism crises, there is a need to examine both their recognition of the importance of measures that assist the organization in times of crisis and also their level of usage.
- Four crisis management practices were identified among Israeli hotel managers: marketing, infrastructure (or hotel)

maintenance, human resources, and governmental assistance.

- With regard to hotel managers in the Israeli hospitality sector, there is considerable correspondence between their perceived practices' importance and their usage.

The Liquidity Crisis and the Indian Hotel Industry: A Hurdle or a Silver Lining?

The state of turmoil in global financial markets has generated new concerns for India: in what ways, and to what extent, will our economy be impacted? Will India continue to be perceived as investment-worthy? And will developments-internal and external-allow different sectors of the economy a good chance for growth?

Where real estate and the hotel industry in India are concerned, the going seems to be good. Within the same week that a Wall Street Giant sold for USD250 million, a 90-odd acre land parcel in the National Capital Region was valued in excess of USD1.25 billion... a sign of optimism and confidence in this sector's future.

In this article, I make an attempt to 'gaze the crystal ball' and see what lies ahead for the hotel industry in India.

In the near term, inflation, growth and liquidity dynamics are expected to make access to debt-based instruments unattractive for most industry players in emerging markets. Real estate, as an asset class, will continue to be under the regulatory microscope especially at current valuations. Investments through dedicated funds and private equity placements will require an enhanced level of due diligence, and this will result in the average time cycle for transactions being extended. Many global funds are likely to re-evaluate their real estate portfolio strategy for India and there are indications of certain fund commitments made in real estate Special Purpose Vehicles (SPVs) having been temporarily suspended. With financing becoming harder to get and hotel projects to take longer to come to fruition, existing players stand to benefit. Hotels constituting the existing market will continue to operate at optimum levels of occupancy, maximise rates and report enhanced profitability.

Existing hotels in India are also likely to benefit from the improved performance of the non-room sources of income, namely

Food & Beverage (including banquet operations), Spa, Corporate Club memberships and other ancillary services. The effective use of technology and best-in-class cost management systems will ensure that profit margins are consistent. Though the industry will face cost inflation in the form of more expensive raw material and labor, an enhanced top line growth, coupled with diligent cost management, should offset the negative impact on profitability. Hotels, by and large, have also successfully made a transition to outsourced services in areas such as security, landscaping, laundry and property management; this will enable hotels to operate at reduced employee per room ratios, thereby providing flexibility with regard to department-level income and expenses.

Our assessment is that an additional 160,000 new rooms need to enter the top 25 hotel markets in India, in the next five years, to bridge the demand-supply gap facing by the hotel industry. Since 2004, potential demand in key hotel markets has grown 20-22% year-on-year. While echoes of global market developments are likely to resound here, the economic fundamentals of India continue to remain sound and the growth trajectory of corporate India is testimony to this. Commercial travel by Corporate India will provide the necessary impetus to the hotel industry. In the last few years, some hotels have been guilty of manipulating the delicate balance between price and value. This has resulted in development of parallel lodging markets and led to erosion of effective capture ratios and displacement of demand from traditional high volume segments such as tour groups, incentives and MICE. We expect a rate rationalization to take place in the market by 2010, and at affordable prices demand indicators continue to remain diverse and broad based.

The extended supply pipeline is likely to further transform the market into a supplier's market and this will, naturally, lead to a continued sharp rise in rates in most cities. The mid-level traveler constitutes a key target market for most hotels in commercial destinations and this segment also exhibits comparatively higher average length of stay patterns. Displacement of this business will be available for hotels with a mid market orientation that can satisfy the value-for-money principle. We estimate that, by 2012, macro demand-supply factors and industry dynamics will present an optimum demand-supply balance and yields will be rationalized. Our experience in India indicates that budget hotels will be able to operate at impressive occupancies, maximize yields through proactive rate management, and build a loyal customer among niche markets like the non-negotiated commercial traveler, airline STPC and extended stay.

Post rationalization, the rate adjustment factor will be comparatively lower for hotels with a mid market orientation and these hotels are expected to present a flatter, but more stable growth trajectory over a long term period. The other advantage a country as vast as India presents is a unique opportunity to do multiple, small format hotels, catering to micro markets. A geographically well balanced portfolio will exhibit stability allowing developers a potential cost advantage from construction and sourcing.

The farm loan waiver announced in Union Budget 2008 and the subsequent qualification for re-eligibility will enable most public sector banks to realign their balance sheets leading to more positive lending. Tax benefits will result in higher disposable incomes and induce leisure related travel within India. Another factor that bodes well for our overall economy is the demographic shift in India's population. By 2020, India will be a nation of 1.2 billion people with an average age of 28. Double incomes and lifestyle aspirations are providing impetus to leisure travel within India that includes a new, but fast-growing segment of demand for niche destinations and unique holiday experiences. In the forthcoming future, we expect to see new destinations on the Indian tourism landscape offering experiential holidays and getaways. According to our estimates, there will be sustained demand for weekend travel at major gateway destinations and these markets will grow in the range of 35-40% annually in the next 3-5 years. Destination travel within India is likely to be an important beneficiary and we expect to see the emergence of Integrated Travel Circuits in the years to come.

To conclude, the hotel industry's visible revival starting 2002, owed to strong domestic travel trends and a positive economic and investment environment, will continue. We expect a good GDP growth rate, positive investment initiatives, ongoing efforts towards infrastructure development and the Open Skies policy to provide an important boost to business travel. The hotel industry, we believe, will witness sustained growth both in terms of occupancy and average rate. The industry has, in the past, overcome the challenges posed by 9/11, Pokhran and SARS. We expect it to remain resilient in the face of the US sub-prime crisis, benefiting instead from a well-performing economy and robust demand from within the sector.

Hospitality Trends in Asia

Looking Ahead at Hospitality Trends in Asia

The future of the hospitality industry in Asia promises great opportunity for continued growth, and this potential is in line with the projected estimates of tourism arrivals to this region in the next few years. The changes in the Asian hospitality and tourism sector were accelerating before the global economic crisis began. With this region emerging from the economic crisis, it is highly likely that growth will continue apace as before, although other regions may remain economically subdued. The Asian region will be significantly transformed within five to 10 years.

According to Michael Enright and James Newton (2005), the Asia Pacific will overtake the Americas to become the world's second largest tourism region, as measured by arrivals, after Europe. Among the major destinations in the region, China is the unrivalled market leader, followed by Hong Kong, Malaysia, Thailand and Singapore. This forecast is supported by the United Nations World Tourism Organization (2009), which sees East Asia, and the Pacific and South Asia growing at annualized rates of 6.5% and 6.2% over the 25-year period up to 2020. These compare with the forecast rates of 3.8% and 3.1% for the Americas and Europe, respectively. This growth is despite the impact of the global economic crisis.

The global financial crisis of 2007 to early 2009 had slowed the expansion that the hospitality sector had experienced in preceding years in Asia. The economic downturn had indeed presented unique challenges, which resulted in the delayed launch of new initiatives, slowed implementation of ongoing projects, and, in some organizations, caused major restructuring.

However, despite the economic meltdown over those two and a half years, the tourism and the hospitality industry is expected to bounce back and enjoy continuous growth in the next few years. Economic indicators, such as the analyses by STR Global (2009), a leader for lodging-industry benchmarking and research, support the notion that while other regions continue to be mired with the aftermath of the global financial crisis, the Asian region has bottomed out and is set to expand. The reasons for the region's economic positive performance now are much the same as before the economic crisis. The governments of the Asian region had taken positive steps to encourage economic development, moved to build the necessary infrastructure, and encouraged local and foreign investment in the sector. These reasons still hold true and will continue to propel the region ahead of other regions

Major Challenges Ahead

Emerging from the crisis of 2009, the tourism and hospitality sector faces major challenges in the next several years. These challenges are related to the quickening pace of change and expansion within the sector in Asia, the ongoing pipeline of projects across Asia, the environmental impacts.

Quickening Pace of Change and Expansion

With the transition of many countries such as China, India, and Vietnam to market economies, there has been significant rapid economic growth in these places. This growth has fuelled higher demand and higher requirements for quality standards for travel services. This trend is for both domestic and international across all demand segments – business, leisure, education, and others.

The tourism scene in Asia Pacific is getting very competitive with different countries coming up with new attractions and offerings to attract tourism dollars. For example, a new Disneyland was announced in 2009 that will be located in Pudong in Shanghai, China. In Singapore, the two resorts, Marina Bay Sands and Resorts World Sentosa, opened in 2010 while Macau continues to improve its casinos and tourism-related attractions in order to keep ahead of the competition. These large-scale projects are integrated projects as they include a range of integrated facilities, which complement one another. A central development theme is that each mega-project is a destination unto itself. They also have the capacity to meet the demand for the mass segment as well as the much smaller high-end segment.

Ongoing Pipeline of Hospitality Projects

A consequence of the expansion of the tourism sector is that many hotel chains plan to open new hotel operations in many countries across Asia over the next few years.

According to STR Global (2010), the Asia-Pacific hotel development scene will continue to grow, as the pipeline helps to gauge how much supply is coming onstream in the next few years. The Asia-Pacific pipeline by chain includes an existing supply of 2.15 million rooms, 171,457 rooms in-construction, and a total active pipeline of 976 hotels comprising 248,156 rooms. Among the key markets, Shanghai, China, reported the largest amount of rooms in the total active pipeline (14,378 rooms). Next is Delhi, India with 6,731 rooms in the total active pipeline. Third is Beijing, China with 5,775 rooms in the total active pipeline. All this will contribute to a promising outlook for the hospitality industry in the Asia-Pacific.

International hotel chains are making concrete plans for expansion. Marriott has 58 hotels now under development, and will add more than 16,000 rooms to its Asia-Pacific portfolio. Shangri-La will be opening 13 new hotel properties in Asia by 2013. For Accor, it is opening 97 new hotels in the near future, which will add around 20,000 rooms in total – a clear sign of its commitment to growing its business in the Asia-Pacific region.

The continuing expansion of hotel room supply in major tourism hubs, such as Singapore and Macau, continues to add hotels, entertainment, high-end food services, and attractions.

Environmental Impacts

Growth is racing ahead in Asia, but the outcome of this is not always positive, as there are often environmental impacts. The hospitality industry is enthusiastic about environmental sustainability as it feels that if it is responsible today, there will be a better environment tomorrow. However, there is a general public perception that hospitality, leisure and travel are unnecessary as some people say that these activities are contributing to environmental pollution considerably.

The industry is very aware of this misconception and should be aware, especially in Asia, where environmental protection and regulation are not as strong in many countries as in the more developed economies. There will be considerable interest, not all welcome, on this issue in Asia. Savvy hospitable organizations in Asia will move the environment to the top of the list of actions under their corporate social responsibility charters (Smith 2008a).

Human Resource Challenges

The tourism and hospitality is a people-business, which demands a vast pool of people dedicated to catering to consumers' and customers' needs and wants. Thus, most governments and entrepreneurs will face significant human resources challenges. These key challenges include competing for advantages and human resource, finding managers to drive their businesses, and providing education and training.

Competing for Advantages and Human Resource

The consequences of current and future hotel and tourism developments result in the frenetic competition for advantages and human resource. Many countries have revealed plans to stay ahead of the competition in terms of its product offerings and meeting the demands of human resource. According to Joachim Willms (2007), five of the top 10 countries which will have the most jobs in the travel and tourism industry in 2017 are from Asia: China (75.7 million), India (28.3 million), Japan (9.4 million), Indonesia (6.8 million), and Thailand (4.7 million). The consulting firm Accenture (Leung 2008) believes that China alone will need an additional 1.6 million employees in the travel and tourism sector in the 10 years up to 2017.

As part of the Singapore government's commitment to grow the tourism sector, the Singapore Tourism Board (2007) has unveiled plans to boost its tourism product and expand the tourism employment to 250,000 in 2015 from a base of 150,000 in 2004. It has projected bold targets to ensure that tourism remains a key economic pillar by tripling tourism receipts to S$30 billion, doubling visitor arrivals to 17 million, and creating an additional 100,000 jobs in the services sector by 2015. These targets will catapult growth in the tourism industry over the next 10 years, and are supported by the S$2 billion Tourism Development Fund. The fund has been set up to support initiatives in these four areas: infrastructure development (developing critical infrastructure to support tourism growth); capability development (enhancing the capability of Singapore-based travel and tourism players and attracting world-class travel and tourism businesses and organizations to set up in Singapore); anchoring iconic and major events (attracting iconic or mega events that will highlight Singapore as a premier destination for leisure, business and services customer segments); and product development (developing strategic tourism products).

The Japan Tourism Agency has also relaunched its previously successful 'Visit Japan Campaign' (Karantzavelou 2008) to boost inbound tourism to Japan, a country where outbound tourists have consistently outnumbered inbound. The recent economic crisis has hit many countries worldwide, and Japan's tourism was similarly affected badly too. JTB Sunrise Tours, which has offered tours to English-speaking travellers for 40 years, says for the industry to grow, tour operators would have to expand travel operations to areas outside the 'Golden Route', which is a five- or six-day tour of Japan. This has traditionally been the most popular inbound tour for first-time visitors arriving at Narita airport. Starting in Tokyo, tourists go to Hakone, Kyoto, and Nara, before departing the country from Osaka. This 'Golden Route' reinforces the fact that Tokyo and Osaka have remained the leading destinations for visitors to Japan for a long time.

But as the volume of tourism into Japan has increased, styles of travel, as well as needs and desires of travellers, are diversifying more to include short stays and experience-based tours. Karantzavelou opined that Japan has a lot to improve to meet diversifying needs and highlighted that the Japanese government must improve the nation's infrastructure to make rural areas more accessible for inbound tourists.

Finding Managers to Drive their Businesses

Finding the people who will staff the expansion of the hospitality sector in Asia is proving difficult. Hospitality enterprises have and will generally be able to recruit and train the vast number of people necessary to staff the lower levels of operations. The tough challenge is to find enough managers, especially senior managers, to drive their businesses. Managers require skill sets that typically require years of formal education to acquire. Generic management is of limited use for the hospitality sector with its intense focus on services, thus managerial education has to be hospitality-specific. With the expansion of hospitality services to second-and third-tier cities across Asia as well as to resort areas, senior managers may not easily be recruited in these locations. Finding managers who can fill these posts and are willing to relocate to these places will be difficult. This problem is compounded by the desire of many Asian organizations to have nationals from their home country head their foreign operations.

According to Berry's (2008) master's dissertation at the University of Nottingham, United Kingdom, it appears that the human resource shortage in the Indian hospitality industry will remain a challenge over the coming years, despite the development of its training and HR programs. Staff turnover remains high and the sector is not the most preferred employer compared with other industries. These problems cannot be ignored.

Providing Education and Training

How is this need for human resource being managed in the hospitality sector by both global and local hotels? Are the increasing number of training courses and professional and degree programs in Asia helping in these areas?

Universities often focus on mid-to senior-level manager education with technical and vocational institutes providing training for sub-managerial positions. Supplementing this supply, hotel chains have established their own in-house training institutes in Asia Pacific. Shangri-La has an institute based in China, with satellite centres in other parts of the region to deliver training locally. Jin Jiang Hotels also has a training institute. Accor, with its training centralized in Evry, France, has a global network of hubs for regional training, including one in Bangkok. Training within these institutes tends to meet in-house demand, mainly for the non-managerial levels that constitute the bulk of staff in hotels. Managerial training is usually outsourced, or undertaken jointly with a specialized provider. Given that training for the junior posts entails less time and expense per capita, the industry is generally able to meet its needs. The major challenge is the supply of senior managers, for whom training often requires years with high cost. Generally, there is a shortage of managers, so recruitment is increasingly from other, nonhospitality sectors. Those with the educational and career records suitable for senior managerial posts in the hospitality sector have been able to demand better positions with branded organizations in desirable locations. To meet demand, educational institutes are expanding their capacity to produce managers for the hospitality and tourism sector. To fast track this, many are entering into joint ventures with established non-Asian institutes so as to produce graduates quicker (Smith 2008b).

In contrast, independent hotel operators located in less desirable, secondary or tertiary cities, for example, have had difficulty in filling their senior posts. Aggravating the problem is the quality of graduates from some Asian hospitality degree programs, whose graduates often fail to obtain suitable employment. The key problem here is the lack of rigor and relevance of the training for the sector, thus employers are reluctant to engage these graduates. A parallel issue is the comparatively low starting salaries offered by some employers for graduates form hospitality-business programs. This, regrettably, encourages fresh graduates to seek jobs in other sectors. According to Dwyer et al. (2009), there was substantial support by the hospitality sector for the view that education and training can foster a more innovative tourism workforce to achieve destination competitive advantage; but it must be recognized that perceptions of poor conditions, poor career paths, and low pay relative to other industries will not attract committed and productive labor. The authors emphasized that hospitality and tourism education must prepare students to play a leadership role in an industry that is undergoing rapid and continuous change. Managers need to know content and have adaptive capabilities to apply their knowledge in changing contexts.

To these views must be added the necessity for managerial expertise that can span Asia with its diversity of cultures and levels of economic development. In a global era of international hospitality operations, organizations must be able to develop and maintain corporate visions across the region. To do this effectively, their senior executives must be adept at cross-cultural management. They must also have a strong sense of business ethics and be able to deliver their organizations' services in different economic contexts.

Trends in the Hospitality Scene

The key trends in the hospitality sector can be identified as the internationalization of hotel operations, expansion of brands by international hotel organizations, broad-based growth of two- and three-star operations in Asia, and the development of low-cost hotels.

Internationalization of Hotel Operations

The internationalization of hotel operations will increasingly take a central role in all aspects of the hospitality sector. Asian hotel organizations, for example, will intensify their drive to become major global hotel operators. Taj Hotels, Resorts and Palaces of India seeks to take its long and successful domestic operational experience global. In North America, it manages several hotels including Taj Boston and The Pierre, New York. The challenge with this approach lies with the ability of the operator to export and adapt its model of hotel operation to very different cultural and business contexts.

Likewise, Jin Jiang Hotels, which is China's largest hotel operator, will leverage its domestic scale of operations to mount international operations. Rather than go immediately global, Jin Jiang Hotels, in contrast, has entered into arrangements for international operators to manage some of their properties such as the Fairmont Peace Hotel in Shanghai. The benefit is that the domestic operator may learn from the international operator before venturing abroad.

As some forays have demonstrated, domestic competence does not necessarily translate into international success, as operating in different countries with new markets requires reshaping of products and services. To help better understand the global challenges and to better prepare for expansion out of their home countries, large Asian hotel organizations are entering into joint venture arrangements both domestically and in other countries.

Expansion of Brands by International Hotel Organizations

Long established international hotel organizations are also seeking greater depth to their operations in Asia. Large organizations such as Accor, Hilton, InterContinental Hotel Group, and Starwood have for some decades operated flagship five-and four-star properties in the primary cities of Asia. Recently, these hotel operators have sought to expand their penetration by rolling out a full range of their brands, particularly at the lower star-rated level. Accor's rollout of its ibis brand is a case in point. In doing so, these operators are demonstrating that they have a good understanding of consumers' demand and operations in Asia.

Broad-based growth of Two-and Three-star Operations in Asia

The expansion of two-and three-star operations in Asia is broad-based. Asian hotel operators are also expanding at this product level. Jinjiang Inn and Taj's Ginger are two brands in the economy sector. There is also considerable ongoing expansion of budget services in airline operations. Established legacy airlines such as Singapore Airlines and Qantas are aggressively expanding the networks of their respective subsidiaries, Tiger Airways and Jetstar. New startups, which include Air Asia, are proving to be successes too.

Development of low-cost Hotels

The global financial crisis has proved to be a wonderful opportunity for budget hotel and air service operators as corporations and individuals downgrade their travel budgets. Having expanded their network of budget properties and services to take advantage of the crisis, it is likely that these operators will have established a solid market share from which they can continue to rapidly expand over the next few years.

Part of the attraction for travellers with low-cost carriers and low-cost hotels is the lower cost, though it would be a mistake to believe that these guests all want to fly cheap and stay cheap too. Some operators will bundle those services, but there will be others who will want to fly cheap but stay expensive. And then there are others who want to fly expensive because it is long haul, but when they arrive at their destination, they will be prepared to stay in budget accommodation. The prospect is a complex set of different combinations of demand. This will prove to be challenging for marketing and price setting.

The advent of economy products and services does not herald the decline of the luxury category. We have seen the retreat of demand for five-star lodgings, flights, and food services with the global financial crisis, but this is short term. The continued growth of the economic juggernauts, China and India, along with that of many other Asian countries, will ensure that there will be many more people willing to pay more.

The addition of economy services to their other services is expanding the suite of brands that some operators must now manage. Over the next few years, there will be a proliferation of brands. The challenge that operators will be avoiding is brand confusion for their customers and quite possibly their own marketing and sales staff.

5

Strategies Behind Crisis Management

Think about Humpty Dumpty being that great project, idea or solution which will propel your organization so far ahead of others in your industry that they will need to spend years just trying to recover from your advancement. Then something happens within or beyond your control. The question becomes—did you pull together the best of the best to discuss Humpty Dumpty's fall before he fell (strategic) or as a consequence of his falling (tactical)?

Dumpty Together Again

This past week I attended a conference of business leaders desiring to take their business to the next level. On the second day, I met a leader who lives in Pensacola, Florida and we began to discuss the oil spill and its impact to the local area. As the leader shared personal photos taken of the beached oil, like many of you, we began to discuss strategies for cleaning up the oil and most importantly its long-term impact on the Gulf Coast, the seafood industry, the tourist industry, the wildlife and possible long-term impact of such a disaster.

And yes we did discuss the politics of the matter – in that this should not have a "we versus them" political spin because it is a "WE" issue. WE are all impacted (or will be impacted) by this disaster ... and perhaps for generations to come. After our discussion, I began to wonder how many businesses go into any type of depth in building a disaster recovery/crisis management strategy on an organizational level as well as on a project-by-project level?

You're probably wondering what disaster recovery/crisis management has to do with Humpty Dumpty. Think about Humpty Dumpty being that great project ... that great idea ... that great solution which will propel your organization so far ahead of others in your industry that they will need to spend years just trying to recover from your advancement. Or the idea which has such a global impact that everything will be better because of the implementation of that idea! Or that new product/service which will increase your stock value by 200%.

This is Humpty Dumpty sitting on the wall – setting the standard for extraordinary greatness! Then something happens within or beyond your control which causes Humpty Dumpty to fall and this fall impacts others on a grand scale.

The question becomes – did you pull together the best of the best (All the king's horses and all the king's men) to discuss Humpty Dumpty's fall before he fell (strategic) or as a consequence of his falling (tactical)? Very few business leaders conduct an in-depth program on crisis management/disaster recovery/risk management associated with the various projects/products/services they desire to introduce into the market. Of course there are many reasons for such actions; however, present history tells us that failing to have a disaster recovery/crisis management plan in place can have negative long-term effects on your business as well as the global economy for generations to come.

Leaders must plan for crises, that is, any dangerous events threatening injuries, deaths and financial trouble which could deeply damage or even close your company. However, if you can muster specific abilities, you can better equip your organization to overcome a crisis.

Recent crises and disasters included events that many once thought impossible. These calamities included terrorist attacks, natural disasters large enough to take out a major city and/or industry, cyber-attacks and corporate fraud. Today's organizations must adopt a mindset of being ready when – not if – a crisis strikes. Crises occur more frequently now; they have become part of doing business. No industry or organization is safe, but you can spare your organization the most serious consequences by drastically changing how it plans and handles crisis management.

Comprehensive risk management goes through stages which require advance planning and proactive investments. First, prevent and mitigate a disaster's damage before any risk occurs. Then prepare a robust response. Third, build recovery infrastructure. Fourth, offer an adequate response by addressing the damages sustained during the event – remember to take responsibility for your organization's part in the crisis. The fifth stage, proper recovery, requires rebuilding infrastructures to provide for the general welfare. The final stage, lessons learned/adjusting other strategies, based on what occurred, what does your organization need to do to prevent this from happening again?

Below you will find Before the Fall Strategies and After the Fall Strategies your organizations can implement to ensure you are able to put Humpty Dumpty back together again.

Strategies for Disaster Recovery/Crisis Management before the Fall

1. *Risk forecasting* – The field requires more precise prediction techniques
2. *Communicating risk information* – Most people assume that low-probability disasters will not affect them. Enlarging the time horizon for disasters helps your employees better assess how they could be harmed. To help the owners of a production facility with a 25-year life span understand their flood risk, show them data indicating that the chance of a "one-in-100-year flood" happening during that 25 years is greater than "one-in-five". Presenting the possibility as a "one-in-100 chance" in a single year is not as compelling
3. *Economic incentives* – Cash can motivate people to protect themselves from disaster, for example, cutting the insurance premiums of Mississippians who buy flood protection.
4. *Private-public partnerships* – Disasters affect public and private organizations, so they should unite in advance to create mutual emergency strategies and defence plans.
5. *Resiliency and sustainability* – Organizations must determine if they will be able to continue to function after a sudden

disaster. This question also pertains to nations, notably developing countries burdened with "low-quality structures, poor land use, inadequate emergency response," and so on Mitroff (2005) recommends that business leader's go through the following Spinning the Wheel of Crisis exercise with their leadership/project teams before releasing a new product or service: The physical prop for this exercise is a large wheel which spins until it hits a flexible needle, which slows and then stops the wheel's motion. Once it stops, discuss the possible crisis which could occur and what actions need to be in place to prevent such a crisis and/or what actions should be taken after such a crisis occurs. This tool should be part of every project manager's toolkit for success. Each segment of the wheel lists a major area in which crises occur:

Economic – This crisis affects the economy Informational – Information gets lost, by break-in or computer error (for example, Y2K, the millennium bug) Physical – A crisis affects your buildings, equipment or products Human resources – Labor issues, fraud or criminal acts generate a crisis Reputational – Rumors and defamation hurt your organization Psychopathic acts – Violence, product tampering or criminal behaviour strike Natural disasters – Hurricanes, fires, floods or mudslides breed crises.

To ensure your organization covers all of its bases, combine elements (for example combine items #4 and #7); what plans need to be in place to ensure a quick and maximum recovery)?

Strategies for Disaster Recovery/Crisis Management After the Fall

Risk-related decision making involves weighing probabilities and benefits versus losses, creating an accurate statistical analysis and considering alternative actions. Follow these principles for perceiving, assessing and managing the risk of extreme events:

Appreciate the importance of estimating crises – While such calculations are filled with uncertainties, organizations need good information to deal with risk Recognize the interdependencies associated with the crisis – Every risk is connected to outside circumstances. Such linked dependencies create dynamic and evolving uncertainties which can mutate depending on events. Keep your risk forecasts up-to-date Understand people's behavioral biases when developing crisis management strategies – People must acknowledge their prejudices to make mitigating them possible. For instance, leaders may put off dealing with possible catastrophes due to a stubborn form of denial called not in my term of office (NIMTOF) Recognize the long-term impact of the crisis/disaster – A catastrophe can create enduring change Recognize transboundary risks by developing global strategies – In disasters, national boundaries are moot. The 2004 tsunami killed people in 11 countries Overcome inequalities in the distribution and effects of catastrophes –Be ready to assist others in need Build leadership for averting and responding to disasters before it is needed – Planning and preparing for disasters is far better than waiting until emergencies strike.

Your post-crisis push is to get back to business; Barton (2007) recommends the following Pillars of Business Continuity:

When disaster strikes, you cannot possibly over-communicate with victims Be in 24/7 contact with shareholders, employees, customers, contractors and vendors Get your off-site IT recovery operations and EOC up and running as soon as possible Make sure the staff receives full salaries and benefits. Give the incident commander authority to pay for "equipment, hotel rooms and consulting services" as needed Document everything, including damages. Plug in your insurance carrier ASAP One and only one spokesperson communicates. Employees should refer all questions to that spokesperson. Avoid policy infractions. Control rumors Designate psychological counselors and make them available for anyone affected Update stakeholders three times daily concerning all activities and progress Stay on top of all suppliers. Make sure they aid in the recovery in a timely manner Make sure the disaster is over before you declare it done. Consider "scenario testing" to ensure that things are again as they should be. Plan a "multi-tiered return to normalcy Assess event fallout. Establish accountability. Reward anyone who deserves it

Now, what about "putting all the pieces together again" – we are living in a time where there is more information available to us in one day than our predecessors had to wait for years to receive. When your organization has trouble identifying solutions to a crisis, do not hesitate to put the best brains together (inside and outside of your company and industry) to come up with the solution.

As an organization, your responsibilities include putting as many Humpty Dumpty's together through creativity and innovation. And at the same time be proactive in your planning and have a through crisis management/risk management/disaster recovery strategy in place just in case he does fall – being proactive in your planning allows you and your organization to survive through unplanned catastrophes/crises. Wisdom would say that your best creative and innovative ideas will come out of how you handle the crisis and what you learned through resolving the issue which caused the crisis/disaster.

When speaking to the business leader last week, I shared that my solution for the oil spillage crisis would be to take the best minds from all the oil companies, colleges and universities, government and even the general public – put them in a room – and have them develop a solution to this crisis as well as develop a standard operating procedure for ensuring that a crisis like this does not happen again. This is how, together, we can put "all the pieces together again" and making Humpty Dumpty stronger and better than he was before!

The Economic Crisis and it's impact on tourism

Nowadays the world is witnessing it's biggest crisis yet This article tries to explain this crisis and presents it's impact on the travel industry.

The consumer himself, to begin with the subject lets do a quick analysis of the crisis:

The crisis can be considered as an illness, this illness started on the stock markets and the credit markets it was a result of a crash the financial system on which the actual economy is based collapsed, as a result all the investments made by people collapsed too then this illness extended and has now reached a global scale, the consumer is the first to suffer from the consequences of this crisis, jobs are being cut down, people get less wages and as a result the family's budget becomes more and more limited and people think twice when they want to have some fun.

Holidays are the primary source of amusement, so one question we can ask ourselves is:

What is the impact of this crisis on tourism?

My question implies that here is an impact what we will try to determine is how big this impact is were going to study it's consequences on the travel industry.

The crisis started in the United States and spread from there, now it is interesting to note that tourism in countries of northern Europe is registering an impact of the crisis, for example the countries of northern Europe are mostly visited by American and British tourists, because of the crisis the exchange rates of pound-euro, euro ?dollar are disadvantageous for British and American citizen.

It is interesting to note that the impact of this crisis aren't yet fully understood, measured because more data, more statistics needs to be gathered. But with the Data professionals have for now we can have a general idea of the consequences of this crisis.

Another impact of this crisis is purely and simply fear, lack of trust and panic, put all these factors together at a major scale and you will be able to paralyze, jeopardize any business any industry.

For instance the traveler is scared of being jobless because of the actual economic situation so he will not plan for any holidays and since there are many people in this situation it leads into a chaotic situation:

Airplane Ticket sales had decreased about 22% in January 2009 now with these number alone we can make a certain number of assumptions:

A decrease of ticket sales will lead in a loss for travel agencies since ticketing is their primary source of revenues, travel agents get their tickets from tour operators so we can assume it will lead in a loss in the business of tour operators, and since tour operators sell packages often including transportation and lodging it will inevitably cause a loss in the hostelry business.

Here we can witness how devastating the crisis really is : (and I'm talking about the travel industry only please consider that there are a countless number of other sectors that are touched too).

The consumers insecurities had consequences on different sectors of the travel industry:

- Ticket sales
- Transportation
- Lodging.

That being said I would also like to mention that unlike other industries tourism has witnessed, experienced crisis and should hopefully be able to counter the current situation.

One positive consequence of the crisis may be the following:

The crisis can allow companies to completely restructure, take new directions, new initiatives, in my opinion the crisis won't be over until trust is restored (people are just too scared to invest their money). But ultimately this crisis will come to an end and that is what companies should prepare for, the current situation is clearly disastrous and difficult but that doesn't mean that it can't be beneficial :

It gives companies time to prepare their next move bring on new projects and maybe rethink their strategies.

But they also have to survive the crisis first, and the government is the key to survive:

Let me explain my point of view, If a new touristic spot opens in a country thanks to this country's government, if the publicity is done accordingly, I mean if people are curious enough to go see for themselves then business could go up not only for the country in itself but also for hotels, restaurants inside this country.

And what tool is more powerful than Internet to do the publicity of such a project on an international scale?

This crisis is the first after the apparition of the web, the web which offers a tremendous choice for the consumer, the web offers multiple alternatives (low cost holidays for example is a perfect parade

As a conclusion I would like to say that the crisis is gradually bringing down the worlds economic system and the tourism, the travel industry are a part of this economic system but to face today's crisis we have a weapon that was not yet discovered at the time of other crisis: The Internet it will of course not solve the worlds problem but if it is used efficiently it can help a business survive and that especially in the tourism industry.

Hotels Could be Hazardous to Your Health

Have you ever been in a hotel during a fire? It's a frightening experience, and you should start thinking about it. For instance, how would you have acted if you had been in one of these fires?

- The Thomas Hotel, San Francisco, Ca 20 DEAD
- The Gulf Hotel, Houston, Texas 54 DEAD
- The La Salle Hotel, Chicago, Ill 61 DEAD
- The Wincoff Hotel, Atlanta, Ca 119 DEAD.

Of course, there have been hundreds more with thousands of deaths, but I think you're getting the drift. The majority of those people did not have to die.

My wife has been in the airline industry for close to 8 years and while accompanying her on a trip recently, I learned how ill-prepared she was for a hotel fire. It's not her fault: it's quite common. Hotels, however, have no excuse for being ill-prepared, but believe me, you cannot depend on the staff in case of a fire. History has shown that some hotels won't even call the Fire Department. I have been a fire-fighter in Los Angeles for over 10 years and have seen many people die needlessly in building fires. It's sad because most could have saved themselves.

What you're about to read is roughly the same briefing I have given my wife on hotel safety. I do not intend to play down the aspects of hotel fires or soft soap the language. It's critical that you remember how to react, and, if I shake you a little, maybe you will.

Contrary to what you have seen on television or in the movies, fire is not likely to chase you down and burn you to death. It's the bi-products of fire that will kill you. Super heated fire gases (smoke) and panic will almost always be the cause of death long before the fire arrives if it ever does. This is very important. You must know how to avoid smoke and panic to survive a hotel fire. With this in mind, here are a few tips:

Smoke

Where there is smoke, there is not necessarily fire. A smoldering mattress, for instance, will produce great amounts of smoke. Air conditioning and air exchange systems will sometimes pick up smoke from one room and carry it out to other rooms or floors. You should keep that in mind because 70% of the hotel fires are caused by smoking and matches. In any case, your prime objective should be to leave at the first sign of smoke.

Smoke, being warmer, will start accumulating at the ceiling and work its way down. The first thing you will notice is THERE ARE NO EXIT SIGNS. I'll talk more about the exits later, just keep in mind when you have smoke, it's too late to start looking for Exit signs.

Another thing about smoke you should be aware of is how irritating it is on the eyes. The problem is that your eyes will only take so much irritation, then they close. Try all you want, you won't be able to open them if there is still smoke in the area. It's one of your body's compensatory mechanisms. Lastly, the fresh air you want to breath is at or near the floor. Get on your hands and knees (or stomach) and STAY THERE as you make you way out. Those who don't probably won't get far.

Think about this poor man's predicament for a moment:

He wakes up at 0230 hours to a smell of smoke. He puts on his trousers and runs into the hallway only to be greeted by heavy smoke. He has no idea where the exit is. He runs to the right. He's coughing and gagging, his eyes hurt. Where is it??? WHERE IS IT?? Panic begins to set in. About the same time he thinks maybe he is going the wrong way, his eyes close. He can't find his way back to his room (it wasn't so bad in there). His chest hurts, he desperately needs oxygen. Total panic sets in as he runs in the other direction. He is completely disorientated. He cannot hold his breath any longer. We find him at 0250. DEAD

What caused all the smoke? A small fire in a room where they store the roll-away beds. Remember, the presence of smoke does not necessarily mean the hotel is burning down.

Panic

Panic (pan ik). A sudden, overpowering terror often afflicting many people at once. Panic is the product of your imagination running wild and it will set in as soon as it dawns on you that you're lost, disorientated, or you don't know what to do. Panic is almost irreversible: once it sets in, it seems to grow. Panic will make you do things that could kill you. People in a state of panic are rarely able to save themselves.

If you understand what's going on, what to do, where to go, and how to get there, panic will not set in. The man in the example I used would not have died if he had known what to do. For instance, had he known the exit was to the left and 4 doors down on the left, he could have gotten on his hands and knees where there was fresh air and started counting doorways. Even if he couldn't keep his eyes open, he could feel his way as he crawled, counting the doors. 1... 2... 3... BINGO! He would NOT have panicked. He would be alive today, telling of his great hotel fire experience.

Exits

The elevator drops you at the 12th floor and you start looking for your room. Let's see... room 1236... here it is. You open the door and drop your luggage. AT THAT VERY MOMENT, turn around and go back into the hallway to check your Exit. You may NEVER get another chance. Don't go into the bathroom, open the curtains, turn on the TV, smarten your appearance, or crash out on the bed. I know you're tired and you want to relax, but it's absolutely essential... no... CRITICAL that you develop the HABIT of checking for your exit after you drop your luggage. It won't take 30 seconds, and believe me, you may NEVER get another chance.

If there are 2 of you sharing a room, BOTH of you locate your Exit. Talk it over as you walk towards it. Is it on the left or right... do you have to turn a corner? Open the Exit door... what do you see... stairs or another door? (Sometimes there are 2 doors to go through, especially in newer hotels.) I'd hate to see you crawl into a broom closet thinking it was the Exit! Are you passing any rooms where your friends are staying? If there was a fire, you may want to bang on their doors as you go by. Is there anything in the hallway that would be in your way... an ice-machine maybe? As you arrive back at your room, take a look once more. Get a good mental picture of what everything looks like. Do you think you could get to the Exit with a blindfold on? This procedure takes less than one minute and to be effective, it must become a habit.

Those of you who are too lazy or tired to do it consistently are real riverboat gamblers. There are over 5,000 hotel fires per year. The odds are sure to catch up with you.

Using The Exit

Should you have to leave your room during the night, it is important to close the door behind you. This is very effective in keeping out fire and will minimize smoke damage to you belongings.

There was a house fire in Los Angeles recently where an entire family died. It was a 3 bedroom house with a den and family room. That night, the occupants had left every door in the house open except one, and it had led to the washrooms where the family dog slept. The house, except for the washroom, was a total loss. When the fire was knocked down, firemen opened the door to find the family dog wagging his tail. Because the door was left shut, the dog and room were in fine shape.

Some doors take hours to burn through. They are excellent fire stops so close every door you go through. If you find smoke in the Exit stairwell, you can bet people are leaving the doors open as they enter.

Always take your key with you. Get into the habit of putting the key in the same place every time you stay in a hotel. Since every hotel has night stands, that's an excellent location. It's close to the bed so you can grab it when you leave without wasting time looking for it. It's important you close your door as you leave, and it's equally as important that you don't lock yourself out. You may find conditions in the hallway untenable, and want to return to your room. If you're now in the habit of checking your exit and leaving the room key on the night stand, you're pretty well prepared to leave the hotel in case of a fire, so let's walk through it once.

Something will awaken you during the night. It could be the telephone, someone banging on the door, the smell of smoke, or some other disturbance. But, whatever it is, investigate it before you go back to sleep. A popular inn near LAX recently had a fire and one of the guests later said he was awakened by people screaming but went back to bed thinking it was a party. He damned near died in bed.

Let's suppose you wake up to smoke in your room. Grab you key off the night stand, roll off the bed and head for the door on you hands and knees. Even if you could tolerate the smoke by standing, DON'T. You'll want to save your eyes and lungs for as long as possible. BEFORE you open the door, feel it with the palm of your hand. If the door or knob is quite hot, don't open it. The fire could be just outside. We'll talk about that later. With the palm of your hand still on the door (in case you need to slam it shut), slowly open the door and peek into the hallway to assess conditions.

As you make your way to the Exit, stay against the wall on the side where the Exit is. It is very easy to get lost or disorientated in a smoky atmosphere. If you're on the wrong side of the hallway, you might crawl right on by the Exit. If you're in the middle of the hall, people who are running will trip over you. Stay on the same side as the Exit, count doors as you go.

When you reach the Exit and begin to descend, it is very important that you WALK down and hang onto the handrail as you go. Don't take this point lightly. The people who will be running will knock you down and you might not be able to get up. Just hang on and stay out of everyone's way. All you have to do now is leave the building, cross the street and watch the action. When the fire is out and the smoke clears, you will be allowed to re-enter the building. If you closed your room door when you left, your belongings should be in pretty good shape. Smoke will sometimes get into the Exit stairway. If it's a tall building, this smoke may not

rise very high before it cools and becomes heavy. This is called "stacking". If your room is on the 20th floor, for instance, you could enter the stairway and find it clear. As you descend you could encounter smoke that has "stacked". Do not try to run through it-people die that way. Turn around and walk up. Now you must really hang onto the handrail. The people running down will probably be glassy-eyed and in a panic and will knock you right out of your socks!

They will run over anything in their way, including a fireman. You'll feel as though you're going upstream against the Chicago Bears, but hang on and keep heading up towards the roof. If for some reason you try one of the doors to an upper floor and find it locked, that's normal, don't worry about it. Exit stairwells are designed so that you cannot enter from the street or roof. Once inside, however, you may Exit at the street or roof but cannot go from floor to floor; this is done for security purposes. When you reach the roof, prop the door with something. This is the ONLY time you will leave a door open. Any smoke in the stairwell may now vent itself to the atmosphere and you won't be locked out. Now find the windward side of the building· (the wet finger method is quite reliable), have a seat and wait until they find you. Roofs have proved to be a safe secondary exit and refuge area. Stay put. Firemen will always make a thorough search of the building looking for bodies. Live ones are nice to find.

Your Room

After you check your Exit and drop the key on the night stand, there is one more thing for you to do. Become familiar with your room. See if your bathroom has a vent; all do, but some have electric motors. Should you decide to remain in your room, turn it on to help remove the smoke. Take a good look at the window in your room. Does it open? Does it have a latch, a lock? Does it slide? Now open the window (if it works) and look outside. What do you see? A sign, ledges? How high up are you? Get a good mental picture of what's outside, it may come in handy. It's important you know how to OPEN your window, you may have to close it again.

Should you wake up to smoke in your room and the door is too hot to open or the hallway is completely charged with smoke, don't panic. Many people have defended themselves quite nicely in their room and so can you. One of the first things you'll want to do is open the window to vent the smoke. I hope you learned how to open it when you checked in. It could be dark and smoking in the room. Those who don't will probably throw a chair through the window. If there is smoke

outside and you have no window to close, it will enter your room and you will be trapped. The broken glass from the window will cut like a surgeon's scalpel. At the Ramada Inn fire, an airline captain on a layover threw a chair through the window and cut himself seriously. Don't compound your problems. Besides, if you break out your window with a chair, you could hit a fireman on the street below. If there is fresh air outside, leave the window open, but keep an eye on it.

At this point, most people would stay at the window, waving frantically, while their room continues to fill with smoke, if the fire burns through. This procedure is not conducive to longevity. You must be aggressive and fight back. Here are some things you can do in any order you choose... if the room phone works, let someone know you're in there. Flip on the bathroom vent. Fill the bath with water. (Don't get into it-it's for fire fighting. You'd be surprised how many people try to save themselves by getting into a tub of water-that's how you cook lobsters and crabs, so you know what happens!) Wet some sheets or towels, and stuff the cracks of your door to keep out the smoke. With your ice-bucket, bail the water from the bath onto the door to keep it cool. Feel the walls-if they are hot, bail water onto them too. You can put your mattress up against the door and block it in place with the dresser. Keep it wet-keep everything wet. Who cares about the mess. A wet towel tied around your nose and mouth is an effective filter if your fold it in a triangle and put the corner in your mouth. If you swing a wet towel around the room, it will help clear the smoke. If there is a fire outside the window, pull down the curtains and move everything combustible away from the window. Bail water all around the window. Use your imagination and you may come up with some tricks of you own. The point is, there shouldn't be any reason to panic-keep fighting until reinforcements arrive. It won't be long.

Elevators

There isn't an elevator made that can be used as a "safe" exit. In all states, elevators by law, cannot be considered an Exit. They are complicated devices with a mind of their own. The problem is people only know one way out of a building-the way they came in, and if that was the elevator, they are in trouble. Elevator shafts and machinery extends through all floors of a building, and besides, with the shaft filling with smoke, there are hundreds of other things that could go wrong and probably will. Everyone tries to get on the elevator in an emergency. Fights break out and people get seriously injured. Smoke, heat and fire do funny things to elevator call buttons, controls and other complicated parts.

Case in Point

Hotel guests in a New Orleans hotel were called on their room phones and notified of a fire on the upper floors. They were in no danger, but asked to evacuate the hotel as a precaution. Five of the guests decided to use the elevator. It was discovered later that the elevator only went down about three floors and then for some reason started going up. It did not stop until it reached the fire floor. The doors came open and were held open by smoke obscuring the photo cell light beam. Besides the five guests in the elevator who died of suffocation, firemen noticed that every button had been pushed, probably in a frantic attempt to stop the elevator.

Fires have killed many people, including firemen. Several New York firemen recently used an elevator when responding to a fire up on the 20th floor. They

pushed 18, but the elevator went right on by the 18th floor. The doors came open on the 20th floor to an inferno and remained open long enough to kill all the firemen. The doors then closed and the elevator returned to the lobby. Hand operated elevators are not exempt. Some elevator operators have been beaten by people fighting over the controls. If you have any idea that there might be smoke or fire in your hotel, avoid the elevator like the plague.

Jumping

It's important I say something about jumping because so many people do it. Most are killed or injured in the process. I cannot tell you whether or not you should jump. Every fire, although similar, is different. I can tell you, however, what usually happens to "jumpers".

If you're on the 1st floor, you could just OPEN the window and climb out. From the second floor you could probably make it with a sprained ankle, but you must jump out far enough to clear the building. Many people hit window sills and ledges on the way down, and they go into cartwheels. If they don't land on their head and kill themselves, they're injured seriously. If you're any higher than the 3rd, the chances are you won't survive the fall. You would probably be better off fighting the fire. Nearby buildings seem closer than they really are and many have died trying to jump to a building that looked 5 feet away, but was actually 15 feet away. Panic is what causes most people to jump. There was a fire in Brazil a few years ago where 40 people jumped from windows and all 40 died. Ironically, 36 of those jumped after the fire was out. Many people have survived by staying put whilst those around them jumped to their death. If you can resist panic and think clearly, you can use your own best judgment.

Calling the Fire Department

Believe it or not, most hotels will not call the Fire Department until they verify whether or not there really is a fire and try to put it out themselves. Should you call the reception to report a fire, they will always send the bellhop, security guard, or anyone else that's not busy to investigate. Hotels are very reluctant to "disturb" their guests and fire engines in the streets are quite embarrassing and tend to draw crowds.

In the New Orleans hotel fire, records show that the Fire Department received only one call, from a guest in one of the rooms. The desk had been notified of fire 20 minutes earlier and had sent a security guard to investigate. His body was later found on the 12th floor about 10 feet from the elevator.

Should you want to report a fire or smell of smoke, ask the hotel operator for an outside line for a local call. Call the Fire Department and tell them your room number in case you need to be rescued. You need not feel embarrassed, that's what we're here for. We would much rather come to a small fire or smoking electrical problem that you smelled than be called 20 minutes later after 6 people have died. Don't let hotel "policy" intimidate you into doing otherwise. The hotel may be a little upset with you, but really... who gives a damn. The Fire Department will be glad you called: you may have saved many lives. Besides, it's a great way for us to meet people! Well, the rest is up to you. Only you can condition yourself to react in a hotel emergency. You can be well prepared by developing the habits we've talked about.

Fire Retardant Fabrics in Hotels and Bed and Breakfasts – Regulation or Sensible Precaution?

Considering that 2006 there has been much controversy in the Uk about the new rules introduced in fire security law. Many in the business see the alterations as over-the-major and element of the 'nanny state'. In this write-up we'll briefly look at both equally what the law calls for and consider the benefits of taking precautions, even when the law doesn't explicitly need it.

Above a lot of ages the Uk government has progressively targeted all forms of fire hazards, with the aim of reducing the number of deaths and injuries caused by fire. In the postwar ages there was a continual rise in these numbers and the government took recognize. The number of deaths from smoke inhalation was of distinct issue, as this rose sharply from the 1950s onward.

The factors for this trend are disputed, but the simple fact that modern fabrics and fillers caused greatly toxic smoke when burning sooner or later prompted the government to regulate the provide of fabric and furnishings, since the a lot more toxic the smoke from a fire the more quickly a person is incapacitated.

It is potentially clear that suppliers and suppliers must comply with government rules on fire retardant fabrics, but in 2006 the new rules changed needs for all organization premises. Fire security law was implemented by the 'Regulatory Reform (Fire Safety) Order 20052. Now, corporations are no lengthier expected to have fire certificates but as a substitute must conduct a danger evaluation to stop fires by reducing danger. The law makes it the responsibility of the organization proprietor to ensure the security of absolutely everyone who uses their premises.

There are precise guidelines for 'sleeping accommodation' which straight utilize to curtain content. Hotels must meet the needs of BS5867 Element 2 Variety B when furnishing a area with curtains. This is a test where a flame is applied to the fabric for fifteen seconds. In summary, this calls for that if the fabric had been to come into immediate make contact with a flame it would have a fire retardant high quality for a limited time by not burning to the edges or falling apart while burning. There are essentially two varieties of flame retardant (FR) fabrics:

1) all those which have been treated soon after manufacture and
2) all those in which the FR high quality is 'built-in'. These are named 'inherent FR fabrics '.

Where a fabric has been treated it must also be in a position to hold its FR high quality soon after repeated washing.

Getting flame retardant fabrics from a respectable firm with items that a lot more than meet the needs ensure fire security and conform to the law. Seem for items labelled 'FR' and request whether or not they meet the security standards for hotel use.

In contrast to the needs for curtains, for bed linen the new rules only state that certain security standards must be regarded for 'sleeping accommodation' as a make a difference of fire prevention. The law does utilize, even though, to all the elements of the true bed (which include head-boards, mattresses, sofa-beds, futons and other convertibles). Potentially a lot less clear is that it also applies to pillows and even throw cushions.

Yet fire retardant bed linen is even now worthy of contemplating as a make a difference of fire prevention, since even when prohibited individuals even now may smoke in a hotel area – specially if they are leaving the up coming early morning. When you are unable to management how a guest behaves prevention is the only confident treatment.

Defending your expense is 1 critical element, however security is even a lot more crucial and safeguarding the lives of guests and employees must make a difference. If as the proprietor you rest in your B&B then your individual security is also at danger. FR fabrics are broadly obtainable for bed linens and price tag just a small a lot more than a regular cotton-product. They could end up saving a lot more than lbs and pence.

Hotel Fire Safety Tips

"Fire!" The very exclamation itself is enough to render the most stout of heart and soul into victims of panic and fear, if not into another fire fatality statistic. For there is something primeval about fire, one of the great dual-edged swords of civilization: when under our control, we can't imagine living without it. When fire is its own master, it is a malevolent and indiscriminate killer.

The threat of fire may be a remote thought for the seasoned business traveler, who stays in a modern hotel, and who assumes every precaution has been taken to ensure that safety is paramount. But the fact is, when staying overnight at even the nicest of establishments, you may be at greater risk than you ever imagined. While there are no hard figures, the U.S. Subcommittee on Science, Research and Technology finds that as many as 85 percent of U.S. hotels lack fire sprinkler systems.

At Greatest Risk

Each year some 32.6 million fires strike Americans at home, in hotels, or at the workplace. That's one fire virtually every second of the day. Fire is the third largest cause of accidental injury and death in this country. Injuries by fire total two million annually, and one out of every eight accidental deaths is from fire.

And the U.S. and Canada have the highest rates of death by fire than any other country in the world. But it isn't necessary to die in the event of fire, even if you are thousands of miles from home in a hotel room with no fire sprinkler system. However, you have to take charge of your own safety. And you have to be prepared in the event the worst happens.

Plan Ahead

Plan your escape from a fire before you are caught in one. Here's what I do-every time.

Before I hang up my clothes or plop down to relax, I familiarize myself with the locations of the fire exits nearest my room. These are generally shown on a map posted on the back of the room door or in a closet. I use the map to locate the two exits nearest my room.

Next I take my key and head out the door. I try to imagine how I would find my way to the nearest fire exit in the dark while crawling on my hands and knees. I count the doorways between me and the fire exit and note any obstacles that could get in my way.

When I reach the exit, I open the door. A locked door will surely be a death trap if a fire were to occur. (By the way, if the door is alarmed, I first notify the hotel security department of my intention to open the door. Then, without letting the door close behind me, possibly trapping me in the stairwell, I take a look inside to get an idea of its configuration and to confirm that the stairwell is free of obstacles that could block my escape.

On my way to or from my room, I find the nearby fire alarms and fire extinguishers or fire hoses. If there are none visible, I'll call the front desk when I return to my room to ask their location. Then I'll go verify their actual presence.

Because it's possible that my path to the nearest fire escape may be blocked during an emergency, I map out a secondary escape route that would take me in the opposite direction as the route I just followed. Again, I note the locations of the fire alarms and extinguishers/hoses.

When I return to my room, I look out the window to see if it would be possible to jump without breaking my neck. In case I'd have to escape that way, I look for obstacles under my window.

I verify the operation of the smoke detector in my room. Typically, a small light on the smoke detector indicates its operation. If I'm unsure that it is working, I call the front desk for assistance.

I figure out how to turn off the fan that delivers air into my room. I find the location of both the entry-and return-air vents and make a mental note of how I could seal them if I were trapped in my room during a hotel fire. Then, because I'd need to let others know I was in my room, I make sure that I can get an outside telephone connection-typically by pressing "8" or "9"-without relying on a hotel operator.

Finally, with an escape plan in place, *now* I relax.

If there is a Fire

If there is any indication or even a suspicion of a fire, call the hotel operator immediately. Give your name, room number, and a brief description of the situation.

Before attempting to leave your room, grab your key. If your family is with you, determine a meeting place outdoors so you will know everyone is safe.

Feel the door with the back side of your hand. (if you used your palm, it might burn your hand due to heat transfer and you would have a hard time using it) If the door or knob is warm, do not open it.

If the door is not warm, drop to your knees and slowly open the door, but be ready to slam it should a cloud of smoke roll in.

If the hallway is clear, head for the exit, not the elevator. Close your door behind you. Take your key with you. Do not stand upright, but crawl or keep low to the floor to avoid smoke and odorless carbon monoxide.

Stay on the same side of the hall as your exit, counting the number of doors to the exit. When you reach the exit, walk quickly, but cautiously down the stairs, and hold on to the handrail as you go. Smoke will sometimes get into an exit stairwell. If you encounter smoke, do not try to run through it. Turn around and walk up. Proceed to a smoke free corridor and cross the building to an alternate exit. If you are unable to leave your room, make every effort to notify someone that you are in your room. If you cannot reach the hotel operator, call the local fire department and identify your exact location. Signal to them by hanging a bed sheet from your window.

If there is smoke in your room, open the window. Do not break the glass unless it is absolutely necessary because heavier smoke may begin to enter from outside.

Fill the bathtub with water. Wet towels and sheets and stuff them around the door and vent which is allowing smoke to enter the room. If the door and walls are hot, bail water on them with your ice bucket to keep them cool·

Place the mattress up against the door and hold it in place with the dresser. Keep it wet. Keep everything wet·

A wet towel tied around your nose and mouth will help filter out smoke if you fold it into a triangle and put the corner in your mouth.

If there is a fire outside of the window, pull down the drapes and move everything that is flammable away from the window.

Do not jump from the room. A fall from this height can cause serious injury. Rather, continue to protect yourself from the fire and signal from your window for help.

Fire Safety in Hotels, Boarding Houses and like Premises

It is important to understand that more than one piece of fire safety legislation and/or fire safety guidance can be applied to any individual premises. For instance take a school the The Regulatory

Reform (Fire Safety) Order 2005 and the Health and Safety (Safety Signs and Signals) Regulations 1996 applies and there could be others. Fire Safety guidance documents including Guide 5 – Educational premises, Guide 1 – Offices and shops, Guide 6 – Small and medium places of assembly or Guide 7 – Large places of assembly may apply and if the school is a boarding school then Guide 3 – Sleeping accommodation could apply.

Fire Safety in new and altered Hotels and Boarding Houses are subject to the Building Regulations and the guidance can be found on my page on Fire Safety in New, Extended or Altered Buildings.

When premises are occupied fire precautions are controlled by The Regulatory Reform (Fire Safety) Order 2005 and this order lays down legal requirements, check them out at the above link.

Fire Safety Guide for England and Wales

The most appropriate guide for Hotels, Boarding Houses and like Premises is likely to be Guide 3 – Sleeping accommodation and can be downloaded at the Department of Communities and Local Government web site. This guide is for all employers, managers and owners of premises providing sleeping accommodation. It tells you about how you might comply with fire safety law, helps you to carry out a fire risk assessment and identify the general fire precautions you need to have in place. It applies to premises where the main use is for sleeping accommodation. The premises addressed in this guide include,

- Guest houses and bed and breakfast accommodation;
- Hotels and motels;
- Hostels, e.g. Y.M.C.A., Y.W.C.A., youth hostels, bail hostels or homeless persons accommodation;
- Refuges, e.g. family accommodation centre's, halfway houses;
- Residential health and beauty spa centre's;
- Residential conference, seminar and training centre's;
- Student halls of residence and areas of sleeping accommodation in other training institutions including military barrack style quarters;

- Those areas of buildings in boarding schools that provide sleeping accommodation; seminaries and other religious colleges;
- The common areas of sheltered accommodation, where care is not provided (where care is provided, see residential care guide);
- Holiday chalets, holiday flat complexes, camping, caravan holiday parks (other than privately owned individual units); and
- Areas in workplaces, where staff sleeping-in is a condition of the employment or a business requirement, as in licensed premises and hotels (but not including tied accommodation such as separate flats, houses or apartments).

This guide addresses:

- Sleeping accommodation for staff;
- Sleeping, dining or other accommodation for guests/ residents; and
- Common areas for residents.
- This guide is not intended for use in:
- Domestic premises occupied as a single private dwelling (which includes private flats or rooms);
- Hospitals, residential care and nursing homes; and
- Prisons and other establishments where people are in lawful custody.

It has been written to provide guidance for a responsible person, to help them to carry out a fire risk assessment in less complex premises. If you read the guide and decide that you are unable to apply the guidance, then you should seek expert advice from a competent person. More complex premises will probably need to be assessed by a person who has comprehensive training or experience in fire risk assessment. However this guide can be used for multi-occupied buildings to address fire safety issues within their individual occupancies.

Fire Risks

Hotels and Boarding Houses are considered to be a high fire

risk, because of the life risk Fires usually occur as the result of carelessness and if some person accidentally or deliberately negates the fire precautions. This can result in serious fire situations causing the possible loss of life and the owner's business being threatened. The risks are similar to those in domestic property however the level of risk varies defendant on the number of staff, guests and as the premises are occupied twenty four hours a day, this increases the risk.

The five principle fire risks are;

- Carelessly discarded smoking materials if it is allowed to come into contact with combustible materials. A lighted cigarette end will take a long time to ignite combustible materials, which may occur in the sleeping hours, thereby increasing the risk. Hopefully the fire detection system would give an early warning of fire, which will not stop the fire but could reduce the damage to negligible losses. The use of signs and the prohibition of smoking in risk areas would reduce the risk and constantly broadcast the dangers to the staff and guests.
- Electrical Appliances are now a standard provision in bed rooms and can be a source of fire if they have been subjected to misuse. Occasionally an electrical faults on electrical apparatus may be a source of fire, especially if they have not been serviced regularly. All electrical equipment should be tested annually and the staff and guests kept informed of the possible dangers associated with the different types of electrical equipment.
- Kitchens can be a high risk dependent on the size and especially if the kitchen is not properly supervised. Full dining facilities increase the risk but this is lessened by having staff in attendance at all times.
- There is a high fire risk is store rooms where bedding, towels, flammable materials and cleaning equipment are stored. Flammable materials in the presence of chemical cleaner may result in a higher fire risk if not store correctly. House keeping and ensuring the store rooms are keep as tidy as possible, will reduce the risk. Also ensure the dangers are discussed at any training sessions.

- Tradesmen on the premises, especially those that use apparatus that is capable of starting a fire, like blow lamps, gas torches, metal angle cutters, etc. One needs to ensure a high degree of supervision during and after their presence. Give the area they have been working in a through inspection and make sure no hot spots or small fires have been missed.

Arson Prevention

Arson is the single most common cause of fire in business premises and 45% of all serious fires are a result of arson. Much of this is not targeted and the vast majority of arson attacks are down to opportunist vandalism. Apart from the need to comply with the law the Responsible Person has a duty to himself and his business to reduce this risk to as low as reasonable possible. Information to assist you, to achieve these aims, go to my page on How to Combat Arson

Training

During training sessions as well as detailing and practicing fire procedures some time should be devoted to emphasising simple fire precautions in an attempt to stop fires happening. Not only is fire training in most premises required under law it also makes sense, half an hour spent before the fire may prevent the fire in the first place and can save lives. For further information go to Staff fire safety training.

Manage Your Hotel Safety

There's plenty you can do to keep hazards at bay!

The last thing you want to think about as you travel the world is hotel safety, especially if you're backpacking. Such is the camaraderie of this way of travel that you'd often rather ignore potential safety risks.

But you will stay in hotels and hostels, and you *will* at times share rooms. Cheap hotels are often of poor construction, and safety and fire norms may not be as strict as you're accustomed to.

Your hotel safety precautions will be different when you're on the road. You probably won't be staying in too many four-star hotels, with room phones, smoke detectors and 24-hour guards. On the contrary, most backpackers stay in hostels, guest houses or backpacker lodges, which often leave much to be desired when it comes to hotel safety, comfort or privacy.

In Dar-es-Salaam I stayed in a six-floor guesthouse and the owners locked it down completely at night to prevent theft. In a fire, it would have been disastrous-every window was grated, every door locked.

Personal Hotel Safety Tips for Women

The difference between cheap hostel beds and a hotel room is that you'll rarely be on your own in a hostel-most are made up of dorms or large shared rooms.

Younger travellers tend to opt for hostels because they're cheaper and more sociable but that doesn't mean there is an age limit.

In Durban one day I woke up to the sight of an 80-year-old man serenely disrobing in full view-as though he'd done that all his life. While some hostels do separate the sexes, many do not.

If this makes you incredibly uncomfortable, don't worry, you'll become more used to unusual situations as you travel. And if you can afford it, many hostels and guesthouses have the option of single rooms, so don't hesitate.

Wherever you are, some basic hotel safety precautions can still be taken. Here are just a few common sense hotel safety procedures:

- Cheap hotels tend to be small. Try to book a room on a low floor (not ground floor) in case of fire.
- Try to get a room that isn't too easily accessible from the street-facing a courtyard is better.
- Make sure the lock on your door works. If it doesn't, use your own. Carry a padlock or combination lock in case your door has a latch-in many countries it will.
- When you first move into your room, check it out -and that means bathroom, behind the curtain, inside any closets and behind doors.

- Look for the fire exits. Make sure you know where they are-and that they're not blocked.
- Once you're sure you're alone, always lock your door when you're inside. It's harder when you're sharing and people come and go at all hours-but do your best. Leave the key in the lock when you sleep, but twist it sideways so no one can push it out and slip it back under their door.
- If for some reason the door won't lock, put something-like a chair-against it and balance something noisy on it. When someone tries to come in they'll wake you up immediately. A small rubber doorstop also comes in handy to keep people out.
- Lock your windows at night if you're near the ground or if there is a balcony. If you think you'll be too hot with the window closed or if there's no fan, make sure you're above the second floor (but preferably no higher than the fourth in case of fire) so you can sleep with your windows open.
- Never open your door unless you know the person behind it. Once a man is in, it's difficult to get him out.
- Avoid being seen entering and leaving your hotel alone. Wait for a group and just walk out with them. No one will know you don't belong.
- Always sleep with a flashlight next to your bed. You never know when it might be useful in an emergency.
- If you're staying in a particularly seedy place-and it may well happen-check for peepholes. I stayed for a week in a brothel in Malawi (and I was lucky to get that room) and I spent most of it barricaded behind my door. I simply didn't feel safe wandering down the halls, and took showers early in the afternoon, when most clients had either gone or not come in yet. This was not hotel room safety at its best!
- When you leave the hotel or hostel, make sure you carry the hotel's card or its address with you. In Zanzibar Stone Town, most guest houses give you a card with a map-the town is built like a labyrinth and you could wander all night trying to get back to your room.

Above all, trust your instincts. If the guesthouse or hostel doesn't 'feel right', leave. Plenty of others are vying for your business.

Hotel Room Safety Keeping Yourself and Your Belongings Safe

Today's backpackers often don't travel light, and that makes hotel room safety a little harder. Some of us rough it, carrying only the bare minimum to survive. Others are 'flashpackers', toting every entertainment or safety gadget under the sun. And some of us work along the way, which means laptops, cellphones, PDAs-many things worth stealing.

The first rule of the road is if you can't afford to lose it, don't take it with you. But if you *must* take it with you, try to keep it safe. Even if people come and go in hostels, there is often a sense of shared vulnerability. Most people are fellow travellers and are equally worried about their belongings.

Still, the same rules apply to hotel room safety anywhere. To keep your belongings safe, follow a few simple hotel room safety tips:

- Keep your eye on your backpack when you check in, especially if the reception or entrance is crowded.
- If there's hotel safe in the room with an electronic lock, put your valuables inside. I prefer not to leave things at the front desk or in the hotel safe-unless it's a large reputable hotel. Small lodges or hostels may not have a main safe-your valuables may end up stashed in the manager's unsecured room or drawer.
- Don't leave anything in full view-temptation is temptation. Anyone can walk off with your laptop while your room door is open during cleaning. And your everyday belongings may be worth someone else's life savings.
- Make sure your windows are locked before you leave. It's easy to slip in and steal.
- Always lock your backpack and fasten it to something solid. What doesn't fit in a room safe-like a laptop-can be locked inside your backpack and fastened to a pipe or railing.

- In a communal hostel, wear your travel money belt to bed and take it to the shower with you. Just throw a towel over it to keep it dry!
- Leave a light or radio on when you leave the room. Anyone who listens at the door will think you're either in the room or coming back soon.
- If you do have expensive gadgets, don't flash them around where other guests or hotel staff can see them.
- Don't leave expensive clothes out to dry or air. A fellow traveler left her high-tech Nike Air-Max trainers on the doorstep-irresistible in a poor country. She spent the next week trekking in her flip flops.

TIP: Talk to other travellers. Word gets around about hotel safety. If hotels are unsafe and theft is rampant, travellers will spread the word! For other types of travel safety, find out how to avoid travel scams.

Hotel Room Safety Devices-or Gadgets!

Despite all your precautions, a bit of help from safety gadgets might be useful. Here are a few of the more popular ones: A wire or cable lock -a length of wire with a lock at the end. You can use it to lock your laptop to the sink or your backpack to the water pipes. It's just nice to have along. One of my favourites is the door stop alarm -wedge it under the door just inside your room. If someone opens the door from the outside, it lets off a shrill siren. It is battery operated, and easy to carry in a backpack. Failing that, a plain rubber doorstop will make it difficult for anyone to get in. Another neat gadget for your hotel room safety is a door knob alarm. It's armed with motion sensors-if someone tries to get into your room, the alarm will ring, usually loudly. Another good piece of safety equipment is the portable door lock. Just slip it into the door frame and presto, your door is locked from the inside. And last but not least, if fear of fires grabs you, carry a lightweight smoke hood. They take up little room and can make the difference between life and death by giving you time to escape.

Accidents happen, but with all these precautions you'll be making sure you put all the hotel room safety odds on your side!

6

Importance of Hotel Safety and Security when Travelling

Professional thieves tend to hang around hotels and resorts, especially the lobbies, looking for tourists and travellers that are easy pickings. Here are some travel tips that may help you feel more secure in your hotel room and when travelling.

Professional thieves tend to hang around hotels and resorts, especially the lobbies, looking for tourists and travellers that are easy pickings. Here are some travel tips that may help you feel safe and more secure in your hotel room when you are travelling, or are on vacation.

- First, the lobbies of hotels and resorts should never be considered secure, even the upscale ones. They are all easy pickings for opportunistic luggage thieves, especially at peak times when the hotel reception staff is extremely busy with new guests arriving and other guests that are trying to check out. Never leave your luggage unguarded unless you know for sure that it is being looked after by a bellman.
- If you are having a bite to eat in a hotel restaurant, especially a buffet, never leave your laptop, briefcase, or handbag unguarded to get a drink or something more to eat. It takes thieves only a split second to make off with them. It is impossible for the hotel staff to be constantly on the lookout for these criminals.
- When booking your room, try to book one that is on the second, third, fourth, or fifth floors, as ground floor hotel

rooms are more susceptible to break ins. Keep in mind that rooms above the fifth floor may not be accessible by many fire engine ladders if a fire breaks out in the hotel.

- Always check to make sure that the door to your room locks properly, and that the windows and sliding doors open, but also lock securely. Most hotels use electronic card keys for their hotel room doors as they offer more security than the standard metal keys.
- Do not carry you key card in its folder if the folder has the room number on it. Write down the room number on a piece of paper, keep it on your person when you go out, and leave the folder in your room.
- Always identify unexpected staff or visitors to your room before opening the door. Call the front desk if in doubt as to the authenticity of that person. It is advisable not to give out your room number to anyone that you do not know and trust.
- It may not be a good idea to hang a 'please clean the room' sign on the doorknob when you go out, as it signals to a would-be thief that there is probably no one in the room.
- Do not assume that your hotel room door is locked just because it closes automatically when you go out. Check to make sure that it has really locked. If your room has a balcony make sure the sliding glass door is also locked, as it may be possible for someone to climb onto your balcony from a balcony beside, above or below yours.
- Do not leave any valuables lying around in plain view in your hotel room. They may be too tempting for some cleaning staff to resist. Place any small valuables in your in-room safe if there is one. Keep in mind that safes that use metal keys are not as secure as the ones that use electronic key cards.
- The next best bet if there is no safe in your room is to lock your small valuables in your largest suitcase when you go out. Locked, hard-sided luggage offers the best security. Some travellers even use duct tape to secure small valuables to the underside of the hotel room furniture.

- Always use your door's deadbolt or chain lock at night before you go to sleep or if you feel like taking a nap.
- There is a small, inexpensive, battery-operated, motion-sensitive, burglar alarm that can be hung on the inside hotel doorknob, or there is a wedge-shaped alarm that you can wedge under the door that accomplishes the same thing. If someone tries to open your door, the alarm will sound.
- There are two less sophisticated methods you could use. You can move a chair in front of the hotel door and place the backrest under the knob, or wedge a standard rubber doorstopper under the door. Either of these two methods is also effective.
- When you pack and get ready to check out of your hotel, do not forget to empty your room safe.
- And last but not least, count the number of pieces of luggage when you check out and make sure that everything has been put in your taxi.

Hotel Security: An Important Selling Point

Managing security in hotels is a delicate balancing act. On one hand, guests want to know that their rooms and possessions are secure and that processes are in place to ensure that any undesirables who wander in off the street are dealt with. On the other hand, they don't want to see blatant signs of oppressive security measures wherever they go. They want to feel they're in a welcoming place with an air of luxury, not a prison.

Security in hotels, as at many public establishments, has also come under scrutiny after heightened terrorist threats across the UK. Viewed as potential targets, hotels are seeking to exercise increased vigilance, including reviewing their existing security systems. Being able to show that high-level security measures are in place is, for some renowned London hotels, now viewed as an important selling point.

Peace of Mind

At the Dorchester, for example, where some of the world's most advanced security systems are set up, head of IT Luke Mellors says the hotel has reaped great benefits from being one of the most secure hotels in London. "It gives us tremendous competitive advantage, and our guests peace of mind," he says.

The Dorchester's surveillance systems are based on technology used to protect military locations and nuclear reactors, and were implemented by Southampton-based security company CSS Security.

CSS was initially established as a locksmiths in the early 1970s by the father of the current managing director, Roberto Fiorentina, who has seen successive waves of new technology ensure that approaches to hotel security are constantly evolving.

"From simple lock-and-key mechanisms, we saw electronics transform access controls," he says. "Then, as computers became widespread, IT people started designing systems. Today, some security systems are based on state-of-the-art technology and software."

One area of hotel security where the latest technology has had a real impact is CCTV, according to Mohammed Ramzan, managing director of Iyonder, a high-speed wireless internet network (Wi-Fi) supplier. Iyonder has worked with numerous hotel chains, including Radisson and Holiday Inn Express, to install Wi-Fi networks that in some cases are being used to support CCTV.

Once a Wi-Fi network is in place, perhaps to give guests internet access, CCTV functionality can be added with no additional infrastructure costs, although hoteliers will have to pay for the cameras and a server to run the system.

One advantage of running CCTV off a wireless network is that properties can position their cameras in locations that have traditionally been hard to reach for hard-wired systems. As long as the network antennas are set up to transmit to a chosen far-flung location, such as the back of a car park, a camera can be installed. Ramzan says that outdoor digital cameras tend to be big and bold and cased in a special housing, while those used inside can be as inconspicuous as required and can even be hidden in clocks or behind wall panels.

The plug-and-play nature of Wi-Fi-enabled digital cameras means they can be moved around easily, to take up a temporary post, as long as there is an electricity plug point nearby to power the camera. This versatility may come in useful if you want to provide extra surveillance services for a conference or social event.

Small digital microphones can also be attached to cameras to enable voices and other noise to be recorded as well. The cameras can be set up to take digital images as often as twice a second, each image being stored on the server with a date and time tag, or they can be adjusted to react to movement or sound.

Easier Searches

In the event of an incident, digital images are also far easier to search through than traditional CCTV recordings. Consider how easy it is to find a specific scene on a DVD compared with a VHS video, and you have a valid comparison. Ramzan notes that, since the squeeze on police resources caused by the London bombings last July, some forces have said that they no longer have to time to sift through endless hours of video footage.

Because the system is based on IP-the basic internet technology-the images can even be viewed remotely. A hotel manager away from his property need only find a PC with a web browser and he can securely access the system to make sure all is as it should be.

The wonder of new technology is not necessarily in the technology itself but in the various applications companies find for that technology.

The PREM Group, for example, which manages a range of hotel chains including the Premier Apartments and Days Inn brands, is developing a system that uses Wi-Fi to track the use of in-room safes, according to Seán Graham, general manager of PREM Group security systems.

The idea came about after the company secured the UK and Ireland distribution rights for the Safemark in-room safe programme, a US-based venture. The business model for this entails leasing standard electronically coded in-room safes to hotels, which charge guests a daily rate for their use.

PREM Group is also offering a warranty of as much as £5,000 for any goods stolen from the safes. Graham says that the company is targeting three-star hotels, properties that traditionally don't include safes in their rooms. Currently, the scheme is based on an honesty system, whereby guests are asked whether they have used the safe or not, and their bill is charged accordingly. This approach obviously depends on the integrity of the guest as, short of examining each room before checkout, there's no way of knowing whether the safe has been used.

The new Wi-Fi version, now being trialled, sees a transmitter on the safe interfacing with the network and recording every time the safe door is opened. The system then automatically updates the guest's bill. "The service aims to make the use of hotel safes a revenue-generating exercise," says Graham.

But the best way to ensure that a safe remains untampered with is to make certain no unauthorised person can get into the hotel room in the first place, and some exciting technologies have emerged aimed at making room access security as robust as possible.

Biometric Systems

A number of lock systems now on the market are based on biometrics-the science and technology of measuring and statistically analysing human body characteristics such as fingerprints, eye retinas and irises, and facial patterns.

US-based security firm ODI Security, for example, has developed a small, discreet fingerprint scanner system that does away with the problem of lost or stolen room keys. According to managing director Rich Slevin, guests checking in need only swipe their finger across a scanner at reception several times to register their details. Specialised software converts the scanned information into digital form and this data is stored on a database.

A record of the fingerprint is kept only momentarily before being transformed into data that describes patterns and matchpoints on that fingerprint. This is used to create a unique algorithm, which is sent to a module on the room door via a network connection. When they reach the door, guests simply roll their finger over a small pad on the module and enter.

Slevin says the system has never rejected a valid fingerprint, and can be adapted to secure in-room safes and even TV sets, to prevent children getting access to unsuitable movies and other programming. The chances of two people having the same fingerprint are about eight million to one. However, Rob Healey, UK marketing manager for system solutions at electronics giant Panasonic, says fingerprints can be damaged if people cut their fingers or work with chemicals or on a building site, for instance. More reliable, he says, are iris recognition systems-because no two people have the same iris patterns, not even identical twins.

Iris Scanning

Panasonic has come up with such a system. Originally developed to offer secure access to banks, laboratories and airports, it has been installed in a number of Japanese hotels. It works in a similar way to ODI's finger-scanning system, but guests are required to look into a small camera at reception. This captures images of an individual's iris-a process that, according to Healey, takes five to 10 seconds. This information is sent to a flat wall-mounted unit, the size of an A4 piece of paper, on which guests look into another small camera-without the need to remove any contact lenses or spectacles.

These technologies have yet to gain widespread acceptance in the UK hospitality sector, perhaps because hoteliers think guests will balk at staring into a camera device for too long. But one cutting-edge access technology that is established in a number of UK hotels is an infrared access device produced by security software firm Guestkey. Installed in the Ritz in Paris and London's Grosvenor House and Berkley, the system uses a conventional pocket-sized plastic laser-coded key. When this is inserted in a lock, infra-red optics decipher the code in the individual key and enable entry.

Guestkey managing director Tony Marsden says about four billion different code combinations are possible with the system, making code-breaking unfeasible. As security information is stored in the lock, regular guests can keep their key but have different rooms assigned to them with each visit.

Advanced Access Control System

Managing director Tony Marsden says Guestkey's infrared optic lock can be configured to pick up unusual behaviour, such as if a wrong key is used or a door is forced or left open for too long. It can even pick up movement in the room when the door is double-locked. If it is connected to a network, this information can be fed to a control centre. Guestkey worked with CSS Security to install such a system into London's Dorchester hotel and integrate it with technology developed by US security company Maxxess, whose systems have been used to oversee whole cities and to protect nuclear reactors.

With these systems in place, anything unusual registered by the lock causes an image from the nearest CCTV camera and a detailed floor plan of that area to appear on a guard's monitor. The guard can then decide what kind of response is required.

Marsden says: "For room access control, this is the most advanced [system] in the world."

Importance of Hotel Insurance and its Features

Choosing the right kind of hotel insurance matters as the occurrence of fire mishaps or any other accidents cannot be guessed. The sudden growth of hotel industry has led to the consideration of insuring hotels by their owners in a serious manner. Any such insurance reflects the needs of the present situation.

If you are planning to insure your hotel, then there are certain guidelines you need to follow. You have to estimate the amount of insurance required. The best way to judge this factor is to compare the insurances offered by banks and lenders to other hotels.

Important Factors: You have to determine the reasons that why exactly you need insurance and what all aspects you expect to cover. Generally, some of the common things that are covered are insurance to buildings, liability, goods and services. It all depends upon the insurance premiums and the scheme you have selected.

Before Insuring: Getting an insurance coverage from a financial institution is not that easy.

Related Coverage

- Kerala Backwater and Its Important Features
- Travel Health Insurance and Its Great Importance
- California City's 2010 Tour Details Regarding Vacation Hotel Features Accomodation And Sightseeings

- Southern California's Incredible Trip Info To Get The Best Of Vacation Hotel Features.

There are certain norms that need to be fulfilled. For example, you should check the wiring of your hotel is perfect or not. Additionally, you should ensure that the structure is stable and is not vulnerable to slightest of the damages.

Insurance Provider: You should choose a provider based upon the years of experience, features available and the coverage offered. The safest way is to go with the one who has got a majority of insurance holders. You can benefit the most from those providers who implement Internet technology.

Compare Features: The best way to choose a provider is to log onto the corresponding website. Similarly, you need to check the features offered by other providers.

Prepare all the information and features in a document for a comprehensive look. This will enable you to get along with a provider who has got best features.

Online Facilities: You may prefer a provider based on the convenience factor. It will be easier for you track down the insurance details on a timely basis. Checking the premiums to be paid and the current status report of your insurance policy matters a lot for you.

Best Insurance for You

Any insurance company offering a wide coverage along with a unique range of benefits will be ideal for you to choose. Also, you need to seek valuable advices from your insurance provider so that you could obtain maximum benefits as long as you are holding policy.

Few Concerns: It is important to check the terms and conditions of a company beforehand. This is because you might have to face issues with certain clauses like payment options and monthly premiums. Getting your doubts cleared in the initial stages alone will benefit you immensely.

Obtain Quotes: You need to request free quotes from all those hotel insurance companies that you have selected on a preliminary basis. Some companies offer customized packages by taking your interests into consideration. The latest trend is to integrate insurance with investments into stock markets. You will benefit the most from such packages even without any risks.

Importance of Security Surveillance

Security Surveillance plays a vital role. Almost all the situations in present days require a complete security & safety plan. Whether a public or private place it is mandatory to plan securities to avoid/ eliminate the calamity.

The security plan must be considered depending on the functions & criticality of locations with detailed information of intrusion detection, video assessment, fire detection access control and actions to be taken by surveillance systems depending on the events. As today's surveillance system is capable enough to react with pre assigned functions when an event occurs.

Vital locations and functions must be monitored using wired and wireless backup communications. Remote connectivity and data backup at the central/remote are the essentials to be considered in situations of present days.

The worldwide increase in terror and theft has become driving force in explosion of CCTV/IP surveillance systems to protect lives and assets.

Attacks on TAJ and Oberoi hotels brought about a jump and a complete re-evaluation of the personnel and asset security requirements to safe-guard a facility. To meet this new threat, video security has taken on the lead role in protecting personnel and assets. Today every state-of-the-art security system must include video as a key component to provide the "remote eyes" for security, fire, and safety.

Attacks on TAJ & OBEROI Hotels, has dramatized the importance of reliable communications and remote visualization of images via remote video cameras. Many lives were saved (and lost) as a consequence of the voice, video, alarm, and fire equipment in place and in use at the time of the fateful attack

The availability of operational wired and wireless two-way communication between command and control headquarters and responders (police, fire, emergency) played a crucial role in life and death. The availability (or absence) at command posts of real-time video images at crucial locations in the hotels during the attack and evacuation contributed to the action taken by command personnel during the tragedy. The use (or absence) of wireless transmission from the remote video cameras in the hotels clearly had an impact on the number of survivors and casualties.

If redundant, backup and IP surveillance solutions were present, the police head quarter might given a full control of the situation and helped in evacuation of survivors and reduce in casualties

IT would be a great help for the police/military to take control of the situation if the cameras were running at different locations on wireless backups which could definitely reduced a casualties and helped out the operation to be cleared in a short time.

Cameras with night vision with a power back in association with wi-fi were present then it might be easy to control the scene and track the victims. By monitoring them the police either outside of the hotel can guide commandos to help evacuating victims or even easily trace & attack terrorists.

Nobody knows where and when this type of situations occurs it is mandatory to plan a surveillance system depending upon the importance of locations.

The function and combination of video into safety and security systems has come of mature as a reliable, cost-effective means for assessing and responding to terrorist attacks and other life-threatening situations. Video is an effective means for decrease in crimes and protecting assets and for prosecuting offenders.

Security personnel today have the responsibility for comprehensive security and safety systems in which video often plays the key role. With today's increase in labor costs and the need for each security officer to provide more functionality, video more than ever before is earning its place as a cost-effective means for improving security and safety while reducing security budgets.

Video offers the greatest potential benefit when integrated with other sensing systems and used to view remote areas. Video provides the "eyes" for many security devices and functions such as:

(1) Motion detectors, Fire sensors smoke detector & alarms,
(2) Watching for presence/absence of personnel in a defined area,
(3) Evacuation of personnel—determining route for evacuation, access (emergency or intruder) to determine response, respond, and monitor response. When combined with fire and smoke detectors, CCTV/IP cameras in inaccessible areas can be used to give advance warning of a fire.

Technologies Which makes difference when integrated properly.

The usage of IP Cameras on network:-This would essentially mean that the images captured can be easily shared on net and would aid in remote viewing. Consider the recent attacks on the crucial landmarks of the country's financial capital. Had the hotels be equipped with the above facilities, many lives could have been saved. The terrorists had ensured that the central monitoring room (CMR) shouldn't be accessed. To ensure this, they had put smoke canisters/tear gas shells in the CMR. When our commandos tried for vigilance they couldn't view anything as the room was badly filled up with the gas. Now, had there been the usage of IP cameras, the commander-in-chief and other operational super commanders sitting at the Police control room could have easily accessed the cameras despite the CMR being filled up with the smoke. That would mean the position of the terrorists and the kind of ammunition they carried. It would also mean evacuation of the innocent hostages from the safest route and saving of a lot of lives of the hostages and commandos.

Night Vision devices:-These devices were there with the commandos and with the terrorists or so is it believed so. But, the latest cameras are equipped with this function. So, even though the lights were put off by the miscreants, we still would have been able to see them and would have an update on their location from time to time.

GPS:-These new aged technologies have aided in the directions. These devices could have been coupled with the existing Wi-Fi network of the hotel and the video images coupled with it can bring the entire position of the anti-social elements on the hand held devices. Can you imagine what wonders that could have done for our commandos?

RFID/Wi-Fi tags:-The new aged tag can be used for giving the identification to the staff and guests. There are memory chips integrated on to them with details such as the codes and the access level where in they are allowed to venture into. So, not just anyone and everyone entering the hotel can go up to 6th floor at Taj where in the VVIP are stationed. Not even by lift. The access criteria can be set via proper software's with administrative controls only. So, somebody who has just come in to have a coffee at Shamiana could only have entry to café and not to the lobby at the floors, despite sneaking the eyes of the security

Video is the critical link in the overall security of a facility but organizations must develop a complete security planby integrating with the differrent technologies rather than adopt piecemeal protection measures. To optimize use of video technology, the practitioner and end user must understand all of its aspects—from light sources video monitors to intelligent video systems and recorders. The capabilities and limitations of video during daytime and nighttime operation. IP and Networking and communications must also be understood.

Travel Managers Underscore Their Strategic Importance

The unthinkable has happened. The world is different for everyone, forever. Our priorities have turned to our faith, our families and our loved ones. What was so terribly important is now very difficult to focus on. Our first thoughts were with those affected, not our own interests. In light of these circumstances, it is difficult to turn our focus to our jobs and our contributions to our companies, but we must.

Well-managed travel programs have eased the stress on both the travellers and their companies. Travel managers all around the country have demonstrated not only their value but also their importance. Consider the following:

Travel managers and their departments were the first place to turn while companies attempted to cope with the situation and their employees. Their initial response, and sole focus, was to identify traveler locations, along with any at-risk situations.

Travel managers coordinated with their key suppliers to bring their travellers home as quickly and safely as possible.

Travel managers are becoming the central point of control for new travel policies, tracking employee movements, and installing and monitoring company security procedures.

If ever there was a time to recognize the strategic importance of travel management, it has been over this past six weeks.

There are important lessons to be learned during this difficult time. Here are a few:

- Travel policies that are followed benefit everyone—all bookings through the designated channel(s) had the greatest likelihood of receiving prompt company communication. Bookings with the preferred suppliers afforded the travel department its best chance to assist the traveler.
- Agency consolidation works—having all travellers book through one source made it possible for these travel managers to quickly ascertain the whereabouts of the majority of their employees.
- Streamlining suppliers helps—information gathering is faster and more accurate when working with smaller numbers of suppliers via defined channels.
- Booking through the designated agency matters—the value of knowing the location of company employees was paramount (especially when compared with potentially saving some money by booking on the Internet, thereby eliminating the company's ability to contact the employee). Employees who booked their hotels through the appropriate channels could be contacted and informed of specific company developments.
- Security changes need a focal point—the point of booking is the most expedient, logical place to affect such changes.
- Preferred vendors are vital—working with some of their best vendor partners, travel managers were able to assist their travellers with hotel rooms, rental cars, etc.
- Internal relationships are important—the ability to work with other departments (corporate security, corporate

communications and IT) impacted the effectiveness of the travel department.

- Disaster recovery planning is crucial—travel managers who planned for emergencies (with the agencies and the internal travel department) were able to quickly react.

Travel managers who have not yet consolidated their programs should note the value points previously described. These advantages, while well known to our industry, can be highlighted to your company in this time of heightened alert. In the near term, travel managers should prepare a gap analysis of their programs, and prepare to present these opportunities to senior management. Attention should be given to all components of the managed travel program, from policy to reimbursement. Travel managers have much to contribute as companies reassess all facets of their business travel.

Travel programs that are consolidated should take careful note of your assistance during this crisis (along with opportunities to improve). Inventory your results in helping travellers, whether in getting a traveler home, assisting with hotel arrangements, or comforting the employee's family. Record the savings as a result of your preferred vendor partners' assistance. Summarize any kind words offered by travellers or their families during this crisis.

When the company's focus returns to your department, be ready to fully detail your role during the difficult times. Ensure that the company at large comprehends the complete extent of your contribution. Be sure to thank each person, including your preferred suppliers, who assisted you in doing your job. You couldn't have done it without them.

As our priorities reorder themselves from tragedy to living our daily lives, we will increase our focus on work and the work to come.

Travel managers, and their industry partners, should be proud of their collective teamwork. There is much to build on, and the stature of travel management can only grow as a result.

Importance of Lighting in Hotels: Setting the Stage

If you are a frequent traveller, then it is more likely that you have observed how the apartments, inns, B&Bs, hotels, and the like set up their lighting fixtures. There are various factors surrounding this, which are given attention below.

Lobby and Reception Area – This is one part of the hotel that acts like a business card, which gives first impressions to the first-time guests. The lights in this area must be very inviting and give a feeling of security, making the visitors want to come back again for the next holiday season.

Corridors – This part must ideally be illuminated properly since this is where people staying in the hotel walk to and fro their individual rooms. It is equally important that the lighting in this space be bright enough for the guests to see clearly their room numbers, thus, preventing them from getting lost around the premises.

Spa and Dining Sections – In-house restaurants and food shops are where the visitors typically go to every mealtime during their stay. Admirably, it is essential for the lights to promote a one-of-a-kind experience to the people eating. On the other hand, the illumination inside the spa must not be too bright or too dark, just enough to give the guests a peaceful and calming feeling.

Although there are still other aspects of a hotel that needs immediate planning and action, still it is an undeniable fact that through using various types of lighting fixtures, the areas inside travel accommodations are enhanced and emphasised.

The Importance of Effective Communication in the Hotel Industry

In any industry, communication has always played a key part in the success of the company. Effective and balance communication have enabled better understanding of each party's objectives and views and therefore streamlined actions and developments leading to success and profitability.

Asset managers' main role is to help align that sometimes vast gap between the interests of hotel owners and management companies. We have recently noted that management companies have increased their transparency as hotel owners have demanded to gain a clearer understanding of how the operators' businesses is going. With everyone looking to cut costs and gain a greater return on their investments, the role of the asset manager is more valuable than ever. There is a much better understanding today with regards to the value of asset management. A good asset manager benefits both parties by being partial, fair and give an 'outside eye' to the business, whether it be by getting insurance costs down, maximizing retail space, promoting sale of real estate and so on.

While asset management is not yet as prevalent in Middle East and Asia, the structure of hotel ownership is changing from hotels being owned and operated by the same parties (either families or hotel chains) to more outside investment fund ownership. Therefore the demand for professional asset managers will increase in order again to better align both parties interest. At this point in time, asset management has been mostly applied to upscale, full-service hotels operated by regional and international hotel companies. The complexity of the market and the specialized and varied service industry will now lead to higher demand for professional asset manager to identify each party's responsibilities and assist them in developing their product while assuring a better return on investment for each.

Although the ultimate responsibility of the asset manager is to maximize profit and value of a specific hotel, the job has evolved beyond a solely "checking the books" function. Asset managers today offer expertise in areas as diverse as real estate, operations, sales, capital expenditures, strategic positioning, marketing and liability. The role of the asset manager has evolved dramatically. We really represent the owner, manage the relationship between owner and operator and act as liaisons. We have a broad range of responsibilities with two objectives: to optimize the performance of the hotel and protect the life of the physical asset. To accomplish this we have to dig in at the property level – how it's run and review capital expenditures. We focus on booking pace, what types of groups are coming into the hotel and anything that is going to impact the profitability of the hotel. This knowledge sharing is to the benefit of owners and operators as asset managers can offer a "fresh eye" perspective to problem solving. And, with a focus on open communication between all parties, the relationships continue to improve. Full transparency between the Asset Manager and the General Manager with open and fair lines of communication will enable a success formula for the development of the property as well as try to define the best equity for the relationship. Balance is mandatory in any relationships and will therefore enable an equitable share of the rewards/profits which will benefit the well being and the sustainability of the long term relationship between the owner and operator. It is also very important for the Asset Manager to understand the capabilities and limitations of the General Managers decisions in order to assess what needs to be addressed at a different level than the property. The partnership the asset manager is creating with the management team of the property, by encouraging suggestions, creative ideas, new developments will also assist in opening up the lines of communications and encourage transparency.

We previously noted that asset managers were seen as referees, with aggressive behaviour and forcing operators to change how they run their businesses. The relationship between the two nowadays tends to work more harmoniously. Operators as well as owners have more financial risk in projects today and are being held more accountable so therefore recruit professional asset managers that are dedicated, passionate and have a wide knowledge of the variety and complexity of the lodging markets. This new approach will lead to open communication between the parties and therefore smooth the way to have their goals aligned.

The growth of the asset manager's role has been considerable in recent years and with the complexity and diversity of new projects around the world, Asset Managers will always play a key role in the partnership between owners and operators. Building effective, fair and trustworthy relationships between both parties are the keys of a successful asset manager as well as bringing his overall wide and diverse experience that will lead the company to profitability and therefore great returns for both parties.

Mr. Sogno is the Managing Director of Global Asset Solution. The company provides expert oversight and owner representation in the hospitality industry (asset management, brokerage, consulting).

7

Front Office and Guest Safety and Security

Security Issues

Security encompasses areas such as security of the property itself, company assets, employees' and customers' personal belongings and valuables, life security, personal security etc.

In all workplaces management stipulates that it is not responsible for valuables and employees personal belongings (their handbags, items kept in the personal lockers, etc.). Yet management must take all possible measures to prevent theft among employees and of employee belongings through its hiring practices and through the implementation of effective management, human resources and operational policies, such as:

- Background checks of selected applicants
- Policies related to employees' entry to, and exit from, the workplace
- Spot checks of locker rooms and lockers
- Effective supervision and control during the work cycle
- Policies related to the discovery of criminal records and wrongdoing among, and by, employees
- Control of people entering and exiting the workplace.

With regard to guest valuables, management informs guests that the hotel is not responsible for valuables left in the room, advising them to secure these in safety deposit boxes provided by the hotel. Besides taking care of security issues related to the people they employ (as outlined above), management must undertake some necessary measures, among which:

- Providing "secure" (safety) deposit boxes and areas to keep valuables
- Policies and practices to ensure the security of these boxes and areas
- Management and operational policies regarding the security of guest rooms
- Management and operational policies regarding the security of public areas
- Security policies and practices for the back-of-the-house areas
- Employment and training of security personnel
- Policies and practices to minimize the "presence" and "patronage" of "shady characters" and criminals, verification of registration and check-in personal data and documentation submitted, and curtailing free movement of unknowns on the premises, as well as direct, free flowing communication with local, national and international security authorities)
- Training of staff in guest and valuable security
- Effective supervision and control procedures.

Some of the security measures taken by hotels:

Key Card Locks

While key card locks on guest rooms are quickly becoming the standard, some hotels still don't take advantage of the added safety provided to guests. Guest room locking systems these days include punch and magnetic key cards which have locks with flash memory and other productivity linked functions. The system can directly be linked with PMS.

Security Guards

Most hotels do not have security guards while some employ them only at night. At Best Western Sterling Inn, we have our own staff of trained security guards working 24-hours every day to provide the best in safety and security for our guests

Defibrillation Units

A life saving device in case of heart attacks, defibrillation units are starting to be deployed among police and emergency personnel across the nation.

Security Cameras

Few Hotels have security cameras with digital technology, intelligent access central system, software interface with CCTV for matching undesirable visitors and criminals, interfacing with motion detectors, pocket lie detectors and spy cameras and use of biometric readers like hand key reader or face recognition system etc.

Fire Alarms

While most hotels now have smoke detectors and fire alarms, Some hotels have a state of the art alarm system with smoke detectors in each guest room and throughout the entire complex that is monitored 24 hours a day, 7 days per week that pinpoints the exact point of the alarm allowing our security staff to respond immediately to the area of any alarm condition.

Emergency Power

Very few hotels have any provision for emergency power in case of an electrical outage while a few hotels provide limited emergency stand-by power to provide elevator service and some lighting. Some hotels has a 2-Megawatt stand-by generator that provides 100% emergency power that can provide uninterrupted guest service during a power outage.

Emergency Manual

Hotels maintain an emergency manual, detailing operations in the event of a variety of emergencies.

Employee Photo ID

For added security, some hotels have employees wearing a photo ID nametag allowing quick identification.

In-Room Safes

In addition to the safety deposit boxes offered by most hotels at the front desks, Some hotels provide in-room guest safes capable of holding a lap-top computer that use the guest's own credit card as the key.

Guest Elevators

Elevators may also be interfaced with a room electronic locking system, where swiping the room card key takes the guest to the floor on which he is staying.

Bomb Threat Security

Precautions and measures that may be taken in the above case:

1. Security nets and body searches for guests not known to the staff.
2. Banqueting suites and other non-public areas should be security checked and locked after use
3. Goods received and bags should be checked and kept tidy.
4. If a bomb threat is received via telephone, the telephonist should note carefully what exactly is said, the time of the call received the accent of the caller and background noise if any. After the alert the GM should stay put in the lobby where he can be reached easily.
5. Duties and responsibility of staff during an emergency should be well-defined.
6. The hotel should work closely with the police to keep them updated.
7. Chamber maids and HK supervisors should be trained to conduct security checks in the guest rooms.

Security Measures for Women Travellers

- Mirrored walls of the guestroom floor elevators so that you can see who is walking behind you
- Well-lit public areas such a s lobby bars
- Valet parking services to avoid the need o a woman to enter the parking lot
- Assigning rooms closer to the elevator
- If a woman traveler is not assigned a room on the special executive floor, hotels most often on request, upgrade her accommodation to that floor without an increase in room

rate. The floor is staffed almost 24 hours a day with a concierge

Importance of a Security System

The guest, who comes to a particular hotel, comes with an understanding that he and his belongings both will be safe and secure during his stay at the hotel. At the same time it is also quite important that the hotel staff and assets are protected and secure. Hence it is very important to have a proper security system in place to protect staff, guests and physical resources and assets such as equipment, appliances buildings, gardens of the hotel and also the belongings of the guest.

The management must take care that the security and safety systems cover the following areas:

- Guest: Protection from crimes such as murder, abduction and health hazards from outsiders, hotel staff, pests, food poisoning etc.
- Staff: Providing staff lockers, insurances, health schemes, provident funds etc. Protective clothing, shoes, fire fighting drills, supply of clean drinking water use of aqua guards, sanitized wash rooms etc.
- Guest luggage: Secure luggage store rooms and proper equipment such as luggage trolley and bell hop trolley should be provided.
- Hotel Equipments: Lifts, Boilers, Kitchen equipment, furniture fitting and building etc. must be protected and for these the security and safety should cover up fire safety equipment, bomb threat security system, water floods security system, earthquake security system, safe vault security system etc.
- Protection of raw materials, goods, provisions and groceries etc. for this the security system should cover proper storage and pest control systems, apart from the application of total material management system.

Types of Security

1) Physical aspect is divided into two parts (a) Internal

(b)external.

a) Internal security
   - Against theft
   - Fire safety
   - Proper lighting
   - Safeguarding assets
   - Track unwanted guests.

b) External Security
   - Proper lighting outside the building
   - Proper fencing of the building
   - Fecing of pool area to avoid accidents in the night
   - Manning of service gates to restrict entry
   - Fixing of closed circuit TV cameras

2) Security aspects of persons

a) Staff
   - Effective recruitment and selection
   - Identification of staff
   - Key control
   - Red tag system
   - Training
   - Locker inspection

b) Guests:
   - Check scanty baggage guests
   - Guests suspected of taking away hotel property should be charged according to hotel policy
   - Guest room security:
   - Provide wide angle door viewer, dead bolt locks, night torch, chains on doors etc
   - Employees should be trained to not give any information abount in house guests to outsiders
   - While issuing a card key ask for key card if in doubt of the guest.
   - House keeping staff should never leave keys expose on unattended carts in corridors

3) Security aspects of systems:
   - Record of all losses and missing items immediately
   - Inventory control should be proper
   - Auditing should be done on a regular basis
   - Proper system for cash disbursements should be made.

The term system implies the operations of the hotel eg: all the equipment used for operation, procedures laid down for operations and policies to be followed. Systems procedures and policies if followed properly shall safeguard the assets and increase life span of equipment as well as avoid any breakdown maintenance.

This would mean the following:

Fix duties and responsibilities: Fix duties of staff members so that they don't interfere with others' work.

Make Surprise Checks

Staff who have access to liquid assets should be made to sign a bond so that in case of theft the concerned person can easily be caught

Hiring of some independent security company to check the security system of the hotel

Safety Issues

When we take the same hotel as example, it is management's duty to ensure "safety" in several areas, such as:

- The structure itself
- Installations and fixtures (check electrical, plumbing, air-conditioning and other installations)
- Public and work areas (e.g. slippery floors, hazardous obstacles in traffic areas), safety of furniture, equipment, appliances, and utensils.

This is followed by:

- Health safety (nontoxic cleaning material and detergents used)
- Good quality air (what we breathe, dependent upon the type of equipment, installations and fixtures used, and regular repairs and maintenance)

- Food safety (a whole world in itself including sanitation, food quality, food spoilage, correct handling procedures, allowable and recommended temperatures, etc.), and checking and control procedures.

An important "preventive measure" is eliminating the possibility of communicating contagious diseases. Even if local regulations do not require it, it is recommended to send food and beverage handlers for a regular medical checkup. Another preventive measure is the formulation and implementation of policies and procedures related to employee accidents which may present a threat to food sanitation.

Culinary staff who cut themselves accidentally at work, as often happens while slicing food products, have to immediately stop handling food, and report to their Executive Chef and to the person in charge of First Aid in their company (Security or Human Resources Department) for preliminary treatment and handling. Healing and precautionary measures are taken before they are allowed back at their job.

There are also some basic "dress" requirements for staff involved in food and beverage preparations: e.g. Chefs' hats (to prevent hair and whatever hair contains to fall into the food), discreet earrings (non-dangling) or no earrings for women, and long hair neatly and securely tied in a bun at the back of the head.

Of no lesser importance is the safety of work tools and work procedures covering all areas, such as stable ladders, secure shelving, safety shoes, well-fitting work garments, clearly written and complete safety procedures and guidelines from management, safety training, and safety installations and equipment, e.g. fire fighting units, regular maintenance schedules for safety equipment and installations, wider traffic areas (to prevent accidents), adequate staffing, and last but not least, continuous effective training in work procedures. All of this necessitates comprehensive planning, the creation of clear policies and work procedures, organization, implementation, training of supervisors and employees, supervision and control.

Fire

Fires in the hotel may result in the injury and loss of life of both the guests and the staff.

Main causes of fire are:

i) Smoking:
   - Smoke only where allowed.
   - Put out cigarettes in the right place.
   - Sufficient ash trays should be provided in eating places and in rooms, but away from curtains and draperies.
   - Educate the guests about fire possibilities due to smoking.

ii) Defective wiring, faulty appliances and motor and worn out insulation

   Such hazards should be immediately reported to the concerned person and such equipment should be immediately repaired.

iii) Laundry Areas: Care should be taken to see that none of the electrical equipment is left on after use

iv) Gas leaks: Precautions should be taken against this especially in kitchen areas.

v) Combustible waste : Combustible material should never b e left near the boiler room

vi) Kitchen : All equipment such as chimneys, exhausts, ventilators, grills, hoods etc. which collect a lot of fume vapour and catch fire easily should be cleaned regularly.

vii) Elevator shafts: These require constant check and inspection. Cigarette butts can ignite the debris and oils that gather at the bottom of elevator shafts.

Types of Fire and fire Extinguishers

Hotel personnel are trained about the fire protection procedure and the types of fire. They must be able to recognize the various types of fire, all fire require air. Air contains O_2 which is necessary for combustion. Fire has been classified in 5 categories depending on how they can be extinguished-

Class A Fire-It is the fire of wood, paper, linen and similar dry materials. They are extinguished by cooling and quenching effect of water. The water reduces the temperature of burning substances below their combustion temperature. These are the most frequent and easiest to extinguish when there is an ample water supply and when water can be directed on the combustible material. Keeping the other combustible material wet will limit the spreading of fire

Class B Fire-These include fires of oil, gasoline, grease and other petroleum product. These fires are extinguished by blanketing the source of burning substances and eliminating the supply of O_2. Petroleum products is lighter than water and will float on water and continue to burn and spread by means of flowing water to other section of the building, hence water is never used for this category.

Class C Fire-These are the fires of pressurized gases. For e.g. L.P.G., most of the gases are lighter than air but L.P.G. is heavier than air. Water is not to be used for this class of fire.

Class D Fire-These are fire of metals having low burning temperature for e. g. Na, Mg etc. This class of fire does not exist in the hotel.

Class E Fire-These are electrical fire. The fire extinguishing agent must not conduct electrical energy which could spread the fire. Electrical fires are usually blanketed and cooled down. Water is a good cooling agent but it also conducts electricity, so it is not used to control or extinguish this class of fire. Electrical fire is usually caused by a part of circuit overheating or by short circuit. Controlling the sizes of electrical fuses and circuit breaker will often minimize this class of fire.

There are 2 systems of fire protection;

1. Portable fire extinguisher.
2. Stationary fire fighting system..

Portable fire Extinguisher

a. Soda acid fire extinguisher-It is used for class A fire. The extinguishing agent is H2O. The fire extinguisher is a cylinder type of pan in which a rubber or flexible hose is attached to the top. When it is desired to use the extinguisher, it is carried to the fire and inverted. A small bottle of acid usually H_2SO_4 is spilled when the cylinder is inverted or turn upside down. Powdered sodas, bicarbonate of soda (Baking Soda) is mixed with H2O when the tank is charge or fills with water. The chemical reaction of acid and soda water creates a pressure which forces the water out of the cylinder or tank. The hose is used to direct the flow of water to the fire. It has 2 disadvantages:-

- It must be kept away from freezing
- Acid causes corrogen problem which reduce the life of the tank or cylinder. The corrogen problem has been minimized by replacing the acid with CO_2 cartridge. Upon the cylinder inversion the cartridge opens and releases CO_2 gas under high pressure. The high pressure gas than forces the water out of cylinder.

b. $CaCl_2$ fire extinguisher-It is also used on class A fire.. $CaCl_2$ is a salt which when added to water form brine which has very low freezing temperature. CO_2 cartridge is used as pressure agent to force H_2O and $CaCl_2$ out of the cylinder to the fire. These extinguishers are used where freezing is a potential hazard

c. Foam type extinguisher-It is used on class B type of fire. The extinguisher is charged with special chemical (Al_2SiO_4), the chemical spread on the burning material and the solution, blanket the fire by excluding O_2.

d. CO_2 fire extinguisher-It is used on C, D and E class of fire. The CO_2 types spray a chemical fog towards the fire. The fog quickly excludes the O_2 from the burning material and blanket the combustible material.

e. D.C.P. extinguisher-It can be used on C, D and E class of fire. The most common extinguishing agent is sodium bicarbonate or plain baking soda. The extinguisher is charged with the dry chemical and a small tank of CO_2 gas. The CO_2 gas exerts pressure on dry chemical and forces it out of a nozzle directly to the fire. The powder strict the fire and the heat from the fire breaks down the chemical which releases CO_2 gas on a large scale which helps in extinguishing the fire.

Stationary Fire Fighting System

a. Automatic sprinklers-It is generally mounted just below the ceiling height with a temperature detector or smoke detector, attached with each sprinkler. The temperature from the fire melts the fusible link on the detector, which opens a water valve. The water is then sprayed on the ceiling and falls on the floor, extinguishing the fire. If the fire area should spread, more sprinklers are automatically opened, thus confining the fire to a small area. The temperature detector can be purchased for different activating temperature. The high temperature detectors are often used in kitchens.

b. Fire Hose System-It is a semi portable system. In this system the fire hose box is permanently located but the flexible hose can be moved to various distances throughout the building. The hose used to fight fire within a building should be of linen type. The linen allows some water seepage through it which will prevent its burning when in use.

Handling Emergency Situations

Apart from fire and bomb threat etc. the front office staff at some point of time have to handle a lot of unusual situations also. Some such situations may be death and illness of guests, theft in hotels etc and many others.

1) Death of a guest in the hotel :
   - Once the information comes to the front desk it should directly be reported to the front office manager.
   - The front office manager will then report it to the GM or resident manager
   - The security manager should also be informed immediately
   - The police is informed and the hotel doctor is summoned who will check and confirm the death
   - Meanwhile the hotel will locate the residential address of the deceased and will inform the relatives.
   - Once the police complete all formalities and activities and gives the permission, the dead body is fully covered and then removed from the room on a stretcher. For this purpose the service elevator and not the guest elevator is used

- A death certificate is obtained from the doctor
- A report should be prepared as to who informed of the death, time, room number and date of death. In case there is any luggage of the deceased in the room a list should be prepared and the luggage should be kept in the luggage room and the person performing this activity should sign this report
- The guest room is locked and sealed.
- After obtaining clearance from the police the room is opened and thoroughly disinfected and spring cleaned and only after permission of the police and subsequent permission of the GM or resident manager the room should be sold.

Some important facts to be kept in mind are:

- Donot enter the room alone always take the lobby manager and security officer with you
- In case you are aware that the deceased was under the treatment of a specific doctor, the same should be called instead of the hotel doctor. His physician will also be helpful in knowing and notifying the incident to the relatives and people known to him
- Donot disturb the body or touch anything before the arrival of the police as this may be a murder or suicide case.

2) Handling accident cases:

- A knowledge of first aid would come very handy in such situations. In general the following points should be taken care of :
- Remove the person who has met with accident from the site of accident {as early as possible and take him to a more comfortable area, use a stretcher in case the need be}
- Call the doctor and if possible give him the details of accident and gravity of the accident.
- Take someone along with you to the site of the accident as you may need help
- Keep alert you must serve the victim immediately by providing first aid

- Try to protect your establishment from any false allegations.

Prepare a full report of the whole accident giving details of the date and time who reported the incident, room no., site of the accident etc. Also make your comments as to the reason of the accident and how could it have been prevented and what action is to be taken to avoid the same in the future.

The Accident Book

- An accident book is usually maintained in all organizations and the receptionist should record all details of accidents which have occurred to employees whilst carrying out their daily activities.
- The book must be kept in a place easily accessible by any injured person or a person bona fide
- Particulars of an accident may be entered here in either by the injured person himself or by a person acting on his behalf
- The accident book when filled up should be preserved for a period of three years after the date of the last entry
- Every employer is required to take steps to investigate the circumstances of the accident recorded and if there happens to be any discrepancy between the circumstances found by him and the entry made, he is required to record the circumstances so found.

Situation of Theft:

Theft is divided into four categories:

I. Theft by employees of the hotel can be avoided by:
   - Work business and personal references should be checked before the employee is hired.
   - A detailed record of all employees who enter the guest room such as chamber maids bellboys room boys maintenance etc
   - All hotel keys should be returned to the department concerned and no employee should be allowed to take keys out of the hotel's premises.

II. Damage of hotel property by the guest can be avoided by:

- The hotel staff should identify the main cause for the damage.
- If the damage is appears to be done intentionally the hotel can ask the guest to pay compensation for the same. For this it is necessary that the front desk is well versed with the cost of the damaged item.

III. Theft of hotel property by the guest:

Can be avoided by taking the following steps:

- Installing automatic locks on the guest room doors
- Appointing a security officer who would walk and take rounds at regular intervals
- Inform guests to use the safe vault of the hotel and not to keep valuables in the guest room
- Keep a watch on walk in as their likelihood of being a thief is more as compared to a guest who has undergone a process of making a reservation in the hotel
- Avoid giving room numbers of resident guests to visitors or over the telephone callers.
- In case the guest loses his key and asks housekeeping to open the room door for them, HK should direct them to front desk
- Master key should be kept under strict supervision and control

Theft by outside visitors can be avoided by:

- being aware of suspicious persons
- regular and irregular schedule of vigil and rounds
- Stagger lunch and rest periods of employees so as to keep one person on duty on each floor at all times
- Instruct eh telephone operator not to connect calls to the guest room incase the request is made by the caller by room number. The receptionist should insist on knowing the name of the guest who the caller wishes to speak to.

- Guest should be informed to keep the balcony door closed to avoid anyone entering the rooms from the balcony
- Closed circuit televisions should be used

IV. Situation of illness and epidemics:

- The receptionist may be called for assistance during sickness of a guest.
- Patient should be advised to consult the house physician but in case the guest has his own physician the same should be called.
- Housekeeping needs to be notified about the sickness and instructions if any
- If the case of serious sickness, the guest should be moved to a nursing home
- During epidemics all precautionary measures especially in food and beverage service area should be followed

V. Handling a drunk guest :

- The guest should be removed from the lobby as early as possible but being careful not to irritate/offend him.
- Preferably taken to the back office or to his room.
- If he behaves unruly, the hotel security must be called.

Safe deposit facility in the hotel for security of guests' valuables:

- It is the responsibility of management to develop and maintain proper safe deposit procedures for its property.
- If this facility is available for guests, notices regarding it should be put up in various conspicuous/noticeable places in the hotel and also should be mentioned to the guest.
- Safe deposit boxes should be located in an area, in vicinity of the front desk and which has limited access. Unauthorized guests or personnel should not be permitted inside the area.
- Front office staff should be well-versed with the procedures regarding safe deposit boxes.

- Strict control should apply to the storage and issue of safe deposit keys.
- At any point of time there should be only one key issued for each safe even if more than one person is using the safe.
- Two keys are required to open a safe deposit box: one being the guest's key and the other being the control key/ guard key put in by the cashier/safe deposit attendant.
- After the verification of the identity of the guest, the safe deposit attendant/cashier should accompany the guest to the safe deposit area where in clear sight should make use of the control key and the guest's key to open the safe.

Sometimes the hotel may not be able to meet the demand for individual safe box; in that case a large box containing the belongings of more than one guest is used. Each guest's belongings are put in an envelope which is sealed. The key to this box is stored in a secure place and a log is maintained which records an entry each time the key is used to open the box

How to Deal with a Drunk Guest

Unfortunately, the out-of-control drunk is not just a cliche; it's often a reality. Often an open bar, free-flowing alcohol and a jovial atmosphere is all it takes for a person to become the rowdy drunken guest. But do not despair; a little quick thinking, a little discretion, and the drunk can be removed from the premises without spoiling anyone's day.

We see drunks everywhere, on the streets in alley ways, sitting in parks, sprawled on the grass at popular picnic grounds, at bars, clubs and so forth. We may laugh at their comical antics, but there is nothing funny about dealing with a drunken guest.

If the event is a wedding, try to find the event coordinator and ask them to observe the guest. Most wedding coordinators have a load of experience handling inebriated guests without the need for force or police intervention. Tell someone, such as the groomsmen or a couple of male attendants, and ask if they could help keep the situation discreet. Ensure that the drunken guest does not drive and attempt to find out their address, phone number etc. See if there is someone you can contact to come and drive this person home. Do not tell the bride and groom unless it becomes necessary, otherwise this will certainly spoil their special day.

Feed the inebriated guest, as food can aid in slowing down the rate at which the body absorbs the alcohol. But no spicy or greasy foods, as you do not want the guest being sick. Try to lead them away from the reception area if possible, into the lobby or another area where guests are scarce. This will aid in preventing any embarrassing antics etc. If the drunken guest drove their own car to the venue, try to get their car keys. Allowing them to drive while inebriated can mean death.

Prior arrangements for inebriated guests is crucial, but if you have failed to overlook this see if there are any hotel rooms available. Try to convince your guest to stay at the hotel or convince them to catch a taxi home. Unfortunately drunken guests can be an embarrassment to many, but you can't wave a magic wand and have them disappear.

Dealing with drunks take finesse and foresight, being prepared for the unexpected. Prior to any home function where alcohol is to be served, realize the possibilities of someone becoming inebriated. There are certain rules of hospitality and one of these is to ensure that a person beginning to show signs of becoming drunk, should not be served more drinks. Tell your nominated guests that drunkenness will not be tolerated and that if anyone shows signs of becoming inebriated, they will be sent home at the drunks expense.

No one needs an exaggeratedly happy drunk or an aggressive drunk at their home functions. Irrespective of if they are quiet drunks or rowdy and annoying others, drunks can be an embarrassment to any get-together. Anyone who is in charge of alcohol should suggest a different beverage when they feel that a guest has overdosed on alcohol. If that person becomes loud or confrontational, there is only one thing to do and that is to call the police. But long before things, get to that point try using the tips below for handling your drunken guest/guests.

1) Try to switch their drinks with something non alcoholic while they are not looking.
2) Offer the drunken guest dry crackers and coffee or orange juice. Do not offer any dairy products as dairy products

aid in producing mucus. Offer plenty of water in lieu of dehydrating the body.

3) Lead the drunk to the bathroom and offer a cold wet flannel as well as a toilet bowl in case they wish to throw up. Now is not the time to be angry unless you wish for the drunken guest to become belligerent or aggressive.

4) The drunken guest pay pass out soon, so getting them to a couch or bed as soon as possible is a good move. But ensure that they are not laying on their back or the stomach. Have them lie on their side and wedge cushions or pillows on both sides of them. If a drunk vomits they have less chance of choking or suffocating, (drowning in their own mess.)

5) Do not leave the drunk unsupervised at any time. They could wander out to the street, railway tracks etc and expose themselves to great danger. Or worse yet, he/she could end up lying in the middle of the road. (A plethora of drunks have been killed due to lying on the side of the road in a drunken stupor.)

6) You can offer a small dose of aspirin to relieve the headache associated with hangovers.

Serving alcohol at any function should be done with commonsense. If you have a friend who repeatedly gets drunks at your gatherings, perhaps a word of advise about the need for counselling may be warranted. If they do not acknowledge that they have a drinking problem, it may be wise to forget their name when the next function comes around.

Importance of Travel First Aid Kit in Travelling

It is a well known fact that all of us have had the opportunity to use a first aid kit at some stage in our lives and carrying one during travelling is all the more imperative to enable you to deal with any health issues.

That is why you should take the time to prepare a kit to have available to you when travelling.

Travel first aid kits are easily made and can inexpensively be put together to be either basic or comprehensive depending on your medical training and how far you expect to be from professional medical help. Here is how to make your own travel first aid kit.

Remember it is adaptable to what fits for you, however here is a list of some typical travel first aid kit items.

The most common ones are the pills and syrups for combating pain, allergies, indigestion and respiratory problems.

Do not forget to carry along your normal medicines that help you take care of the odd allergy or help boost blood sugar levels as these are proven items and you must carry them along with the other travel first aid things. You may also want to include cough medication, or if you suffer from asthma, an extra inhaler etc

While some of the medicines and pills for the various ailments are par for the course and must be taken, it is equally important to carry along other travel first aid items like antiseptic soaps, bandages, scissors, tweezers and other aids to help you cope with any emergency during the journey

The idea behind the travel first aid kit is to manage any medical exigency in mid journey. You have to ensure that your cell phone is fully charged and there are enough torch lights, lighters in stock.

Maintaining a Safe and Secure Environment in Hotels

Safety Aspects

Under the heading of safety, it is necessary to consider the welfare of visitors and members of staff using the reception area, and of course, this is related to the reputation and prestige of the organisation. A person who is placed at risk through the negligence or carelessness of the hotel may well become annoyed and be unlikely to stay, make recommendations or indeed return. As well as not returning themselves, an irate guest is likely to publicise their low opinion of the hotel, which could lead to a certain loss of future trade. In service industries especially, personal recommendations (or the opposite) can mean a significant increase (or decrease) in customers.

It is wise, therefore, for the hotel staff to try to predict exactly where an accident could occur and remove the hazard. Most visitors will be engrossed in their business transactions or travel worries or relaxed and enjoying their holiday, and may overlook hazards and take risks without realising that they are doing so. Visitors are always unaware of potential hazards such as an unexpected step up or down, swing doors that fly open violently and steep stairs. Hotel staff who will be aware of these potential dangers should take care that visitors are also made aware, and any careless or 'dangerous' behaviour is stopped, before accidents happen.

The Health and Safety at Work Act 1974

In larger organisations, there may be an employee who's function is to promote, investigate and comply with all aspects of health and safety and the requirements of the Act. In smaller establishments, the health and safety role may be part of another role, that of owner, receptionist or manager. Whichever type of hotel a receptionist works in, she should have some knowledge of the Health and Safety at Work Act 1974 and follow its guidelines in all aspects of her work.

Extract

'It is the duty of the employer to consult representatives of the employees with a view to the making and maintenance of arrangements which will enable him and his employees to co-operate effectively in promoting and developing the health and safety at work of the employees and in making sure that the measures are effective...'

'Every employee has a duty while at work:

a) to take reasonable care for the health and safety of himself- and of other persons who may be affected by his acts or omissions at work.

b) as regards any duty or requirement imposed by his employer or any other person or under any of the relevant statutory provisions to co-operate with him so far as is necessary to enable that duty or requirement to be performed or complied with.'

In other words, it is the employer's duty to provide and maintain a safe environment in which employees may work. It is the duty of the employees to take reasonable safety precautions and to co-operate with the management in making the organisations's premises a safer and healthier place in which to work.

For more information about the Act, visit the Royal Society for the Prevention of Accidents web site.

The Receptionist's Role

The genuine accident is really very rare, most result from oversight or carelessness, and it will never be possible to eliminate accidents completely. However, if the receptionist takes accident prevention seriously and is aware of the possible hazards then she may help to make her organisation a safer place in which to work.

In general terms, the receptionist should be aware of the conduct of staff and customers who move through reception. In a busy reception area, many mishaps can be caused by 'bumping' into someone.

Personnel become absorbed in a report or some important papers while walking across the reception area. They may push open glass doors without looking to see if someone is on the other side and a person struck by a glass door could suffer serious facial injuries. Staff should be made aware of how their conduct can be a potential hazard and this should be enforced during regular training sessions. The receptionist could draw the attention of visitors to such situations by displaying a warning notice or special warning posters.

Another potential safety hazard is that of discarded cigarettes. Although certain parts of hotels, such as bedrooms and some dining rooms are non-smoking areas, the reception and surrounding lounge areas are usually not. Therefore the receptionist should ensure that plenty of ashtrays are provided and pleasantly request all visitors to use them if they smoke. Cigarettes left smouldering on the edges of tables or window-sillls are a fire hazard. A regular check on ashtrays to ensure cigarettes are thoroughly extinguished will provide for a safer and pleasanter reception area.

The receptionist may do a tremendous amount to make her establishment a safer place in which to work and to welcome guests, by warning the management of potential danger spots and by her own vigilance.

Hazard Spotting

Hazards can occur because of bad maintenance of equipment and hotel fixtures and fittings, or because of poor working practices- the following should help you spot possible hazards before accidents happen.

Electric Appliances-these should be regularly maintained by an electrician and fuses checked. There should be no trailing wires. Plugs must be earthed and no sockets or adaptors should be overloaded and all appliances should be switched off at the end of the day and the plug removed when machines are not in use.

Entrances and Fire Exits -these must be kept clear of obstructions such as boxes, parcels awaiting collection, etc. Glass doors need a bright notice asking users to take care to avoid striking anyone approaching from the other side. Large glass partitions/doors need some form of patterning or decoration to alert people to their presence.

Flooring -frayed carpets, torn or badly worn lino, raised floor tiles, and highly polished floors can all bring about falls. Action should be taken when weather hazards-ice, etc, cause the entrance hall to become slippery.

Heating System-radiators should not be obstructed. Many systems are devised to direct heat to a large area and restricting this dispersal to a smaller part of the room may cause dangerous overheating.

Storage Areas-filing cabinets, shelves, luggage storage and cloakrooms should be checked frequently, because stored items may change hourly. A logical method should be adopted in order to avoid accidents caused by heavy boxes falling or even small containers tipping and causing a much larger volume of goods to overspill.

Gangways and Corridors-should be kept clear at all times to avoid staff and visitors tripping and falling. They should also be clear to aid the quick passage of people during emergency exit procedures, and of course should not block emergency exits. Hotel deliveries should not be left in the reception area or in corridors for these reasons.

Procedures in the Event of an Accident

Following procedures promptly in the event of an accident can help to reduce injury, damage, undue stress and unfavourable guest relations. The receptionist in a small to medium-sized hotel will often be the person called upon in the event of an accident, even if the accident did not occur in the reception area. Therefore, all receptionists should be well versed in the correct procedures and be able to deal calmly and efficiently with whatever arises. The following is a general list of procedures which should help to deal with any accident.

Attend promptly	When advised of an accident, attend to it straightaway-delaying may cause further damage or injury. Never go to a scene of an accident alone-you may be able to deal with a minor accident alone, but another person can act as a witness or help minimise disruption to other guests.
Assess injury and/or damage	It is important to calmly assess the incident to see what must be done first.
Call for assistance eg ambulance, hotel maintenance, other first aider, etc	If you have an injured person, they should be your first duty as below, therefore ensure you have other people to attend to getting specialised help and minimising the danger and disruption to other guests and staff.
Comfort, calm and treat the injured person	It is important to give confidence to the casualty-be calm, talk and listen, and reassure the person. See First Aid for further procedures.
Keep alert	It is important to assess the whole situation, it is your duty to protect and serve the guest and the hotel. Is the casualty in further danger? Is there danger to other guests/staff? Was someone negligent-could this happen again?
Make written report	Once the casualty has been dealt with and the incident is over, complete accident report form and report to hotel manager.

Accident Report Book

An accident book must be kept in every organisation which employs more than ten persons. It can be obtained from Her Majesty's Stationery Office (HMSO) and the receptionist should record all details of accidents and events which have occurred on the premises which requires either treatment or advice, or which could, in the future, develop into a condition needing medical attention. This book could be used as evidence in a court action for compensation, eg to confirm the exact date of the accident, the extent of the injury, and the treatment obtained either directly or by referral to a doctor.

The book must be kept in a readily accessible place and the reception office, central to all departments and easily accessible to guests, is the ideal place. A completed accident book must be kept for a period of three years after the date of the last entry. Employers are required to investigate the circumstances of every incident and record any discrepancies found.

Accident Report Form

The following is an example of an Accident Report Form on which details of injuries, diseases and dangerous occurrences are notified. This is required under the Health and Safety at Work Act 1974 and has to be sent to the local authority which is concerned with the safety of employees and visitors.

Security Aspects

The subject of security covers such items as:

- Protection of the hotel's property against damage and theft
- Protection of visitors' property against damage, theft and loss
- Safeguarding of information regarding business matters and visitors' details.

The reception counter is the 'front line' to which all such urgent matters are brought and an answer has to be given immediately about the correct procedures to be adopted. An index of all possible incidents and the action to be followed should be maintained. It is necessary for instance to know when the internal security staff can deal with a problem and when to dial 999 to reach the police quickly.

There will possibly be an alarm system linked either to the local police station or to the internal security office. This alarm should be used whenever a situation arises with which the receptionist is unable to cope and the safety of staff or that of the guests is endangered. Hotel management do not expect receptionists to take risks to protect property or guests, but if the receptionist observes someone acting in a suspicious manner, it is vital to act quickly to alert those in the building who can deal with it.

A receptionist has access to much information regarding the hotel, its security measures and its guests and this should never be divulged to people outside the hotel, or even to staff in the hotel who do not need to know these details. Information regarding such details would be invaluable to the prospective burglar!

A hotel has people coming and going at all times of the day and night, and reception staff should be ever vigilant from their central vantage point.

Security Procedures

There are many situations within a receptionist's working day where it will be necessary to be security conscious. It is easy to be complacent in working habits, which can lead to an opportunity being seen and seized by a thief. A common example of this is a member of staff leaving a cash drawer open, allowing a customer to remove cash from the till when the cashier turns away.

Daily work patterns may also present an opportunity for a thief. When we work in an area we become familiar with our surroundings, used to seeing things in a certain place and floowing procedures in a certain way. It is often these patterns that are observed by potential thieves and which can lead to break-ins, thefts and fraud. Being aware of potential breaches of security and knowing how to report them or the action to take is an essential starting point, and follow the basic security practices listed below:

- Handle all cash transactions away from the customer and other unauthorised persons, preferably out of their sight. This is especially true when counting the float.

- Never handle cash without some sort of receipt or authorisation to justify the transaction and remember you must always follow a company's policy concerning the handling of cash.
- Keep security issues and procedures confidential-you can never be sure who might overhear you discussing a sensitive issue.
- Never accept or return guests property, unless it has been properly recorded. You should always follow your company's procedure.
- Keep your own belongings, such as handbags or wallets, secure and out of sight in a locked compartment or drawer.
- Keep alert to anything or anyone looking suspicious-an occupied car parked outside the building for a long period of time, boxes or ladders placed near to windows, fire exits left open.
- Keep keys, especially master keys, under close supervision. Room keys should never be in easy reach or sight of callers at reception.
- When visitors arrive for staff or guests, check that they are expected before giving them directions on how to move around the hotel. Never allow visitors to enter a dangerous or restricted part of the establishment unescorted. Whenever practical ask visitors for identification.

Lost Property

Hotel guests bring varying amounts of personal property with them, depending on the purpose and length of their visit, and hotels usually encourage guests to deposit valuables in the hotel safety boxes. Some hotels have small safes fitted in each room and guests use a room key and code to access their valuables. Despite these measures, guests still lose valuables and other items of property.

The receptionist can be responsible for causing much good will or the worst kind of ill-feeling by the way in which lost articles are handled. Each hotel should have procedures in place for dealing with all lost or mislaid items and many use a policy similar to the following:

- All articles found in guest rooms are recorded and kept in a lost property area usually in the housekeeper's quarters.
- The record of items found will include a complete description of the article, time, date, place, and name of finder.
- All articles found in the lobby, main dining room or lounge areas are recorded and kept in a lost property area in reception, for a period of time-usually 24 hours.
- Any unclaimed articles are then sent to the lost property area in the housekeeper's quarters.
- All articles of value are recorded and placed in a safety deposit box held in the reception area.
- The housekeeper will hold unclaimed articles for a period of time-three months. At the end of the period, unclaimed articles are returned to finder who will be expected to sign a receipt.
- All employees receiving enquiries for lost articles will check with the housekeeper and receptionist.
- Guests claiming lost property are required to describe fully the lost article and sign a receipt for its return.

Following a policy such as that above will help maintain a good relationship between guest and hotel staff.

Suspicious Items or Packages

In any area of work there may be times when an unattended item, package or bag raises suspicion. This could lead to an emergency, and, if not handled correctly, may result in danger or injury to people in the area.

In recent years there has been an increase in the number of bombs and incendiary devices used by terrorists in pursuit of their particular cause. Evacuations, or closure of shops, transport systems and public areas are no longer an unusual occurrence, especially in large cities. Often these evacuations occur as a result of a hoax, and, although no explosion or fire takes place, businesses often suffer significant damage through the loss of income or delays caused by the need for an evacuation.

It is important to treat any suspicious item seriously. Be aware of the dangers it potentially contains and be prepared to inform people of your suspicions quickly and calmly.

A suspicious package which is not dealt with immediately may result in serious injury to people in the area or serious damage to the building. It is an essential part of your daily work to keep alert to dangers from suspect packages and follow laid down procedures when dealing with the problem.

Recognising a Suspicious Item or Package

It is impossible to give precise guidance about where a suspicious package may be placed, or what size or shape it might be. However, the following might raise your suspicions:

- Something that has been left unattended for some time, such as a briefcase next to a chair, or a suitcase left in a reception area.
- Something that looks out of place, like a man's holdall in the ladies' cloakroom, or a full carrier bag near a rubbish bin.
- In fact, anything that sticks out in your mind as somewhat unusual.

On Discovering a Suspicious Item

On becoming suspicious about an item or package, it is important to ensure the safety of everyone in the vicinity.

- Do not attempt to move or touch the item. The action of moving or disturbing the item may be enough to start a reaction leading to an explosion or fire.
- Remain calm and composed. Try not to cause panic by shouting an alarm or running from the item. People and property can be injured through a disorderly or panicked evacuation.
- Report the matter to your supervisor or the police immediately. Check your establishment's procedures to find out who you should inform.
- If possible, cordon off the area and move people away. It may be difficult to do this without causing people in the area to panic, but it is essential that no one attempts

to move or touch the item, so you will need to warn people to keep clear.

- At some point it may be necessary to evacuate the building, or the part of the building nearest to the suspect package. This may be a decision taken by your supervisor, or the police if they are involved. If it is thought necessary to clear the area, follow your hotel's procedures for the evacuation of the building.

Summary

Maintaining effective safety and security measures should be the concern of everyone working within an establishment and is an essential part of good business practice. The safety and security of everyone who works in, or visits, the premises, should be of the utmost importance in the minds of employers and employees if accidents are to be prevented and the wellbeing of the business assured.

There may be staff within an organisation employed as Health and Safety Officers and as Security Officers, whose main role will include all aspects of protecting people on the premises, eliminating potential hazards and lapses in security and looking after the security of the building and the property contained within it. However, it is the responsibility of each and every employee to take reasonable care of their own health and safety and for that of colleagues and visitors. Safe and secure working practices should always be adhered to and any unsafe conditions or systems should be reported to management at the earliest opportunity.

The hotel receptionist is in a position of trust and huge responsibility-dealing closely with guests, their records and property, handling large amounts of cash, cheques and credit card payments and being a front line representative for the hotel. Therefore, the receptionist should follow and promote the highest standards of safety and security, and remember that profitability can be affected both by the immediate loss of property or damage to the hotel and by bad publicity, which can damage the business through loss of custom.

The maintenance of a safe and secure environment requires a positive and active approach from all employees.

First Aid

First aid is the aid given in an emergency until medical aid can be obtained. Many people actually endanger the lives of casualties through ignorance of the correct procedures. Basically it is the task of the first aid person to prevent a casualty from becoming worse before he receives medical attention. Every hotel should have a number of first aid boxes, and one of these will be kept in the reception area, nearby should be a basic first aid booklet to act as a reminder for correct application of bandages, splints, etc. There should also be a list of persons on the staff who hold a first aid qualification (with internal extension numbers), as well as external numbers for local doctors, opticians and dentists, and the nearest hospital dealing with casualties. The initial action to be taken by the first aider is to give confidence to the casualty. She or he will do this by being calm, talking and listening to the casualty and reassuring the person. She must always be gentle and careful in handling and move the injured person as little as possible. It is essential that the first aider protects the casualty from the cold with blankets but does not apply extra heat (such as hot water bottles) as this will draw blood from vital organs to the surface of the body. Any open wounds should be covered with sterile dressings. Therefore in summary, the receptionist should:

- Keep calm
- Reassure the patient
- Move the casualty as little as possible
- Keep warm with blankets
- Cover wounds with sterile dressings.

Basic First Aid Procedures

Minor Bleeding	• Wash the wound under running cold water. • Apply a clean sterile dressing. • Bandage firmly to keep the edges of the wound together. • Where the cut is to an arm or leg ask the person to sit down and raise the limb to help stop the flow of blood.

Burns and Scalds

- Place the burn under cold, slow running water-this reduces pain and heat and is the best immediate treatment.
- Remove restricting articles rings, bracelets, etc, in case swelling occurs.
- Do not remove burnt clothing.
- Do not apply ointments.
- Cover the burn with sterile dressing such as lint to prevent infection.

Fainting and Unconsciousness

- Check for any injuries caused by falling.
- Place the person into the Recovery Position. • Check that the airways (nose and mouth) are clear.

Fractures

- If a fracture is suspected-keep the patient warm and as comfortable as possible.
- Do not give anything to eat or drink.
- Do not move unless patient is in danger.
- If patient needs to be moved strap or splint the limb.

Heart Attack

- If a patient is showing symptoms of a heart attack-pale complexion, sweating, pain in an arm, vomiting-call an ambulance.
- Then-loosen any tight clothing
  - Check the pulse
- Reassure the patient
- Keep warm and as comfortable as possible

Nose Bleed

- If this occurs as a result of a fall or a blow, medical aid must be sought, until this arrives-loosen clothing around neck and chest.
- Ask casualty to sit forward and breathe through the mouth and pinch the soft part of the nose.

- After 10 minutes, release the pressure-if bleeding does not stop-repeat treatment.

Resuscitation Procedure

This should only be applied if the patient has stopped breathing.

- Check that airways are clear
- Lie patient on his back
- Check pulse at neck
- Lift patient's chin by putting one hand on the forehead and the other under the neck-this will bring the tongue away from the back of the throat.
- Pinch the patient's nostrils together.
  - Take a deep breath and place mouth over patient's. Blow gently-no force is needed. Continue breathing in this way, watching the chest, it should lift with the air going into the lungs and fall with deflation. Check the pulse to make sure the heart is beating.

These procedures are for guidance only and should only be performed by a skilled first aider. Don't get caught out-take a first aid course now if you are working or intending to work as a hotel receptionist.

The First Aid Box

The first aid box must be of the approved type to be used at work and there should be sufficient contents for the number of employees and visitors in a particular area.

Summary

Within the normal course of the hotel receptionist's work, she may be required to deal with an accident or an emergency resulting in someone sustaining an injury. Often these injuries are not life-threatening, but occasionally they may be serious enough to warrant the person involved being taken to hospital, or being unable to carry on their work for that day.

Although other members of staff may be first aiders, because of the central position and the fact that a member of the reception team is always on duty, it is important for receptionists to have at least a basic knowledge of first aid. This knowledge can really only be gained by attending a first aid course and keeping knowledge updated through refresher courses.

If you are already working, your hotel may welcome your request for first aid training and organise this for you. If not, first aid courses can be taken through any adult education centre or by contacting such organisations as the St John Ambulance Brigade or the British Red Cross.

Whether or not you are a trained first aider, it is important that you have a knowledge and understanding of the hotel procedures in the case of an accident and comply with HASWA guidelines for recording and reporting any accident.

As has already been stressed, the success of a hotel is very dependent on how guests are treated. Any bad publicity caused by the mis-handling of an accident can adversely affect the number of guests wishing to stay at a hotel.

Fire Safety

Fires occur each week on premises where staff are working and customers or visitors are present. Many, fortunately, are quite small and can be dealt with quickly. Others lead to tragic loss of life, personal injury and devastation of property.

The commonest causes of fires are misuse of electrical or heating equipment and carelessly discarded cigarettes. People are often the link needed to start a fire-by acting negligently, by leaving rubbish around, or by being lazy and taking shortcuts in work methods.

There are three ingredients needed to make a fire:

Fire Hazards

Fire hazards can exist wherever there is a combination of fuel, heat and oxygen. As part of your responsibility in ensuring the safety of yourself, colleagues and customers you need to be aware of some of the most common causes of fire.

Rubbish-fires love rubbish. Accumulations of cartons, packing materials and other combustible waste products are all potential flashpoints.

Electricity-although you cannot see it, the current running through your electric wiring is a source of heat and, if a fault develops in the wiring, that heat can easily become excessive and start a fire. Neglect and misuse of wiring and electrical appliances are the leading causes of fires in business premises.

Smoking-the discarded cigarette is still one of the most frequent fire starters. Disposing of waste correctly will help reduce fires from this source, but even so, remember that wherever cigarettes and matches are used there is a chance of a fire starting.

Flammable goods-if items such as paint, adhesives, oil or chemicals are stored or used on your premises they should be kept in a separate storeroom and well away from any source of heat. Aerosols, gas cartridges and cylinders, if exposed to heat, can explode and start fires.

Heaters-portable heaters, such as the sort used in restaurants and offices to supplement the general heating, can be the cause of a fire if goods come into close contact with them or if they are accidentally knocked over. Never place books, papers or clothes over convector or storage heaters, as this can cause them to overheat and can result in a fire.

Fire Fighting Equipment

Fire extinguishers in the workplace, are designed to be used for small fires only and there are different ones depending on the type of fire.

All fire fighting equipment is designed to remove one of the three factors needed for a fire-heat, oxygen or flammable material. Fire extinguishers are filled with one of the following:

Water-this type of extinguisher provides a powerful and efficient means of putting out fires involving wood, paper and fabric.

Dry powder-these extinguishers can be used to put out wood, paper, fabric and flammable liquid fires, but are more generally used for fires involving electrical equipment.

Foam-the pre-mix foam extinguishers use a combination of water and aqueous film, and are effective for extinguishing paper, wood, fabric and flammable liquid fires.

Carbon dioxide-these extinguishers are not commonly in use, but can be used in situations where there are flammable oils and spirits, and in offices where there is electronic equipment.

Fire fighting equipment is essential in areas where there is a potential risk from fires and it is also essential that equipment is:

Maintained regularly and kept in good condition-the fire brigade or your supplier will carry out annual checks and note on the extinguisher when the check was carried out.

Kept unobstructed at all times-the equipment must be visible and readily available. Obstructions can prevent easy access and may result in unnecessary damage to the equipment.

Available in all areas of work-the most suitable extinguisher should be available in each area.

Used by trained operators-fire extinguishers can be noisy and difficult to control-it is important that the user knows the best way of utilising the extinguisher to tackle a fire in the most effective way.

Fire in Reception

In a reception area, there are two main hazard areas. The electrical equipment and paper used on a busy reception desk and the seating or waiting area for the general public.

Much of the electrical equipment used on a reception desk remains in use twenty-four hours a day. Care must be taken to ensure that the wiring and connections are in good condition and maintained according to the manufacturer's instructions. If the reception area closes for any period of time, then all equipment which is not left permanently switched on, should be switched off and unplugged.

Waste paper should not be allowed to collect in quantity. It should be placed in appropriate bins which must be regularly emptied.

It is important, that when clearing ashtrays, the contents are not tipped into the paper bins, as cigarettes which are still warm can ignite paper. The lounge area of reception needs to be checked regularly to make sure that no cigarettes have been left smoking and unattended. Areas where there is upholstery or wood, like chairs and curtains, need to be checked especially carefully. Any open fires should also be checked regularly and can be made extra safe by placing fireguards around them.

Discovering a Fire

It is important for all receptionists to be alert to potential fire hazards in their organisation and be fully aware of procedures in place to prevent fire. In case of fire, the receptionist should be aware of the positions of all fire extinguishers and should know the drill for evacuating the premises.

If a fire is discovered, this sequence of events should be followed:

1. sound the alarm immediately
2. call the fire brigade
3. secure the guest list
4. evacuate the area
5. assemble in the designated safe area for roll call.

Sounding the alarm-the function of the alarm is to warn every person in the building that an emergency has arisen and that fire evacuation procedures may need to be put into action.

Calling the Fire Brigade-there will be a designated person to call the fire brigade-often a receptionist or telephonist. Some organisations are connected directly to the fire station which is alerted as soon as the alarm rings.

When calling the fire brigade, be ready with the following information:

- your hotel's address
- your hotel's telephone number
- the precise location of the fire.

Securing the guest list-the receptionist will be responsible for securing and removing the guest list-the fire brigade needs this list to check that no one is left behind in the building. Every hotel will have strict procedures concerning this.

Evacuating the area and assembling outside-when evacuating the premises:

- switch off equipment and machinery
- close windows and doors
- follow marked escape routes
- remain calm, do not run
- assist others in their escape
- go immediately to an allocated assembly point
- do not return for belongings, no matter how valuable.

Fighting Fires

Fighting fires can be a dangerous activity, and is generally to be discouraged. Personal safety and safe evacuation must always be a primary concern. If a fire does break out, it should only be tackled in its very early stages and before it has started to spread.

The following points should be noted before tackling fires:

- Evacuate everyone and follow the emergency procedure to alert the fire brigade. Tell someone that you are attempting to tackle the fire.
- Always put your own and other people's safety first-never risk injury to fight fires. Always make sure you can escape if you need to and remember that smoke can kill. *If in doubt, get out.*
- Never let a fire get between you and the way out. If you have any doubt about whether the extinguisher is suitable for the fire, do not use it-leave immediately.
- Remember that fire extinguishers are only for 'first aid' fire fighting. Never attempt to tackle the fire if it is beginning to spread or if the room is filling with smoke.
- If you cannot put out the fire, or your extinguisher runs out, leave immediately, closing doors and windows as you go.

Summary

Knowledge of the basic rules of fire prevention and the procedures in case of fire have an important place in the training of receptionists. With her knowledge of, and her communication with, all departments in the hotel, the receptionist is in a good position to be aware of any potential fire hazards and should report these to management or the health and safety officer. She should also become familiar with the type of equipment and chemicals used in specific areas and the location of the various types of extinguisher.

In the event of fire, the receptionist should follow the evacuation procedures and all actions should be calm and purposeful so as to reduce the possibility of panic and encourage people to leave the building in a controlled manner. The receptionist will have a position of responsibility in the case of an evacuation and must remember to take the guest register with her to inform the fire brigade of the building's occupants.

These pages can only serve as an introduction to fire safety procedures, and all receptionists should make sure they attend all fire training courses offered by their employees. For more general information about fire safety and fire organisations-click on the fireman above!

In a hotel, the safety of a great many people can rely on the prompt and efficient action of the staff in the event of a fire.

One in Five Accidents in Hospitality

According to recent research, about one in every five recorded public liability accidents take place in hotels, pubs and nightclubs; while slips, trips and falls cause the most public liability accidents.

This is according to InjuriesBoard.ie-an independent statutory body which assesses the amount of compensation due to a person who has suffered a personal injury-in a recent report. In addition, the body totted up the total cost of the country's public liability awards at €65.4 million in the 24 months to December 2008. Nineteen per cent of such accidents occurred in hotels, pubs and nightclubs.

Accidents in privately owned establishments accounted for 56 per cent of the overall total. Females accounted for 70 per cent of the 2,860 public liability awards during this period – more than twice as many (2.3 times) as males. This is a direct reversal of data for workplace accidents where females account for just 30 per cent of awards.

Patricia Byron, the chief executive of InjuriesBoard.ie, said: "With almost one fifth of these accidents occurring in the hospitality sector, it is vitally important that hotel, pub and nightclub owners do not cut back on their investment in health and safety. It may be tempting for some of them to do so, but this kind of approach can backfire, particularly when they are operating in such a competitive and accident prone sphere."

Measures Should be Reviewed

She added: "As this review highlights, the factors which give rise to accidents in public places are many and varied. It is timely for public and private sector organisations alike to review the measures they have in place to prevent accidents across retail, hospitality, leisure and public spaces. "Accident prevention is always important and ensuring your customers enjoy a safe environment can save money in the long run. Consumers must also take responsibility for accident prevention and be vigilant to the risks they face.

"In an example given by InjuriesBoard.ie, a 45 year-old office administrator, was attending a relative's wedding reception and whilst dancing on the temporary dance floor that was provided by the hotel, the heel of her shoe became wedged in a ridge of the floor and she tripped and fell.

The fall caused the woman to fracture her left wrist. She underwent a number of physiotherapy treatments and the movement and strength of her wrist is still limited. The woman's claim was processed within the nine month time-frame and the woman was awarded almost €37,000. As she was unable to work for 12 weeks, this amount included Loss of Earnings as well as other fees and expenses necessarily incurred.

What the Statistics Show

The research indicated that slips, trips and falls account for 67 per cent of personal injuries in a public place. Other causes include being struck by a falling or flying object (11 per cent), five per cent were from being injured by machinery, burns/scalding accounted for two per cent and food poisoning was the cause of one per cent of public liability accidents.

Patricia Byron concluded: "To date, more efficient

administration by InjuriesBoard.ie is delivering €100 million in savings each year compared with the prior adversarial system.

We believe that improved accident prevention measures can deliver substantial additional savings as well as facilitating lower insurance premiums for consumers and for business."

Loss Prevention and Security

Guest safety and security are an integral part of the hospitality industry. Another term for safety is "loss prevention.1' A loss prevention and security program is also a means of protecting a hotel's resources—both people and property—from accidental loss, damage, or injury. With the exception of large convention hotels, loss prevention and security was not part of the hotel departmental structure until the 1960s. However, by the mid-1970s, most hotels either had established loss prevention and security programs or were contracting with outside firms Co provide full-time security.

LOSS PREVENTION

Guest Room Safety

Generally, guests suffer the same types of injuries as the staff. A good safety program can prevent the most common types of injuries to both employees and guests. One that involves all employees can have a great impact on public safety.

The most common accident that guests have is a slip or a fall in the bathroom, particularly in the bathtub or shower. This occurs not only because the area is slippery, soapy, and wet, but also because the shower handle, towel rack, or soap dish sometimes do not remain fixed when the guest grabs them for support.

In the past, chemical etching of the tub's ceramic surface was recommended in order to provide a firmer grip. However, laboratory tests have indicated that this is of little value when the tub is wet or coated with a slight soap residue. Because of the potential for tripping on their edges, rubber bath mats contribute to falls and should not be used. Sticky sprays, good only for one shower or bath, are impractical for hotel use.

Although safety strips are not appreciated by some guests, who feel that they are unsanitary or can collect bacteria, they are the only known practical solution for tub surfaces. Negative reactions can be reduced by properly cleaning them, periodically replacing them, and selecting attractive colours and designs.

Alerting the guests to hazards by printing safety messages on soap wrappers, urging guests to be careful of falls in the bathroom and explaining that abrasive strips have been installed to promote safety, also may assist in minimizing the risk of a fall.

The installation of sturdy soap holders and grab bars is also important. Soap holders should do two things: (1) allow drainage and (2) keep die soap from sliding out. They should be fabricated and installed to withstand a 300-pound pull or push from either direction. Soap holders that do not meet these requirements should he phased out.

The next most common accidents are cuts received on sharp metal shower edges, burns from hot water, and bumps and bruises involving children. Some guest accidents happen because a guest is unfamiliar with the hotel surroundings: Guest accidents also may occur because of unstable televisions, unidentified glass doors, rough furniture edges, tripping hazards (oversize bedspreads, dangling extension cords, etc.), defective furniture, and loose furniture parts.

These accidents suggest the need for consistent vigilance in two departments—housekeeping and engineering. The executive housekeeper should encourage room attendants to look actively for potential hazards as they clean and to suggest safety improvements. As you learned in the last chapter, the housekeeping department is responsible for replacing torn linen; housekeeping staff should also be on the lookout for oversize bedspreads, broken or loose furniture, frayed cords, or other unsafe conditions in the guest rooms.

Cords should be secured or positioned out of the major lanes of traffic in the room. Room attendants also should check for loose, damaged, buckled, or frayed carpeting as they vacuum. Faulty lighting, burned out bulbs, trash, uneven floor surfaces, loose tiles, and cracked plate glass are other hazards.

The engineering department must establish standards for safety and must develop a system to identify, log, and correct emergency and nonemergency situations. For example, the engineering department should make sure that all large panes of glass are marked with safety decals and that all identified defects are taken care of promptly.

Safety in Public Areas

Injuries occurring where guests congregate are primarily rails due to loose carpets, separated seams, poor lighting, ice and water, and tripping hazards, such as vacuum cleaners, carts, and cords.

Water and ice spills on uncarpeted floors should be cleaned up immediately. Warning signs must be used while floors are being mopped in public areas. Rubber runners both inside and outside the lobby in rainy or snowy weather can reduce slipping hazards. Elevator safety is also essential. Establishing an inspection schedule for elevator safety maintenance and putting "Out-of-Order" signs on or near elevator doors on each floor at the first sign of elevator trouble are important steps in maintaining guest safety.

Obstacles must be removed from passageways and attendants1 carts, and other obstructions must he kept as near the hallway walls as possible. All personnel should be on the alert for people in front if they are pushing a cart. Ladders, toolboxes, and other equipment must be removed immediately after repair work is finished to avoid creating additional hazards.

Most guest accidents out-of-doors involve falls. Typical accidents include tripping over curbs; stumbling in holes, cracks, or rough areas of pavement; and slipping on ice or snow. The engineering department can prevent many of these accidents by replacing burned-out bulbs immediately; repairing damaged pavement, sidewalks, and curbing as quickly as possible, and clearly marking those areas that need attention; keeping outside areas clean and free of trash; and clearing ice and snow as soon as possible.

Safety in Banquet Areas

Many accidents in banquet areas happen because preparation for such a function involves many critical steps in a very short period of time. The major types of accidents in banquet areas are falls over carpeting and chairs. Other types of accidents include falls off platforms, down stairs, and over wires, and on food or liquid spills.

Swimming Pool Safety

Accidents in the hotel swimming area include slipping on wet tile; head injuries due to diving into the shallow end of the pool; drowning; cuts from broken beverage glasses on pool steps and sharp metal edges on railings; and allergic reactions to chlorine. Good housekeeping practices for the pool area include proper cleaning, posting and enforcement of safety rules, prompt repair, and regular maintenance. A safety option is to employ a trained and certified staff of lifeguards. This option provides for consistent cleaning, enforcement, and repair of the swimming pool.

Loss Prevention Committee

Loss control is the development of standards and procedures that are designed to protect the guests and the assets of the hotel from unnecessary loss. A key component of loss control is a loss prevention committee. The responsibilities of the loss prevention committee include, but are not limited to, a review of past accidents and security problems; an elimination of present hazards and security problems, and development of policies and procedures to control them; and prevention of future hazards through attention to employee suggestions and new technology. It is important that a cross section of employees participate in the committee's monthly meetings and that the committee have management authority. The committee should include at least five members, each of who is a representative from each of the following categories: management, supervisory personnel, and hourly employees.

In the interest of safety program coordination, the general managers of larger properties often appoint one committee member as a safety manager— usually the chief engineer or director of security. The selection should be based on organizational and technical skill, as well as availability.

The most important function of the safety manager is to be acquainted with all required codes, laws, and regulations in order to ensure complete compliance throughout the property.

Committee meetings should be limited to one hour, and an agenda should be prepared and distributed in advance to ensure that the meeting is well organized and productive. As an ongoing follow-up procedure, each member of the loss prevention committee should communicate pertinent information to superiors and employees.

A successful loss prevention and control program depends on full commitment from management. If the general manager actively participates in loss prevention and control, prevention, other employees will follow suit. It is the general manager's responsibility to integrate safety, security, and property conservation\ into all areas of hotel operation.

The department head or supervisor is responsible for implementing a loss prevention and control program. Depending on-the size of the hotel, the Hotel Inspection.

To keep guest and employee accidents to a minimum, it is essential to detect unsafe actions and conditions in advance. While this is not necessary in every department, a department head or a supervisor in each department of the hotel should perform inspections of their areas at least once a month.

An inspection should include the physical structure (floors, doorways, etc.); equipment in the laundry and kitchen areas; power tools in the engineering department; cleaning and transportation equipment in the housekeeping department; observation of any unsafe work practices or poor work habits by employees; and conditions of all public areas, such as lobbies, function areas, and so on.

The department heads conduct-inspections with a checklist developed by the department and approved by the safety and, security committee. The checklist should emphasize the high accident areas of housekeeping, food and beverage, and engineering. Typically, the checklist focuses on tips for the safe operation of equipment; proper lifting; keeping the working area clean; wiping up spills; wearing safety equipment; sanitation; careful packing of moving equipment; and tripping hazards. A tips list should be developed for each group of employees that includes food service; food preparation; housekeeping; banquet service; stewarding; laundry; engineering; receiving; parking; bell staff; door staff; front desk; and clerical areas. Upon completion of the monthly inspection, each department should begin correcting the identified hazards, and the checklist should be submitted to the safety and security committee for follow-up purposes.

Accident Investigation

An accident can be defined as an unforeseen and unplanned event or circumstance. Although every accident may not result in an injury, accidents stop the work flow and have some economic impact on the hotel's business. The purpose of an accident investigation is to examine the cause of an accident and to prevent the occurrence of similar incidents in the future. Each accident should be treated as a signal that the potential exists for greater damage or injury and should be investigated thoroughly.

Accident investigation also demonstrates management's concern for guest and employee safety; pinpoints areas in current operations or safety programs that need revision or strengthening, and provides education regarding safety. All hotels should have a written policy regarding accident investigation and reporting.

An accident investigation should be completed within 24 hours, when the facts are still fresh in the minds of those involved, witnesses haven't had time to influence each other, the physical conditions arc unchanged, and corrective action can be initiated to prevent others from being injured. The only exception to this 24-hour rule would be if a person has been injured and needs immediate medical attention or is too emotionally upset to discuss the incident. If the accident is severe, the hotel's insurance representative should be advised immediately.

When conducting an accident investigation, the investigator, who usually is the department head or supervisor, should keep several points in mind:

1. Let the injured party tell the story.
2. Take the injured party back to the scene of the accident.
3. Determine what the injured party was doing just before and at the time of the accident.
4. Although verbal reenactment of the accident can be valuable, never allow anyone to repeat an unsafe act physically.
5. Avoid placing or accepting blame.

While allowing the participants in the investigation to talk freely, keep them focused on the issues but don't ask leading questions.

There are typically separate forms and considerations for employee accidents and for public liability accidents. When properly completed, each form should give department heads and supervisors key information that they will need to stay informed and to plan future action. It is most important to record all incidents that could result in claims, that could recur, or that could result in another incident involving a guest or an employee. If no injury is reported, in many cases a hotel will assume that no further action needs to be taken. For example, a guest falls while taking a shower. He reports the fall to the front desk. Since no apparent serious injury resulted from his fall, the front desk takes no action and the guest continues on his travels. Three months later, the hotel receives a claim for hip surgery, based on the guest's fall in the hotel. Without any report, documentation, or investigation of the incident, defence by the hotel against the claim could he difficult.

All incidents—both those reported formally to management and those learned of indirectly by management—should be documented for two reasons: (1) to identify what action needs to he taken by the hotel in order to prevent recurrence and (2) to provide a defence for the hotel against groundless allegations of negligence.

The Security Department

The role of the security department is a difficult one. Incidents often involve on-the-spot decisions made under stressful circumstances. The rapport established by a security department employee with an upset guest can profoundly affect the guest's perception of the hotel and may affect the course of subsequent legal action. A minimum standard of reasonable care, as defined by management, must be maintained at all times. (2) A professional and effective security department ensures the comfort, safety, and security of guests, employees, and the corporation's assets, and provides an indirect contribution to the hotel's financial success.

Director of Security

The director of security, who reports to the general manager or resident manager, is responsible for implementing hotel security policies and procedures in coordination with the general manager and all department heads. Depending upon the size of the hotel, the director of security is usually supported by a staff that may include an assistant director and security officers. (3) For more details on the responsibilities of a director of security.

Security Planning

Every hotel must assess its vulnerability in order to tailor a security plan that will meet its needs. There are multiple factors to consider, such as limiting access; monitoring activity; misappropriation of assets; employment guidelines; guest relations; contracts with outside security firms; use of force; arrest; employee locker control; guest room security and safety notices; bank deposits and escort of funds; lost and found; baggage storage; key control; unregistered guests; reporting incidents; and record keeping. (4) To keep track of these various factors, hotels generally conduct a security audit, such as the one shown in Appendix 5-1.

Unruly Guests. 0 When using hotel facilities, guests and visitors should be required to practice standards of conduct that will not interfere with the comfort, safety, and security of others. This is especially important in lounges and other public facilities. Unruly guests or visitors should be handled politely and firmly. Every effort should be made to remove unruly persons from public areas before prolonged discussions or interviews can occur. A private office or a secluded area should he used both to avoid exposing other guests and visitors to any confrontations or unpleasant scenes, and to avoid any possible allegation of failure with respect to the unruly person's right to privacy.

Use of Outside Security Firms. 0 In some cases, such as with VIP guests or exhibits of valuable merchandise, patrons or guests may request the services of an outside security firm or armed security guards. Management should secure a special release in such cases. The release covers security firms hired directly by exhibitors, conventions, and show management. The presence of gaming facilities in a hotel, like those that contributed so much to Barron Hilton's success, present very specialized security issues.

The outside security, firm must provide the hotel with satisfactory evidence of liability coverage in the amount of not less than $2 million per occurrence, including, but not limited to, premises, operations, personal injury (including assault and battery), contractual liability, and professional liability. The outside security firm also must agree to indemnify and hold harmless the hotel from any liability involving the security firm (including specific incidents involving weapons), and from any and all legal fees and costs.

Key Control. 0 While disposable key cards and electronic guest room locking devices have eased some of the security problems inherent in the hotel industry, key control is still a concern. The security department must coordinate with the front desk department to ensure that guest room keys arc issued only after identification and registration have been verified. Strict control of master keys, or those keys providing access to all guest rooms that are not double-locked, and emergency keys, or keys that open all guest room doors, even when they are double-locked, is a concern of the security department.

Another way to enhance key control is to make sure that, upon check out, a conscientious effort is made to retrieve guest room keys by all persons having contact with the departing guest, including the bellman, the cashier, the doorman, the maids, security personnel, and the garage attendant.

Emergency Plans

Emergencies such as bomb threats, floods, earthquakes, tornadoes, fires, hurricanes, gas leaks, loss of utilities, riots, and elevator evacuations, while unexpected and, in most cases, out of the control of the security department, can and should be anticipated.

Depending on its location, a hotel is at higher risk for certain disasters, such as an earthquake or civil unrest. In such cases, the general manager, in coordination with local authorities, should develop an emergency plan tailored to the specific hotel. Different plans should he developed for different emergency Situations. One of the most important features of an emergency plan is the delegation of specific responsibilities so that hotel staff know who to turn to and what is expected of them in the case of an emergency

In the following chapter, several departments are covered that are important to the success of a hotel. Typically, these departments are covered in courses in a hotel management curriculum and thus are only considered briefly in this text.

Summary

A loss prevention and security program is a means of protecting a hotel's resources—both people and property. Generally, injuries to the public mirror those among staff. The most common guest accident in the bathroom is a slip or a fall. The next most common accident is a cut from a sharp object or a burn from hot water. Injuries can occur in the guest room because of unstable appliances, glass doors, rough edges on furniture, and damaged carpet. The prevention of injury to the guest must extend to the internal and external public areas as well.

The loss prevention committee can be used to improve safety for both employees and guests. A key component in any loss prevention program is regular inspection of the facilities. If an injury to an employee or a guest occurs, a thorough investigation of the accident must take place as soon as possible. Employee injuries can he minimized through employee training.

The head of the security department is the director of security. Key to the responsibilities of the director of security include the security audit, implementation of hotel security policies and procedures, and preparation of emergency plans.

Hotels use Crisis Management, Communication to Ensure Safety During Emergency Situations

Ensuring the safety of their guests and employees is the top priority for hoteliers. Whether operating a beachside hotel, ski resort in the Rockies, or urban skyscraper, natural disasters and emergency situations are a reality. Hoteliers who display a heightened approach to crisis management and communications are better prepared for such frightening scenarios.

Hosting hundreds of travel writers this past September for the Society of American Travel Writers convention, Bermuda's Fairmont Southampton and Fairmont Hamilton Princess hotels were not going to let a looming hurricane dampen the annual conference. As Hurricane Erin prepared to bear down on Bermuda with winds up to 85 miles per hour, hotel employees readied to execute an expeditious plan for the safety of the employees and guests. All team members assumed specific duties from locking down balcony furniture and providing candles to securing doors and windows.

Fortunately, little damage was incurred by the low-level hurricane. But the hotels were ready for the worst, said Janet Eger, manager of communications for Toronto-based Fairmont Hotels & Resorts. Eger said the company takes pride in its overall strategic approach to crisis management.

"Safety is a top priority," she said. "Fairmont has been extremely proactive in crisis management and planning with an effective program in place."

Fairmont recently underwent an aggressive six-month, crisis-communications-training program with key executives in five countries. As part of the program, a variety of scenarios depicting emergency situations were revealed via video to address appropriate action plans and how to implement with precise coordination and communication.

"It ensures that our executive team is aware of what our core values are, and where our moral compass is," Eger said. "It is not only important how we executive our actions during a crisis, but it's also important that we communicate what we are doing to ensure the safety of guests."

Among other things, the training program outlined how to activate an operations post, devise a working media center and designate a crisis team with specific roles and responsibilities. Systems are tested and drilled for a variety of circumstances relevant to a particular property.

And while one can't plan for a crisis to happen, one can plan how to deal with a dangerous situation. Preparedness is the key, according to Benny Stephens, vice president of design and construction for US Franchise Systems, which franchises Hawthorne Suites, Microtel Inns and Suites and Best Inns and Suites. "The most important thing is to ensure that your people are aware of the procedures and are well-trained in the areas of safety," Stephens said.

The company's proactive approach includes intense training of standard operating procedures in addition to adapting appropriate building safety requirements.

From a physical standpoint, each property is designed to meet and exceed numerous life-safety requirements such as fire-protected stairwells, sprinkler systems and automatic fire alarm systems as deemed by national code and local authority.

Dana Ferrer is marketing manager for commercial fire-alarm-panel manufacturer Notifier, which is based in Northford, Conn. The company's horn/strobe system alerts property-level personnel when a fire emergency has been detected. The hotel's point person then implements the property's emergency operating plan to protect its employees and patrons.

"Obviously, safety is the No. 1 priority to a hotel," Ferrer said. "Our company works with hotels as part of its overall building security system."

Evacuation routes and emergency exits are another critical component to a property's safety plan. Sag Harbor, N.Y.-based Dortronics Systems manufactures electric-locking systems for commercial use.

Bryan Sanderford, national sales manager, said the purpose is to offer reliable and secure exits to facilitate quick evacuation during an emergency.

"The whole idea of our product is to provide an extra layer of security and the means to be safe while allowing people to get out in a fire emergency situation," Sanderford said.

The magnetic locking systems are tied to a property's fire alarm. When a fire alarm is triggered, the emergency doors automatically open, allowing patrons immediate access in and out of the building.

While technological improvements enhance a hotel's security, there is no substitute for a sound set of policies and procedures.

Stephens said USFS hotels use an emergency procedures manual, which has been an effective tool at its 500 plus properties.

The comprehensive manual was designed to assist franchisees during dangerous scenarios including earthquakes, tornadoes, power failures, armed robberies and bomb threats. It features checklists, specific processes and action plans, signage requirements and evacuation procedures.

Stephens said proper training is critical to ensure consistency and understanding of the plan. Routine fire drills with employees and guests allow an opportunity to play out action plans and reinforce a prepared environment.

Fairmont's Eger said in any emergency situation, open lines of communications are key to maintaining a sense of control and coordination.

"Keeping people up to speed is the way to alleviate panic," she said. "When people have the information, they are less likely to jump to unnecessary speculation."

Hotel Emergency Procedures

All hotels are required by law to provide their guests with a list of specific emergency procedures. Because one of the most common emergency situation in a hotel is a fire, emergency procedures typically include a detailed map of the floor the room is on and an outline of the route to the closest exit. Emergency preparedness also includes a list of what to do once you've evacuated the hotel as well as what to do in the event that you're prevented from evacuating.

Evacuation

Hotels often post a room-specific evacuation map on the back of the door to each room. The nearest exit is marked, as are all other exits on the floor in case the closest one is blocked. Hotels that don't put individualized maps in each room are required by law to provide general floor plan maps. Front desk staff may highlight the nearest stairwells and exits to a guestroom on a paper copy.

Emergency evacuation procedures begin by moving to exit when an alarm sounds, even if you suspect it's a drill. Before opening the door, you should feel it for heat and look for smoke coming underneath the door. Barring any smoke or flames, hotel procedures dictate that you should exit via the safest, shortest route possible.

If there's heavy smoke, you should stay low to the ground. Never use elevators during an emergency evacuation; they may become stuck mid-descent, or the shaft may fill with smoke. Also, the fire department may need to use the elevators to assist immobile people.

Becoming Trapped

Emergency procedures for becoming trapped in an area or room inside a hotel begin by first closing as many doors as possible between you and the fire and then sealing the area by placing water-soaked towels and sheets over all vents and door cracks. Use the phone, if it works, to call 9-1-1 and report the fire and your location in the building. Hanging a sheet or a noticeable item of clothing from the window signals your location, whether or not you're able to use the phone to call for help.

Breaking windows or opening them more than a few inches can invite flames and smoke from other openings inside. Fresher air is always near the floor, so protocol dictates that you stay low. In addition, placing a wet cloth over your mouth and nose helps you breathe better in a smoky environment.

Follow Up

Often, but not always, hotel emergency procedures request that evacuated guests gather in a predetermined area—usually in front of the hotel. It's important to report yourself to the person who's taking roll call of all of the guests on the register so rescue workers won't go into the burning building looking for someone who has already evacuated.

In situations where it's unclear whether or not the fire department has been called, you should call 9-1-1 if there's a way to do so. If you believe someone is trapped in the hotel, never attempt to go back inside. Rather, tell a member of the police or fire department.

What Should Hotels Do in a Blackout Emergency?

A hotel blackout can be a source of fear, panic and chaos if not handled properly. Blackouts happen suddenly, catching both employees and guests off-guard. The key to addressing a hotel blackout as hotel staff is to act as if you have not been surprised by the blackout. Follow the procedures your staff team has outlined for blackout emergencies to the letter, and keep guests as informed as possible throughout the process.

Demeanor

"Professional Management of Housekeeping Operations" by

Thomas Jones writes that staff demeanor in the event of a blackout is of utmost importance. Guests will be looking to you not only for the practical steps of dealing with problem, but for your overall attitude about the situation. Staff should remain calm and seek updated information via walkie-talkie, radio or other cellular device. Staff will be expected to know what's happening moment-by-moment, and should be able to provide these details as calmly as possible.

Report

The manager on duty should call the company that supplies his hotel's power and verify whether this is a neighborhood-wide blackout, or simply an issue with his hotel. As he learns these details, he should have a spokesperson relay these facts to hotel guests via loudspeaker. The nature of the problem will modify the steps to be taken. If an evacuation is not absolutely necessary, hotel guests should stay where they are until the power is turned back on.

Action

When the details of the blackout are gathered, guests should either be instructed to stay put or evacuate. If the power will be back on shortly, it is best for guests to stay exactly where they are, as moving about the hotel in the dark could be dangerous. If the blackout could possibly be a signal of a larger electrical problem, or is unexplained, it is best that guests evacuate. Your hotel should have an evacuation plan for other disasters, such as fires, and should follow this plan exactly as it is written.

Blackouts & Other Signs of Alcoholism

Blackouts are among the most terrifying symptoms of alcoholism. Entire segments of time simply disappear, leaving you with no memory of what you said or did. If you experience blackouts in connection with your alcohol consumption, you should acknowledge that you have a problem and seek help immediately. But blackouts aren't the only signs of alcoholism; knowing what they are and how they affect your life can be the first step on the road to recovery.

1. Cravings

  - o Alcoholics often have an overwhelming need to drink, and when they start drinking, they have an extremely difficult time cutting themselves off.
2. Secrecy
  - o Alcoholics may drink alone and take steps to hide evidence of their drinking, such as hiding the bottles in a hard-to-find place.
3. Tolerance
  - o It often takes an increasingly larger amount of liquor for an alcoholic to feel intoxicated, and/or he may drink simply to feel "normal."
4. Withdrawal
  - o If an alcoholic stops drinking, he may suffer from withdrawal symptoms such as vomiting, shivering or breaking into a cold sweat.
5. Reverberations
  - o Alcoholism often has an effect on other parts of the alcoholic's life. Work performance may suffer, troubles at home may increase, and friends or family members may drift away.

Emergency Department

"Accident and Emergency" and "Emergency room" redirect here. For other uses, see Accident and Emergency (disambiguation) and Emergency room (disambiguation).

An Emergency Department (ED), also known as Accident & Emergency (A&E), Emergency Room (ER), Emergency Ward (EW), or Casualty Department is a medical treatment facility, specialising in acute care of patients who present without prior appointment, either by their own means or by ambulance. The emergency department is usually found in a hospital or other primary care center.

Due to the unplanned nature of patient attendance, the department must provide initial treatment for a broad spectrum of illnesses and injuries, some of which may be life-threatening and require immediate attention. In some countries, emergency departments have become important entry points for those without other means of access to medical care. The emergency departments of most hospitals operate 24 hours a day, although staffing levels may be varied in an attempt to mirror patient volume.

History

The first specialized trauma care center in the world was opened in 1911 in the United States at the University of Louisville Hospital in Louisville, Kentucky, and was developed by surgeon Arnold Griswold during the 1930s. Griswold also equipped police and fire vehicles with medical supplies and trained officers to give emergency care while en route to the hospital.

Department Operation

As patients can present at any time and with any complaint, a key part of the operation of an emergency department is the prioritization of cases based on clinical need. This is usually achieved though the application of triage.

Triage is normally the first stage the patient passes through, and most emergency departments have a dedicated area for this to take place, and may have staff dedicated to performing nothing but a triage role. In most departments, this role is fulfilled by a nurse, although dependant on training levels in the country and area, other health care professionals may perform the triage sorting, including paramedics or doctors.

Most patients will be assessed and then passed to another area of the department, or another area of the hospital, with their waiting time determined by their clinical need. However, some patients may complete their treatment at the triage stage, for instance if the condition is very minor and can be treated quickly, if only advice is required, or if the emergency department is not a suitable point of care for the patient. Conversely, patients with evidently serious conditions, such as cardiac arrest, will bypass triage altogether and move straight to the appropriate part of the department.

The resuscitation area is key in most departments and the most serious patients will be dealt with in this area, and it contains the equipment and staff required for dealing with immediately life threatening illnesses and injuries. Patients whose condition is not immediately life threatening will be sent to an area suitable to deal with them, and these areas might typically be termed as a *majors* or *minors* area. Such patients may still have been found to have significant problems, including fractures, dislocations, and lacerations requiring suturing.

Children can present particular challenges in treatment and some departments have dedicated pediatrics areas and some departments employ a *play therapist* whose job is to put children at ease to reduce the anxiety caused by visiting the emergency department, as well as provide distraction therapy for simple procedures.

Many hospitals have a separate area for evaluation of psychiatric problems. These are often staffed by psychiatrists and mental health nurses and social workers. There is typically at least one room for people who are actively a risk to themselves or others (e.g. suicidal).

Fast decisions on life-and-death cases are critical in hospital emergency rooms. As a result, doctors face great pressures to overtest and overtreat. The fear of missing something often leads to extra blood tests and imaging scans for what may be harmless chest pains, run-of-the-mill head bumps, and non-threatening stomachaches, with a high cost on the Health Care system.

Nomenclature

During the 1990s, an effort began to change previous naming conventions to the more accurate term *Emergency Department* (ED), which is a term increasingly used by members of the speciality internationally.

Historic terminology still exists across the world, especially in vernacular usage. For instance, terms such as the previously accepted formal term 'Accident and Emergency' or 'A&E' are still widely known in countries such as the United Kingdom and its former territories, as are common informal terms such as 'Casualty', or 'Casualty Department'. The same applies to 'Emergency Room' or 'ER' in North America, originating when emergency facilities were provided in a single room of the hospital.

In the cases of both 'ER' in North America and 'Casualty' in the United Kingdom, the continued prevalence can be to some extent linked to the existence of long running television dramas bearing those respective names. The term "Urgency" instead of "Emergency" is used in some Latin American countries. Emergency Departments are known as *"Servicios de Urgencia"* and they function in a similar fashion to European Emergency Departments.

Signage

Regardless of naming convention, there is a widespread usage of directional signage in white text on a red background across the world, which indicates the location of the emergency department, or a hospital with such facilities.

Signs on emergency departments may contain additional information. In some American states there is close regulation of the design and content of such signs. For example, California requires wording such as "Comprehensive Emergency Medical Service" and "Physician On Duty", to prevent persons in need of critical care from presenting to facilities that are not fully equipped and staffed.

In some countries, including the United States and Canada, a smaller facility that may provide assistance in medical emergencies is known as a clinic. Larger communities often have walk-in clinics where people with medical problems that would not be considered serious enough to warrant an emergency department visit can be seen. These clinics often do not operate on a 24 hour basis.

United States

Many U.S. emergency rooms are exceedingly busy. A survey of New York area doctors in February 2007 found that injuries and even deaths have been caused by excessive waits for hospital beds by ED patients. A 2005 patient survey found an average ED wait time from 2.3 hours in Iowa to 5.0 hours in Arizona.

One inspection of Los Angeles area hospitals by Congressional staff found the EDs operating at an average of 116% of capacity (meaning there were more patients than available treatment spaces) with insufficient beds to accommodate victims of a terrorist attack the size of the 2004 Madrid train bombings. Three of the five Level I trauma centres were on "diversion", meaning ambulances with all but the most severely injured patients were being directed elsewhere because the ED could not safely accommodate any more patients. This controversial practice was banned in Massachusetts (except for major incidents, such as a fire in the ED), effective January 1, 2009; in response, hospitals have devoted more staff to the ED at peak times and moved some elective procedures to non-peak times.

In 2009, there were 1,800 EDs in the country.

United Kingdom

All A&E departments throughout the United Kingdom are financed and managed publicly by the NHS of each constituent country (England, Scotland, Wales and Northern Ireland). As with most other NHS services, emergency care is provided to all, both resident citizens and those not ordinarily resident in the UK, free at the point of need and regardless of any ability to pay.

Historically, waits for assessment in A&E were very long in some areas of the UK. In October 2002, the Department of Health introduced a four-hour target in emergency departments that required departments in England to assess and treat patients within four hours of arrival, with referral and assessment by other departments if deemed necessary. Present policy is that 95% of all patient cases do not "breach" this four-hour wait.

The 4-hour target triggered the introduction of the acute assessment unit (also known as the medical assessment unit), which works alongside the emergency department but is outside it for statistical purposes in the bed management cycle. It is claimed that though A&E targets have resulted in significant improvements in completion times, the current target would not have been possible without some form of patient re-designation or re-labeling taking place, so true improvements are somewhat less than headline figures might suggest and it is doubtful that a single target (fitting all A&E and related services) is sustainable.

Critical Conditions Handled

Cardiac Arrest

Cardiac arrest may occur in the ED/A&E or a patient may be transported by ambulance to the emergency department already in this state. Treatment is basic life support and advanced life support as taught in advanced life support and advanced cardiac life support courses. This is an immediately life-threatening condition which requires immediate action in salvageable cases.

Heart Attack

Patients arriving to the emergency department with a myocardial infarction (heart attack) are likely to be triaged to the resuscitation area. They will receive oxygen and monitoring and have an early ECG; aspirin will be given if not contraindicated or not already administered by the ambulance team; morphine or diamorphine will be given for pain; sub lingual (under the tongue) or buccal (between cheek and upper gum) glyceryl trinitrate [nitroglycerin] (GTN or NTG) will be given, unless contraindicated by the presence of other drugs, such as drugs that treat erectile dysfunction.

An ECG that reveals ST segment elevation or new left bundle branch block suggests complete blockage of one of the main coronary arteries. These patients require immediate reperfusion (re-opening) of the occluded vessel. This can be achieved in two ways: thrombolysis (clot-busting medication) or percutaneous transluminal coronary angioplasty (PTCA). Both of these are effective in reducing significantly the mortality of myocardial infarction. Many centres are now moving to the use of PTCA as it is somewhat more effective than thrombolysis if it can be administered early. This may involve transfer to a nearby facility with facilities for angioplasty.

Trauma

Major trauma, the term for patients with multiple injuries, often from a road traffic accident or a major fall, is sometimes handled in the Emergency Department. However, trauma is a separate (surgical) specialty from emergency medicine (which is a medical specialty, and has certifications in the United states from the American Board of Emergency Medicine).

Trauma is treated by a trauma team who have been trained using the principles taught in the internationally recognized Advanced Trauma Life Support (ATLS) course of the American College of Surgeons. Some other international training bodies have started to run similar courses based on the same principles. The services that are provided in an emergency department can range from simple x-rays and the setting of broken bones to those of a full-scale trauma center. A patient's chance of survival is greatly improved if the patient receives definitive treatment (i.e. surgery or reperfusion) within one hour of an accident (such as a car accident) or onset of acute illness (such as a heart attack). This critical time frame is commonly known as the "golden hour".

Some emergency departments in smaller hospitals are located near a helipad which is used by helicopters to transport a patient to a trauma center. This inter-hospital transfer is often done when a patient requires advanced medical care unavailable at the local facility. In such cases the emergency department can only stabilize the patient for transport.

Mental Illness

Some patients arrive at an emergency department for a complaint of mental illness. In many jurisdictions (including many U.S. states), patients who appear to be mentally ill and to present a danger to themselves or others may be brought against their will to an emergency department by law enforcement officers for psychiatric examination. The emergency department conducts medical clearance rather than treats acute behavioral disorders. From the emergency department, patients with significant mental illness may be transferred to a psychiatric unit (in many cases involuntarily).

Asthma and COPD

Acute exacerbations of chronic respiratory diseases, mainly asthma and chronic obstructive pulmonary disease (COPD), are assessed as emergencies and treated with oxygen therapy, bronchodilators, steroids or theophylline, have an urgent chest X-ray and arterial blood gases and are referred for intensive care if necessary. Non invasive ventilation in the ED has reduced the requirement for tracheal intubation in many cases of severe exacerbations of COPD.

Bibliography

Bolshevism, Germy: *Coping with Tourists: European Reactions to Mass Tourism*, Oxford, Berghahn Books, 1995.

Bryson, McDowell: Concierge: *Key to Hospitality: A Training Manual*, New York, Wiley, 1992.

Burkart, A and Medlik, S: *Management of Tourism*, The, London, Heinemann, 1975.

Burns, P., : *From Communist to Common-weal: Reflections on Tourism Training in Romania,* Tourism Recreation Research, 1998.

Clark, Mona: *Interpersonal Skills for Hospitality Managers,* London, Chapman Hill, 1995.

Conroy, B. : *Quality in Education and Training for Tourism*, London, Tourism Society, 1997.

Cooper, Chris: *Geography of Travel and Tourism*, The, London, Heinemann, 1987.

Cukier, J. : *Tourism Employment in Bali: Trends and Implications*, London: Thompson, 1996.

Donald, M.: *Customer Service in the Hospitality and Tourism Industry*, Englewood Cliffs, Prentice Hall, 1994.

Douglas C: *Practical Tourism Forecasting,* Oxford, Butterworth Heinemann, 1996.

Elio, C.: *The Hospitality Law Desk Reference,* Miami, Southern Beverage Journal, 1994.

Fowler, Peter: *Heritage and Tourism: In the Global Village*, London, Retailed, 1993.

Ghimire, Krishna: *The Native Tourist*: Mass Tourism within Developing Regions, London, Earthscan, 2001.

Goeldner, C. R: *The Evaluation of Tourism as an Industry and a Discipline, Paper Presented to,* International Conference for Tourism Educators, Guildford, University of Surrey, 1988.

Hoffman, Edward: *Project Management Success Stories: Lessons of Project Leaders*, New York, John Wiley & Son, 2000.

Ireland, Lewis: *Quality Management for Projects and Programs*, Upper Darby, PMI, 1991.

Jakle, John: *Tourist, The: Travel in Twentieth Century North America*, University of North Nebraska, 1985.

Kotler, Philip: *Marketing for Hospitality and Tourism*: New Jersey, Prentice-Hall, 1998.

Larkham, P J: *Building a New Heritage: Tourism, Culture & Identity in the New Europe*, London, Routledge,1994.

Lawrence, E. : *Technology of internet business*, Wiley, Australia, 2002.

Lock, Dennis: *Project Management*, New York, Wiley, 1996.

Marcussen, Carl H. : *Internet Distribution of European Travel and Tourism Services*, Research Centre of Bornholm, Denmark, 1999.

Medlik, S. : *Tourism, Past, Present and Future*, London, Heinemann, 1981.

Nijkamp, Peter: *Sustainable Tourism Development*, Aldershot, Avebury, 1995.

Nijkamp, Peter: *Sustainable Tourism Development*, Aldershot, Avebury, 1995.

Peters, M: *International Tourism*, London, Hutchinson, 1969.

Prentice, R: *Conceptualising The Experiences of Heritage Tourists*, 1997.

Richards, G. : *Tourism in Central and Eastern Europe: Educating for Quality*, Tilberg, Tilberg University Press, 1996.

Rocco, M.: *An Introduction to Hospitality Today*, Orlando, Educational Institute, 1998.

Schwaninger, M: *Trends in Leisure and Tourism for 2000 - 2010*, Prentice Hall, 1989.

Swarbrooke, J. : *Tourism and Leisure Education in the United Kingdom*, Tilberg, Netherlands, Tilberg University Press, 1995.

Umbreit, T. : *The Role of Education in the Tourist Industry*, Salt Lake City, University of Utah, 1987